ESSAYS ON BIBLICAL THEOLOGY

Hartmut Gese

ESSAYS ON BIBLICAL THEOLOGY

Translated by Keith Crim

AUGSBURG Publishing House • Minneapolis

Contents

Preface

The lectures on biblical theology contained in this volume were delivered during the past five years, some of them more than once. I have been reluctant to accede to the often expressed wish that they be published, as it seemed to me better, because of the inner connections among the various themes, to delay publication until I could achieve a certain completeness. For these are themes of a biblical theology that should be viewed as a whole, even when only one aspect is being discussed at a time. Thus one lecture can be seen to support another, and what can only be alluded to in one is more fully developed in another. The first lecture is of an introductory nature, and is intentionally elementary. The last one leads us beyond biblical theology into hermeneutics and deals with a highly urgent practical problem. Between them are six lectures on basic questions of biblical theology, and finally one dealing with the understanding of the prologue of John's Gospel in terms of tradition history, as an example of the relationship between the Old and New Testaments. In any case it is unavoidable that each lecture be complete and independent in itself, and should remain so for the reader, although they overlap at points where one aspect intersects another. I first intended to edit out repetitions, but decided not to do so, because I did not wish to destroy the form of the lectures, each of which was to be read for itself. It was important that the lecture form remain, because only so does their nature as sketches become apparent; this is appropriate in the present situation for a historic and theological view of that whole which is presented in the Old and New Testaments as a unity.

I

The Biblical View of Scripture

NYONE WHO WANTS TO SPEAK of a biblical view of Scripture must first consider the question of what the adjective "biblical" means in connection with the concept "view of Scripture." Scripture in this context, of course, means the Bible. We can speak of the view of Scripture held by the church, or by the early fathers, or by the reformers, or of our view of Scripture, but what does it mean to speak of a "biblical" view of Scripture? It means the view that the Bible has of itself as Scripture, or which it developed of itself. Before we attempt to derive a view of Scripture from some systematic, dogmatic, or practical point of view from outside the Scripture, we should try to arrive at a proper view of Scripture in terms of the Bible itself. This means that we must approach this important question historically. It is in this manner that the question should be asked and answered.

The Unity of the Bible

The Bible lies before us as a collection of books and writings, which fall into two distinct divisions, the Old and the New Testaments. Indeed the usual view is not so much that it is a unit composed of two parts, but rather two totally distinct collections. Since anyone who speaks of a view of Scripture has first the one and then the other part in mind, it is absolutely necessary to deal first

9

of all with this problem of the relationships and connections between the two Testaments. "Scripture" can only mean these two,
and these two *together*. How are we to define this connection?
What is the *one* Scripture—or is there really such a thing?

It is widely held that the Old Testament is a holy Scripture that
had already taken on a fixed form in pre-Christian times. To be
sure, the New Testament refers to it and is related to it as a sacred
Christian Scripture, but, it is thought, it should be regarded as the
Jewish sacred Scripture. In the history of the church there have
been many attempts to evaluate the Old Testament on the basis
of the New Testament, and these have run the gamut all the way
to total rejection. It is certain, however, that in all the writings of
the New Testament the Old Testament is regarded as the one holy
Scripture, and its validity is by no means regarded as limited.

This is carried so far, to cite two extreme examples, that in
Romans 10:5-9, where Paul contrasts the righteousness that comes
from the law with that which comes from faith, this new and
different righteousness through faith is supported by a quotation
from the Torah (Deut. 30:12-14). The Deuteronomic teaching that
the law is not something that is foreign, but that it is quite near to
us in our mouths and hearts, is for Paul "the word of faith which
we preach" (10:8). Even more striking is the way in which this
apparent contrast is presented in Matthew. In the introduction to
the passages in the Sermon on the Mount which contrast the new
righteousness with the old ("You have heard that it was said to the
men of old . . . . But I say to you . . .") it is emphasized in 5:17-19
that Jesus did not come to abolish the law; yes, not an iota, not a
dot will pass away from the law, and anyone who thinks he can do
away with the least commandment will be the least in the kingdom
of heaven.

The New Testament is full of controversies with the teachers of
the law over the interpretation of the law and the new righteousness,
but in these controversies the Old Testament is never abandoned to
the opponents. Instead they are accused of a false interpretation or
a false use of the Old Testament. Unless we are willing to reject
a priori the New Testament's interpretation of the Old as forced

and tendentious, or at best, unimportant—and that would have far-reaching consequences for the content set forth in the New Testament's interpretations—it is not open to us to regard the Old Testament as a second-rate Scripture which found its legitimate continuation only in later Judaism.

There have been various attempts to find the correct relationship of the Old Testament to the New. Some have thought of it as a duality under the schema of promise and fulfillment. But for one thing, this looks at only one side of the Old Testament, and in addition the promise lies totally under the shadow of the fulfillment. The Old Testament is even more strongly felt to be something that can be dispensed with when it is seen as containing the typological foreshadowing of the New. What is the importance of this foreshadowing when the fulfillment of truth is there before our eyes? If, however, the Old Testament is regarded as merely the historical documentation of the preparation for the New, it is by that token degraded to a sort of prologue which has no direct meaning of its own. It is totally impossible to decide on the one hand that there are two fundamentally independent holy scriptures, and then on the other hand to try to establish a necessary relationship between these two separate entities, without sacrificing the absoluteness of the New Testament.

The question cannot be answered, because it has been incorrectly framed, and proceeds from false presuppositions. There is no Old Testament that was complete prior to the existence of the New Testament, and there is no revelation that was concluded prior to the New Testament. The Old Testament grew and developed in a long process, which in the last analysis can be understood as the process of canonization. First it was the Torah that was completed as holy Scripture and accorded canonical status at the time of Ezra in the new liturgical form of worship centering around the word of God. (We will have to look at this more in detail.) But at the same time there already existed the framework for a second part of the canon, the prophetic tradition, which was closed at the end of the prophetic period in the third century B.C.

Even then the formation of the Old Testament was not yet complete. A great wealth of materials, above all the collection of Psalms, which was closed at about this same time, and the wisdom literature, which had its beginnings in pre-exilic times, the apocalyptic literature, which had become an independent form, and special forms of post-exilic presentations of history, yes all this and much more had not yet been brought together as a third part of the canon, because the growth process of tradition history had not yet been completed. The New Testament does not refer back to a completed Old Testament, but it calls the available form the "law and prophets" after the names of the completed parts (Matt. 5:17; 7:12; cf. Luke 24:27) or "law, prophets, and Psalms" (Luke 24:44).

When the New Testament came into being, however, it not only continued this development of the Old Testament in the formation of the New Testament tradition, but also completed it insofar as no further Old Testament tradition can develop or assert itself alongside that of the New. The New Testament therefore for the first time constitutes the Old Testament as such by placing itself at the end of the biblical transmission as the *non plus ultra* and therefore the goal, and thus bringing all that had been before, that is, the so-called Old Testament, to a conclusion.

We are dealing with a single process of the development of the biblical tradition, and there can be a distinction between Old and New Testaments only insofar as we can distinguish in this process between that which has not yet been completed, has not yet reached its goal, and the *telos,* the end and goal. The New Testament does not stand in contrast to a completed Old Testament, to which it must build artificial bridges. Rather the New Testament was preceded by a development of Scripture, that is, a history of revelation, to which it itself belongs.

Where did the usual concept of a self-contained, completed Old Testament come from? There are various major and minor reasons for this, which we cannot go into here in detail. Only the most important ones will be mentioned.

1. The Greek language of the New Testament sets it off from the Old. But already long before this the Old Testament tradition

had been separated from the Hebrew language. On the one hand there was the transition to the Aramaic language of the Persian Empire—due not entirely to external factors—and on the other hand there was a transition to the Greek language, for example, in the Wisdom of Solomon. Here too there were internal factors at work. The transition to the world languages did not mean that the Hebrew spiritual tradition was lost in the process. Every reader of the Greek New Testament senses the Hebraic thought which lies behind it, and only when viewed against this background does the tremendous spiritual accomplishment of the language of the New Testament become apparent.

2. It is said that the literary form of the New Testament is basically different from that of the Old. This is certainly true of the apostolic letters and for the totally new form of the Gospels. The former is connected with the activity of the apostles and the definitive mission to the world-wide Roman empire, and the latter is the form taken by the testimony to Jesus Christ. The difference in form is in both cases determined by the content and is necessary. On the other hand, the last form to develop in the Old Testament—apocalyptic—is continued in the New Testament, not only as the final proclamation of Jesus in the so-called synoptic apocalypse (Mark 13 and parallels), but even as an independent book. And within the framework of the gospels, letters, etc., we find again all the important late forms of the Old Testament tradition.

3. Most important, however, is the third argument: the Jewish Masoretic text of the Old Testament. In spite of the flourishing of Old Testament literature at the time of Jesus (we might think of the discoveries at Qumran), the Judaism which rejected the Christ event remarkably enough terminated the formation of the Old Testament tradition. In the refounding of Judaism after the catastrophe of A.D. 70 a final canonizing of the Old Testament took place, in which the third part of the canon (which had still remained open) was reduced by leaving out everything that was disputed and could

still be excluded. Especially the wisdom and apocalyptic materials, that had such close affinities with the New Testament, were dropped. A specific theory of canon, which placed the final limit in the time of Ezra, attempted to contrast the Old Testament, as a definitively complete entity, to a quite different tradition on a different level, that of halachah and aggada, which led to the Talmud and Midrash. In this view of the matter there is clearly a gulf between the Old and New Testaments, and from this point of view it is possible to speak of "inter-testamental" literature and even of Old Testament apocrypha.

It must be pointed out that the Reformation church, by separating out the Apocrypha, did not render a service to a total view of the biblical tradition. This step was caused by the fact that the church, in contrast to the early church before the time of Constantine, had lost the Hebrew Old Testament and had to receive it back from the synagogue. The humanistic scholarship of that time, which here as elsewhere was constantly on the lookout for non-genuine or forged material, was obliged to declare the missing books of the Christian Old Testament apocryphal, and this verdict was accepted by Luther, even though his theological sensorium found much of value in these apocryphal books. Since the historical discoveries of the nineteenth century, and especially since those at Qumran, we know of no further scholarly reason for removing the Apocrypha. But it is precisely from that time on that the Bible Societies seem to have determined to protect us from the Apocrypha.

Luther felt that he was forced to undertake a similar, though less drastic process of elimination in the New Testament. Hebrews, James, and Revelation, which at times had been in dispute in the early church, he placed at the end of the New Testament without assigning them a number, and he declared in the introductions to these books that they were non-apostolic. Soon after the time of Luther, however, no more doubts were permitted in reference to the canonical character of these writings. In spite of this, in all editions of the Luther Bible they stand at the end, although now numbered.

Tradition History

This recognition of a unified process of tradition of the Old and New Testaments viewed as a whole has brought us closer to the biblical view of Scripture. We must now consider this process, first by looking more closely at the phenomena of tradition history and then at the course it followed.

Formerly the inspiration of the Bible was pictured in abbreviated and schematic form as the inspiration of the authors of the various writings. The concept of authorship itself, however, was for earlier generations a much broader and more comprehensive concept than it is for us. In a time when authorship was not determined by originality and so-called intellectual property but by a firm base in tradition history and by the beginning and continuation through a bearer of the tradition, designations of authorship must have been understood in a completely different manner, especially since only rarely was a text simply written down, but rather it developed in a lengthy process of taking on written form.

Let us begin with the final stage. Almost all biblical texts give evidence of a long process of development. This can be divided into an oral tradition before the text was written and a further stage in which the text was worked over after it had been fixed in writing. The prehistory of the oral tradition is not merely what might be called a stage prior to "actual inspiration" when the text came to be written, a stage that happily was superceded at the written stage, but it is the highly significant point of origin of the text, which leads us directly into living events.

We have, for example, in the Old Testament a large number of decalogues. The classic decalogue itself is a result of centuries of work and tradition. In spite of this, additional ones came into being in order to formulate new understandings of the truth in the framework of this tradition of the revelation at Sinai, but without wanting to overshadow the classic decalogue. The long development of the decalogue tradition took place in the life of Israel in continuity with the Sinai revelation. It must be significant that the oldest, or at least an old, formulation was not simply transmitted, but that the process continued until finally a form crystallized that could be recognized as final, without excluding the development of secondary forms. That the Elohist and Deuteronomist present this form of the decalogue in the account of the revelation at Sinai is completely true to the nature of the process. Only a one-dimensional, superficial, self-styled objective concept of reality could raise the objection that this decalogue was not revealed at all. That would be to overlook the fact that the revelation to Moses contained that truth which now could finally be expressed and unfolded in that power which in the living experience of Israel found its expression in the decalogue.

The older transmission of Israel's history depended entirely on that form which is called saga, and which, in contrast to written historical accounts, is at home in oral tradition. That is, saga arises and lives on in the process of telling and listening. In this life experience of structured recollection, the people of Israel became aware that God was directing their history. It would be foolish to demand that the biblical account present an obviously objective history. What we have here is the experiencing of history, history lived out in belief and unbelief. History is something that is experienced and not something in itself.

Moreover, the life situation of proclamation precedes the written formulation of the prophetic word. The Psalms are first of all songs of Israel's cultic life, and even prior to the wisdom texts there was the instruction given by the wise and the extensive work of transmission involved in the collection and preservation of these intellectual insights. The Gospels recount events which first had to be grasped and reflected on by the apostolic tradition in all their depth and meaning. Indeed, it was necessary for the literary form to develop before these events could be presented, and then finally presented in quite different forms, according to their various aspects and the particular stage of transmission.

The oral prehistory of biblical texts points us to developments in the life of Israel which stand in the closest possible relation to the mystery of inspiration. Revelation took place in events in the life of the people. The fact that the Bible is not an instructional book but a book presenting life as it is lived, bearing testimony, and proclaiming its message, is closely related to this reception of truth in the midst of life as it is being lived.

When a text became fixed in writing, its formation was by no means concluded. With a few exceptions, it was subject, as written word, to the further living process of transmission. Only those things were preserved which in this written form proved useful in life. So collections of Torah and of laws, of songs, and of wisdom texts came into being in order to be of service in life situations in specific areas. Even the history which grew out of the life of the people in Israel, the historical tradition that was fixed in written form, was not created for the archives, but in the process of its transmission it was again and again added to, selections were made, and new shape was given to it.

The prophetic traditions fall into two very different groups. Inasfar as the prophetic word found expression in historical events and was fulfilled in them, the tradition took its form from the experience of these historical events, the form of saga, of the so-called prophetic legends, such as those of Elijah and Elisha. But when Israel was conquered by the first great world empire, Assyria (Assyria was only the beginning of the world empires that included Babylon, Persia, the empire of Alexander, and the Roman empire), and judgment fell on Israel as a historical state with its existing forms of cult, law, etc., then the prophetic word which announced this judgment, this total change from existing external situations to true and genuine existence, was handed on in absolute precision. The people knew that this judgment was not completed in the contemporary historical catastrophes, but that it continued to be valid, and even in the future it would not permit Israel to be content with a superficial, external form of life, but would continue to exhort the people to change and to repent. By the nature of the material, the collection of prophetic oracles that had been fixed in writing continued to be renewed, added to, and brought up to date.

How did this many-sided, many-faceted, productive process of documentary transmission take place? First we should mention the additions which can be easily recognized as such. Often they were simply intended to make the original statements understandable in later situations, or were new interpretations, the updating of the traditional material. These customary designations are not entirely happy ones, and in any case it was more than an occasional modernization that took place in the course of transmission. Behind this there was progress in the history of revelation, an unfolding of the truth. Out of the old material of the world of the Davidic kingdom with its conception of the king in Zion as the son of God, as seen in Psalm 2 or Psalm 110, there developed in the Psalter the proclamation of the messianic king.

The process of tradition history corresponds to a process of revelation history. That is much more than a modernizing or an application to new situations. The truth which was originally intended and expressed took on new dimensions, and of necessity, if it was to be truth, it had to be expressed in these dimensions. Thus entire complexes of tradition can, through being reworked and having material added, function in an entirely new perspective. For example, the many apocalyptic additions in the prophetic writings bring the light of this later tradition to bear on the transmitted material.

It might be asked why, in this course of transmission, the old was not simply rejected, to be replaced by the new, but on the contrary, the old was preserved and only placed in a new light. This is connected with the fact that the history of revelation which is the basis of this transmission process is not a journey toward a truth that at last will be discovered, but is the truth from the outset, not a static truth of a timeless doctrine, but the truth which lays hold of men and women and transforms them, which creates true being. It is extremely impressive to note how the tradition intentionally preserves the old at new stages. For example, the priestly account of creation in Genesis 1:1-2:4a was supplemented by the so-called Yahwistic description of the primeval world. The old truth did not become untruth or half-truth. No, in spite of the new, greater, and more profound perspectives, the old truth was preserved and continued to perform its function in the whole, just as no one can eliminate a person's childhood from his life, simply because the age of childhood has been left behind. The old truth is not past truth, but it continues to be present.

In this magnificent conservative tradition Israel was schooled not to forget the old language and the old reality, and was challenged to become the full Israel. In the Psalter the newly-won knowledge of the truth of eternal life in fellowship with God (Ps. 49; 73, etc.) stands alongside psalms in which the worshiper wrestles with God for deliverance from death, and where knowledge of eternal life is lacking. Why weren't the older psalms eliminated? Because they were not untrue. Even later psalms could speak the old language, and the knowledge of eternal fellowship with God is not a new article in a creed which advances beyond the old, but is the result of this wrestling for deliverance from death.

Such profound insights are not items of information that are simply to be transmitted. They are services of commitment, transitions, breakthroughs that men and women must achieve, acts in which the self is transformed. The powerful accomplishments of the wisdom tradition which the Book of Job attained stand in contrast to the old wisdom of the three friends. It is not that this old wisdom is false, but that the judgment which the friends pronounce on Job is false. The validity of the old wisdom remains, and for that reason it is worked out and presented in such poetical and rhetorical completeness. It is only after this wisdom is recognized as representing the eternal, inviolable, righteous order of the world that the transcendence expressed in Job can be seen—fellowship with God over against all well-being, all experience of salvation—transcendence in the experience of being justified beyond any worldly security. But in order to become Job, it is necessary first to be his friends.

This brief discussion of the growth of tradition history could give the impression that this process went forward through the centuries without interruption or tension, with no particular inner or outward difficulties. As we hold the results of this development in our hands, we are impressed by its completeness and fullness, and we wonder how this fits with the tortuous course of Israel's life. We must bear in mind that this process of tradition as a living process, rooted in that change-filled life, is what produced this completeness and fullness. Amid all the changes, the hardships and difficulties of Israel's life, Israel's upbringing took place, and the proper formation of the tradition was the result.

It was precisely the catastrophes in the history of Israel that were helps in the formation of the tradition. The catastrophic collapse of the kingdom of Northern Israel led to the Deuteronomic movement, which was able to combine the materials transmitted in the North with those of the South. The exile in Babylon led to a particular formation of traditions grouped around the so-called Priestly Writings. It was this that first opened up for all Israel the priestly knowledge formerly inaccessible to the laity. There were certainly many mishaps and misfortunes in the long history of tradition, but because the formation of tradition is an organic process these wounds were healed and wholeness restored. The completeness and fullness of the process of tradition results from the fact that it is a process of growth.

The Pauline corpus in the New Testament is a collection of the apostle's letters. Certainly not all of his letters are included here. Wouldn't it be helpful to have one or more of his other letters? Think what important and invaluable things may have been lost through chance. Were a number of letters deliberately omitted from the collection? The Pauline corpus is not a mere collection of the preserved literature, any more than the Bible as a whole is. It is not an edition of all the apostle's letters. The living process in which the apostolic writings were read again and again in the churches and exchanged with other churches produced the biblical Pauline corpus. Thus it was the expression of the apostolic message in letters and its reception when they were read that brought the corpus into existence.

The Pauline writings are the product of the life of the church. Even in the unlikely event that a letter of Paul were rediscovered, we could not give it canonical status, no matter how interesting it was, because it would be only a sermon that had remained unheard. Anyone who is offended by the view that the Pauline corpus contains so-called "non-genuine" letters has not understood the nature of the process of tradition, the living growth that always brings forth a whole. It was necessary for Paul's letters to be supplemented, rounded out by members of his school, even if, yes, precisely because various aspects of the apostolic message find expression here (e.g., on the one hand, Ephesians, and on the other, the Pastorals). It was not necessary to supplement them because the apostolic preaching was deficient, but because the genuine letters alone clearly did not reflect the full effect of the apostolic proclamation, and because the personality of the apostle Paul, which those who received the genuine letters had before them, had a far-reaching effect. Thus we can say that it is precisely because the tradition corresponds to a revelation that occurred in life-events that the completeness and fullness exists.

To be sure, this has also its negative side. There is no way to measure how much traditional material disappeared and was lost in the course of more than a thousand years. The Qumran library, for example, gives us an impression of the diversity of the literary riches that existed. This should not bother us. The strict choice, through which only those materials survived that were the bearers of life in the light of revelation, is what produced the wholeness. Only in this manner could the whole take form.

Once we recognize that the events of tradition history took place in living settings, we will conclude that we can identify those areas of life that correspond to the areas of tradition. We can, for example, connect the priestly teaching of Torah or law with the priestly realm of tradition, and so forth. The strands of tradition which were formed in this manner often reveal specific concepts of authorship. In complete contrast to our concept of authorship, the traditional material is not considered "intellectual property." As the transmitters receive and hand on, they are also responsible contributors to the process, but they are not authors. It is in keeping with the nature of the material that the founder of such a school of tradition is regarded as the author. Accordingly we can understand that the Mosaic Torah must be regarded as revelation given to Moses, even when its formulations and the structure of its content date from a later time. When the Pentateuch says, "Moses spoke," this expresses a real truth which cannot be properly dealt with by the objection, raised by our limited way of thinking, that this is unhistorical.

Let me mention an extreme example. Among the strands of prophetic tradition in the eighth century B.C., Isaiah is the only representative of Jerusalem. The great importance of the prophetic proclamation that took place in Jerusalem in connection with the specific traditions of the city resulted in the formation of an Isaianic school that was able to grow over the following centuries. It is exciting to note how the content and the interpretations in the first 39 chapters of Isaiah were formulated in this centuries-long process of listening to Isaiah's original proclamation. In the book of Isaiah we now have in Chapters 40-66 a section (clearly marked off by the historical section in Chapts. 36-39 as a supplement or a second part) which contains a different tradition of an exilic prophet, with a postexilic addition. This tradition is anonymous, due to certain considerations of content and form, and we usually call it simply Second Isaiah.

It would, however, be naive to assume that this material came to be written in the Isaiah scroll only by chance, because, for instance, there was room there for it. There may well have been innumerable chance happenings in the long history of tradition, but they would have in any case been smoothed out through the ongoing broad stream of tradition. In the period when Second Isaiah was supposed to have been added so accidentally to Isaiah, there must have been hundreds of Isaiah scrolls. No, this material was placed there deliberately. It is shown to be relevant by the fact that Second Isaiah continues the Zion tradition of Isaiah, and further by the important and close linguistic similarities between First and Second Isaiah. Above all, various redactional strands in Isaiah show close relationships to Second Isaiah on the one hand, and to Chapters 56-66, Third Isaiah, on the other. That is to say, it was appropriate to add the tradition of Second Isaiah to that of Isaiah and to complete the whole as "Isaiah the Prophet."

When the New Testament identifies the author of a passage in Second Isaiah as "Isaiah the Prophet," this is completely in keeping with the data of tradition history and true to the material involved. It is nonsense to interpret these statements in modern categories and claim that to recognize a part of the book as coming from Second Isaiah is to contradict the New Testament. Note how carefully the tradition itself stresses this distinction through the historical section in Isaiah 36-39. It would have been easy to incorporate Second Isaiah much more closely into the book of Isaiah, and indeed even later essential material was so incorporated. It was important to set off Chapters 40-66, but not to separate them from the Isaiah tradition.

We have now cited enough examples to clarify the phenomenon that is incorrectly termed pseudepigraphy. This is not a case of perpetrating a literary deception under the name of a false author. On the contrary a connection that is important in terms of tradition history is given appropriate expression. The Isaiah apocalypse, Chapters 24-27, which in content and style is so closely bound to the rest of the Isaiah tradition, is Isaianic just as the Torah of the Pentateuch is Mosaic, or the Epistle to the Ephesians is Pauline. When a so-called non-genuine letter imitates even the details of the customary epistolary form, this is not deception, but it is using the only possible form in which this specific tradition can appropriately be given expression. That many misunderstandings arise here is due to our use of modern categories and a mode of thought that is completely foreign to ancient thought in general and the biblical tradition in particular.

We might mention here in passing another difficulty in the biblical texts that is closely connected with the matters we have been discussing. This is the so-called *vaticinium ex eventu,* the foretelling of an event after it has already taken place. As an example we may take Zechariah 11:4-17, the shepherd allegory. The prophet, and there is no doubt that Zechariah is meant, presents under the symbolic action of herding sheep with the two staffs "Grace" and "Union," which are then broken, the course of history from the time of Ezra to the reigns of Alexander's successors. The purpose of this is not to ascribe to Zechariah prophetic powers he did not possess, but to portray the transition from the Persian to the Hellenistic period as completed through Zechariah's prophetic actions. Zechariah, standing as he did at the end of the prophetic period, was able to write the first apocalypse concerning the end of the old aeon. The dynamic of the apocalyptic tradition reached far beyond any application to the then-existing Persian empire. And the fact that this tradition continued past the time of Alexander into the Hellenistic period by means of the stages of tradition represented in Second Zechariah (Chaps. 9-11) and Third Zechariah (Chaps. 12-14) is in keeping with this.

Thus the *vaticinium* expresses an apocalyptic understanding of a complicated period of transition: God's revelation in the apocalyptic vision of Zechariah is what brings about this transition of the successive world empires. The *vaticinium* expresses this insight and does not ascribe to Zechariah in retrospect knowledge that he did not have. Here too our modern way of thinking falls short, because it is trapped in an inflexible concept of reality and is unable to sense the subtlety of biblical language and the depths of experience expressed in the text.

At the end of our discussion of the phenomena of the biblical tradition history, someone may raise the objection that all this assumes a quite complicated analytical knowledge which a modern biblical scholar might work out, but which would be foreign to the simple folk of ancient times. Behind this frequently-heard objection there lies a little of the romantic view of the naivete of the ancients. Some are eager to see the apostles as simple fishermen and the Pauline congregations as simple Corinthian dock workers. Even if we only look, however, at the externals of the upper-most layer of the texts in question, this view is called into question. It is clear that the simple person of that time was much more intellectual than we give him credit for. What kind of people must they have been who sang the New Testament hymns to Christ in their worship services! How much intellectual power the congregational letters of Paul demand of those who heard them read! But we may leave all that aside. The texts themselves can make us aware of these analytical matters. We find many different means used to identify the layers and additions in the texts.

For example, the Deuteronomic law contains a double framework of speeches. The inner and older of these addresses Israel in the singular as "thou," while the outer and younger uses the plural, "ye." Why this change in number, except to distinguish clearly between the later layer and the earlier? But there is more. In the singular parts there are individual sentences in the plural, and conversely, singular sentences in the plural sections. This variation in number has two functions. One is to emphasize sentences and call attention to them, and the other is to identify interpretative glosses. There is a large range of possibilities for marking such additions. There was thus no attempt to conceal the complicated structure of tradition history, but it was to be recognized. And it was! When we study the New Testament's exegesis of the Old Testament we find an overwhelming number of sublime and difficult insights into the Old Testament. There is no ground at all for speaking of a naive use of Scripture.

Revelation History

We have examined the structure of the Bible as determined by tradition history, and we have seen that one total process of tradition history formed the Bible and gave structure to it. Behind this process and constituting its basis we can recognize the course of history of revelation. I will now attempt to sketch it in broad strokes, because only by understanding it can we understand the structure of the Bible.

God's revelation of himself to humans is neither timeless nor restricted to one point in time. It begins in a historical *kairos* and travels a historical path, just as truly as we are historical beings. This path has a goal, and revelation reaches its *telos* in this process of self-revelation to human beings. This history of revelation is the secret of the history of Israel.

We can designate as the starting point of this revelation history the event, which in terms of tradition history is the heart of the Old Testament, the revelation at Sinai. In contrast to all previous human experience of a divine world and divine order, in contrast to all mythological conceptions of God, God reveals himself as a person as "I," "I am YHWH," reveals himself to his human partner, the "thou," whom he binds to himself and to whom he binds himself, "I am YHWH, thy God." As a full revelation of himself, it is revelation in a relationship which is exclusive in nature.

The primordial Israel at Sinai is an international confederation of tribes, constituted as such by this revelation. From Sinai on they knew that they had been rescued by this God out of total slavery to the most powerful nation in the world, that Israel was born out of the exodus miracle of deliverance from the waters of chaos. And in the Sinai revelation Yahweh identified himself with the God who had called forth the patriarchs from the world of the nations and promised them a future. God's revelation of himself to Moses as the representative of Israel contains within it the gift of a life under God, which is described in the mosaic tradition as law, an instruction in the true way of life.

The gift of the land is the gift of historical existence, and its crown and conclusion is the capture of Jerusalem by David, who confers on Israel national identity in the full sense. Zion, Jerusalem's cultic mountain that belonged to David's family, was chosen by God as his sanctuary, and in the cultic representation of the ark of the covenant, the God who on Sinai only appeared to Israel takes possession of a piece of land, by taking up his dwelling in the midst of Israel. And the Davidic king, enthroned on this Zion, in God's heritage (the heritage of land) exercised as God's son full earthly lordship.

Revelation has opened up a new existence, and Israel has become a political state, the most important state between Egypt in the West and Mesopotamia in the East. God dwells in this world, and the divine lordship on Zion is expressed in political power. The cult of the divine state on Zion brings this before the eyes of all the world. Israel's full exercise of power in history, moreover, leads to participation in all the fullness of the human culture of the time. Just as all cultic hymns must be traced back to David, so must all science and wisdom be traced to Solomon. Israel was now a participant in all the riches and splendor of human culture.

But the disclosure of what life is went further and led deeper. Israel, unable to conform to the life of the world, fell into poverty and impotence, and when by the Assyrian conquest the first great empire in history was established, an overwhelming transformation took place. In the prophetic movement revelation destroyed the primacy of life in the world by pronouncing judgment on the existing forms of state, law, and cult, all that was merely external and collective. In their passing through judgment, what is real and true was revealed, the truth that lives beyond what is present to our senses, that is, responsible, conscious acceptance of the revelation. The result of this judgment is the so-called deuteronomic tradition.

Out of the prophetic proclamation came the law that brought each individual to a life decision, which demands total commitment of the self, of all one's heart and soul. Corresponding to this newly achieved consciousness is the comprehensive collection of traditions in the history of revelation, the deuteronomic combination of the ancient historical traditions of J and E, and the creation of the so-called deuteronomic history. It is possible to say that the deuteronomic movement produced the basis of the Bible. Each individual was to be made aware of the revelation, and the head of the house had to teach it to his family. The revelation became doctrine.

The process by which revelation became law was not completed in the deuteronomic law. The final destruction of the state of Judah, the destruction of the Temple, the painful experience of the exile resulted in that concept of law which in the symbolism of the cult sought to make the worshiper aware of all of creation, all history, including the transcendence of being, and sought to establish fellowship with God through atonement. Only in a final, total commitment of life is the holiness of God revealed. Just as Deuteronomy presents law under the aspect of action, the priestly code presents it under the aspect of being.

With the priestly code the transmission process of the legal material was complete, and through its combination with Deuteronomy and the older materials the Torah became the Pentateuch. In postexilic Judah, that small province in the Persian empire, the first part of the Bible attained canonical status. What did this mean? Ezra assembled everyone who could understand—men and women, clean and unclean—not in the Temple, but in the great square at the water gate in front of the Temple. Ezra stood on a platform, he opened the book, and all the people rose. Ezra praised God, and all the people answered, "Amen, amen," and prayed to God. After this solemn liturgical beginning, Ezra read aloud from the book of the law and explained its meaning, so that what was read could be understood (Neh. 8). Becoming canonical is the liturgical event of the proclamation of the word. Here arose the form of worship characterized by reading the word and by a sermon, which has continued to our own day. From its beginning, the Bible has been a book used in worship.

Basically, by the time of Ezra the outline of the prophetic tradition had already been established. It found final expression in especially rich manner in the Isaianic stream of tradition already discussed above, in the Jeremiah traditions in keeping with the Deuteronomic tradition, in Ezekiel, in keeping with the priestly traditions, and in smaller collections. But from the time of the first apocalypse in Zechariah's night visions on, the final stage of prophecy underwent a transformation to apocalyptic, the revelation of the end of time, of the final goal of the eternal kingdom of God, when all power that opposes God will be swept aside in the new creation, and Israel, now including all mankind, will attain in the heavenly Zion final communion with God. This final historical perspective of revelation was included in the formation of the prophetic tradition, before it came to an end in the third century B.C., and as a second part of the canon was placed alongside the first to provide historical instruction and guidance.

As early as the Persian period the scholarly understanding of the world-order in Israel's wisdom literature had been transformed into experience of transcendence: wisdom became theology. The eternal nature of God's fellowship with the human "I" was recognized, and this in turn had great influence on the spirituality of the Psalms. Transcendence was recognized as a feature of creation which was identical with the revealed law. The personification of wisdom, placed before creation as pre-existent and seen as the son of God, reigning with him (Prov. 8:22-31) was the eternal Logos, who in God's revelation took up his dwelling on Zion (Sir. 24:1ff.).

Just as the Torah became wisdom literature, so also the apocalyptic which had developed out of prophecy took on the character of wisdom. In messianic terms, the concept of the son of God developed into that of a martyr on the one hand (Zech. 13:7-9), and on the other into the concept of the transcendent son of man who presides at the final judgment and brings about the consummation of the world. The end of the Old Testament took place in grandiose fashion, formally in the flowing together of all three great streams of tradition—Torah, prophetic apocalyptic, and wisdom, and in terms of content in the presenting of all those concepts which constitute the many-sided Christology of the New Testament, which is no less than the theology of the Old Testament, which gave expression to the events of the New Testament. The fullness of time had come.

Jesus of Nazareth entered into that historical realm which had been prepared by the history of revelation, and he accomplished in his life the messianic establishment of the kingdom of God. The proclamation of the Good News, the miracles of healing and the forgiving of sins, his associating with sinners and his establishing of peace and reconciliation, the revelation of what was hidden and the final proclamation of the Torah, the choosing of the twelve as representatives of the true Israel and the crossing the boundary between Israel and the heathen—this is what the New Testament interprets as the new aeon. This activity in full responsibility before God, in the acceptance of God's promises, had as its answer the sentence of death that is pronounced on all humanity, announced here by the high priest Caiaphas and the Roman prefect Pontius Pilate.

In this most evil, shameful, painful death of the true Messiah, in this prototypical suffering, however, the great turning point was reached. In the death of Christ the final depths of human existence were plumbed, and that which is holy is united with the most extreme suffering of death. Through this death of the son of God, the light of a new creation shines forth. According to the New Testament then, the *telos* is reached, the path of revelation is at its end. The so-called Old Testament is completed by the events of the New Testament; it is brought to its goal.

Two phenomena of the Old Testament, which has been brought to completion in this manner, must be looked at here:

1. There is no absolute, fixed limit of the third part of the canon. The rapid conclusion brought about by the events of the New Testament overtook the maturation process of tradition history. The early church acted appropriately when it remained content with an approximate limit. When we look at the New Testament, the Apocalypse of Enoch is really a part of Scripture, because it is not only alluded to, but in Jude 14-15 it is cited as holy Scripture. But the fullness of apocalyptic tradition is included in the New Testament Apocalypse of John. In the latest writings of the third part of the canon there was at least a partial Christian textual redaction. Nothing shows better that a unified tradition process encompasses both Old and New Testaments than the fact that, at the end of the Old Testament, tradition history and canonical history overlap.

2. With one voice the early church taught the inspiration of the pre-Christian Greek translation of the Old Testament, the Septuagint, to a degree scarcely accepted today even by the Roman Catholic church. Even though this verdict of the early church is not binding on us today, we should still pay attention to it. What lies behind it? Not primarily the disputes with the Jews, but the frequent adoption of the Old Testament by the New in the form found in the Septuagint, or in a similar form. Did the inspired New Testament fall victim to a false translation? No, at least since the discovery of the Qumran texts we know that the text of the Old Testament had not yet taken on a final and fixed form at the time of the New Testament. Several textual traditions could still exist side by side, and the Septuagint is witness to a highly respectable form of the text. The Masoretic text of the Jewish redaction after A.D. 70 represents the quite specific choice of a textual tradition and not simply the "original" text. For example, the book of Jeremiah in the Septuagint is about one-eighth shorter, and therefore preserves an older form from tradition history. Even in the history of the text, there is no break between the Old and the New Testaments.

The New Testament is the apostolic witness to the *telos* of revelation history. The concept of "apostle" presupposes the final event of the resurrection in that an apostle, as a witness to the resurrection, has verified the resurrection, and has met the risen One. (Paul's apostleship was based on his corresponding experience on the road to Damascus.) In terms of tradition history, the New Testament is the product of the apostolic tradition, naturally not in the sense of the modern concept of authorship, but in the sense of the biblical concept of tradition. (Cf. 2 Peter 3:2, where the *apostolic* New Testament is placed alongside the *prophetic* Old Testament, including Moses.) The apostolic tradition does not consist in the words accidentally spoken or written by an apostle, but in the total effect of his apostolic testimony. Thus the Gospel of John is to be understood as the witness of the apostle as finally composed by the Johannine school.

The extremely rich gospel tradition was limited by the early church in this sense to four gospels, and it is highly significant that the church did not produce a composite gospel but retained the four-fold gospel, which reflects the living process of transmission, and includes an especially early form, the Gospel of Mark, even though it served as the basis for the Gospel of Matthew on the one hand, which adopted fully the Old Testament tradition, and the Gospel of Luke on the other hand, which was written for Gentile Christians who were not so much at home with the details of the Old Testament. Luke consistently described the path of the gospel to the center of the inhabited world, Rome, and the Apocalypse of John, bringing the whole of Old Testament apocalyptic to its goal, pursued the road to the end of time.

The New Testament contains in addition only the Pauline corpus and the epistles of the apostolic "pillars," as Paul called them once (Gal. 2:9, Jude is the brother of James), which are late in tradition history. The exception is the second letter of Peter, which hardly is the product of even a distinct Petrine tradition. It looks back at the New Testament (1:19-21; 3:15-16). It is the seal of the whole, and the fact that this conclusion appears under the name of the foremost apostle Peter and is presented as his will and testament (1:12-15) is fully in keeping with the truth of tradition history: the New Testament is the *apostolic* testimony.

Here we have a conclusion and a boundary. All subsequent church tradition, no matter how much it was the work of the Holy Spirit, and no matter how highly it is prized, lies basically on another plain. The biblical history of tradition has reached its end, because the New Testament claims that the history of revelation attained its goal in the death and resurrection of Jesus.

Let us sum up this discussion of the biblical understanding of Scripture. We have seen that the Scripture is historic in nature and that it understands itself as the testimony to the history of revelaion as it developed in the living process of tradition history. And this lively form is truly the Scripture's own, no matter how much trouble our un-reason has with it. True, the Scripture is doctrine, but it is much more than a timeless book of doctrine. True, the Scripture serves for our edification, but not if we try to peel off the historical shell from the edifying kernel. Only a sense of Scripture that accepts its character as history and as revelation history opens up the full meaning of Scripture, and in each individual word of Scripture the perspective of the total way of God is present as a part of an organic whole.

In the light of tradition history, it is nonsensical to try to find a so-called canon within the canon, a concept that completely contradicts the essence of the canon. Quite apart from the fact that any such choice involves one-sided theological presuppositions, it is a misunderstanding of the historical character of the Bible, which is contained in the *history* of revelation, the process in which truth unfolds. It confers an absolute character on traditions that demand to be understood only in the most intimate relationships with and dependence on other traditions.

Nor does a fundamentalist understanding of Scripture do justice to the Bible. Without a sensitivity to the scriptural modes of thought in terms of tradition history it is easy to carry biblical traditions and points of view over into the world of a limited understanding of reality as merely so-called facts. Then all one can do with the Prophet Jonah's whale is try to determine its zoological species, while the scarcely perceptible depths of ultimate human insights are lost to view, and what the New Testament meant by the "sign of the prophet Jonah" is no longer visible.

Those who want to be critical overlook in an uncritical manner the manifold connections of every part with every other in the organic witness of the Bible. And those who want to be especially "believing" run the danger of no longer seeing the depths of biblical faith and insight which transcend the world of "facts." We must take care not to obscure the biblical witness in either of these ways. We want to preserve the fullness and depth of the Bible and to be open to its totality and mystery.

II

Death in the Old Testament

HISTORICAL OBSERVATIONS ARE MORE IN DISPUTE TODAY than ever. And when we are concerned with human affairs, someone usually questions whether historical knowledge and insights can give us valid answers. The people of the Old Testament are basically different from us in every respect. Their thoughts and language, their feelings, their psychic makeup, their collective life and much more separates them from us who are living today. Is it possible for ideas handed down to us from those who had such a different mentality to be of significant value?

I want to begin with a brief examination of this basic question because it is the custom today to cast doubt on the value of historical knowledge. But it seems to me that it is precisely this belittling and rejecting of historical knowledge that represents a very unmodern, non-contemporary attitude. Paradoxically enough, modern persons are confronted to an astounding degree by the possibility of historical knowledge. This is due less to the refinement of scientific techniques than to the inner alienation, estrangement, and freedom from tradition of those who feel the historical distance so keenly. It seems to be the case that our present-day possibility of attaining historical knowledge is the equivalent of the direct passing down of intellectual values in earlier times. This would mean that if we do not expand our present consciousness—which to a crucial extent has become devoid of content—to encompass the general consciousness of humanity we will fail to accomplish one of the decisive tasks confronting the modern world.

Inner historical knowledge corresponds to the lost traditions, and this is also true of our contact with the Bible. What was simply given through tradition in earlier times we must deliberately work out. Anyone who thinks it is possible to avoid doing so is thoroughly mistaken about our present situation and fails to see that the demand for freedom from and independence of tradition is the specific, historical result of tradition. For this reason we cannot rest content with evaluating the nature and reality of death in terms of supposedly modern intellectual reactions, but must incorporate into our knowledge the experience of this reality that has been handed down to us from the past, even though, or rather precisely because it has been gained in such varied ways.

These are general considerations and are not specifically theological. But when we remember that Christian theology stands or falls by its relation to the biblical tradition, then we can see in this necessity of being in relation, in this identity of objective and historical relationships, the pattern for what is today more important than ever—that in our experience of life we do not remain in the narrowly circumscribed circle of dull (and today often anxiety-ridden) experience. Rather we must learn to listen and to make the message of the biblical witnesses a part of our consciousness. It will not do for theology, in a too narrowly understood missionary zeal, to restrict itself to what seems to fit within the limited horizon of our self-styled modern contemporaries and declare superfluous and outmoded anything from our tradition that doesn't fit within those limits. For the possibility of narrowing our horizon to the point of blindness is real, and in this process truth would be lost. Confronting the biblical message can only result in a broadening of our consciousness, a liberation from the narrowness and stuffiness of our experience of life. The truth makes us free. This is why people seek the truth, but cannot force the truth to fit human standards. I hope that the following discussion will demonstrate how historical and objective understanding belong together.

Assumptions: Mythical Thought and the Old Testament

The people of early antiquity, including those of the early parts of the Old Testament, belonged to a collective whole, an extended family, or a kinship structure, in a manner that we can scarcely imagine. The social structures that supported life were based on kinship structures, which, even when they were artificial, were felt to be real, organic, natural, and not in any sense artificial. The feeling of identity of the thinking, acting individual is largely rooted in the familiar community, the clan or tribe, which is the comprehensive unit which thrives or perishes. The individual was so embedded in collective life that it is necessary to say that the group was the primary unit of life, and the individual could be so thought of only in a derived sense.

The problem of death, which is always the death of an individual, existed therefore in a different and apparently very attenuated form. The individual's close relationship to the family continued even after death, and in some ways was even increased by death. As an organism the extended family exists by virtue of the children proceeding from their parents, and is expressed in veneration of parents, who in turn are children who venerate their parents, so that reverence and awe are concentrated on the dead ancestors all the way back to the original parents from whom the living are descended.

To be placed in the family grave, that is, to return to one's ancestors (Lazarus rests in Abraham's bosom, Luke 16:22) is not only a comfort at death, but in the relation of the individual to the group it is the goal of the individual's life, in which the final refuge is reached. Much worse than death therefore is burial in "foreign soil" (cf. Amos 7:17). Through burial in the family tomb the individual returns to the great collective from which he or she came, as a child returns to its mother. The burial cave becomes the great mother, and Job can say, "Naked came I from my mother's womb, and naked shall I return" (1:21). We are familiar with the prehistoric graves that show that early humans felt the necessity of artificially placing the corpse in the fetal position so that the body would show the spiritual event of the return to the pre-natal state.

In addition, the life of a community in a land can only be established by a grave. This explains the great significance of the acquisition of the cave of Machpelah as hereditary grave (Gen. 23) for all those who are descendants of Abraham and Sarah, the great mother. Already in this act the basis is established for possession of the land, the gift of Palestine as a part of salvation history. It is possible to imagine a conflict with the original conception of God's gift of the land in the historical events of the exodus from Egypt and the occupation of the land, as described in the so-called tradition of the conquest and settlement. It might seem so to our restricted way of thinking but not for the formation of the biblical tradition.

In Genesis 50 we read about how the great funeral of Jacob, the eponymous hero of Israel, was performed in reverse analogy to the exodus. All the Egyptian court and the army of chariots and horsemen accompanied the deceased to the Holy Land. This becomes a symbol in reverse of the exodus, but in an anticipation that corresponds to the truth. Life in the land first became possible through a grave; through a grave the group put down roots in the land. The grave is the maternal origin and the final refuge. All this may seem quite foreign to us, but at the deepest level it is not foreign at all. Depth psychology has made us aware of psychic levels that go back to that human existence of the distant past. We must pay attention to them, for they are a part of us, and only when we care for them properly do we remain mentally healthy.

Another point. The ancient mind did not share our biological concept of life. We divide the world into the dead realm of minerals and the living realm of plants, animals, and humans. But the ancient world had an animistic view of life, of the "spiritual" world, so that the dead world includes stones and plants, and the living world animals and humans. The one divine power of life, the breath of the spirit, is at work in every living individual. Life is more alive than our life, and what is dead is not so dead as our "dead." Life is always whole and healthy, and the severely ill person has already entered the sphere where death is at work, the underworld.

According to this way of thinking a dead person is never thought of as nonexistent, but rather has entered a non-living existence that is under and behind the living existence, with its creative power. The dead person exists in the uncreated (chaos) existence of the depths, which is at the basis of all life. Desecration of a corpse is much worse than death, because in it the integrity of the dead person is disrupted in an external, though not in a deeper sense. The one who dies returns to the origin of things, but he is not nonexistent.

For mythological thought this underworld of death and of origins becomes the basis of the world of life as the overworld. In this way there arises a distinctively transcendent concept of a realm beyond, from which all life comes and in which it ends, while the overworld is under the lordship of the cosmic gods of light, in contrast to the dark womb of the depths. Being is thus dependent on this prior being, is surrounded by it, and finds in it its beginning and end.

The secret and unfathomable power of the depths demands its own cultic institutions. At least one particular cult should be mentioned here, that wide-spread substratum of mythical religion, the cult of heroes, that is the worship at the graves of primordial men, the final projection of the line of ancestors, the heroes of ancient times, whose human bodies contained divine powers. These powers that had once been possessed by humans secure for those born later the possibility of life, space in the land, and protection of life. In the cult it is possible to come into contact with, or at least secure the saving effects of these possessors of the greatest fullness of life (cf. their designation as *rephaim,* i.e., "healers") and bravery *(nephilim,* "fallen [heroes]"), of the ideals of the highest and strongest efficacy of human life. The Old Testament knows of such traditions, but its relation to God does not leave room for a cult of heroes any more than it leaves room for idolatry.

This way that primitive societies had of understanding human existence, so different from our concepts and so foreign in the way it viewed death, by no means ignored the problem of the death of the individual. Because of the individual's strong sense of security in the extended family that lives on without dying, we would expect a lessening of the problematical nature of death. Nevertheless the ancient myths show us that death, the cessation of one's participation in the cosmos of light and order, was felt as *the* central problem of human existence, as the basic anthropological fact that does not fully correspond to the order of the cosmos.

The myths contain a wealth of examples of how certain people who were close to the essentially divine attribute, immortality, missed the chance to attain this immortality. The oldest extant great epic of humankind, the Gilgamesh Epic, has the quest for eternal life as its theme. Gilgamesh had the plant of life in his hands, but it was stolen from him by a serpent, while he, worn out by his wanderings, washed in the waters of the deep.

The Adapa Epic tells us that Adapa, the wise and pious man, the example for everyone, was supposed to obtain immortality. But when he was taken into the heavenly assembly he declined to eat the bread of life that was set before him or to drink the water of life, because, having been deceived by Ea, the god of wisdom and abyss, he feared that he would be poisoned.

Aqhat, the royal hero of an ancient Syrian epic, rejected the offer of the goddess Anat, the Syrian Athene, to grant him immortality in exchange for his all-conquering bow, because, like Adapa, he was unable to trust this offer.

> What does a man have at the end?
> What does he have at last?
> White hair covers my head;
> my pate turns gray.
> And I will die the death of all men,
> yes, I will certainly die.

According to this mythological view of humanity, humans are always shut off from eternal life in a tragic manner, foreign to their nature, and contradictory of the deeper, ideal order of things. In the myths humans have a tragic view of life. They see themselves as caught in a deep conflict. By their consciousness they share in the cosmic order and thus in the sphere of the immortal gods of the world of light, but with their earthly bodies they are subject to death. In myth this concept can be expressed quite crassly by etiologies that tell that death originated by accident and that the person was deceived into becoming a victim—so contrary does death seem to the order of creation.

The wife given to the first man, if we reconstruct the pre-Israelite tradition that lies behind Genesis 3, acting in ignorance of the order of creation, gave the man the forbidden fruit, by which he gained his consciousness (knowledge of good and evil, that is, complete, total knowledge), but by so doing he brought death on himself, because it is only in respect to self-consciousness that humans experience death. In the Greek myth of Epimetheus and Pandora we still find an echo of this tradition, even though here it is not a question of death but of all the sufferings of life.

The Old Testament did not shove to one side the experience of existence gained by early humans. This mythological tradition is no fantasy, but a bitterly serious experience, even though expressed in the categories of early human thought. We incorrectly regard these categories as childish, because in childhood we repeat mythical stages of consciousness. The Old Testament adopted the being and consciousness of early cultures but redirected them in their essential elements. We can say that the truth of this experience of being came then to be fully perceived for the first time.

The woman who was man's counterpart, not a stranger, but a part of himself, knew very well what she was doing. It is expressly stated that she knew the prohibition. So the man is not confronted by some external desire, but by a temptation in the center of his being. "The woman saw that the tree was good for food (physical desires), and that it was a delight to the eyes (emotional desires), and that the tree was to be desired to make one wise (intellectual desires)" (Gen. 3:6). It is the intellectual dimension that brings the decisive temptation. It speaks to the morality at the center of the self, our highest nature.

Moreover, Adam was not taken by surprise; it is stressed that he was present. It becomes clear then that the origin of human death is not a tragic event, not an unfortunate disturbance of the order of things, but a human decision, human will, the essence of human desire, that is, to participate in the world of divine consciousness, even though it is not appropriate for the human as an earthly being to do so. People contain within themselves the dreadful conflict; it is not a misfortune imposed on them from outside.

That is to say, in the Old Testament, people identify with themselves and recognize the apparent "error" in the world order—death—as something within themselves, as guilt.

A supplement to the so-called story of the fall (Gen. 3:22-24) shows that the exclusion of Adam and Eve from access to the tree of life, of which the myth of Gilgamesh had so much to say, is not to be traced back to some human misfortune, but to the will of God himself. The man and woman are directed by God out of the despair of their longing for immortality in paradise back into their earthly fate, that is, the realm of history where God's saving will is at work.

The same supplementer also portrayed in Genesis 6:1-4 the fact that human access to eternal powers by way of a chthonic culture at the graves of legendary heroes is contrary to God's will. The heroes born of marriages with angels are humans subject to the ordinance of human death. The human longing and striving for salvation cannot be satisfied in the mythic experience of life through the cult of either heavenly or subterranean powers. People are directed to God, that is, in contrast to the mythological concept of God, to the God who has revealed not only some ordinances and commands, but *himself* in relationship to his human counterparts. The biblical revelation brings humans to themselves in that each one is called to be a "Thou" to the revelation of the divine "I."

Three Stages of the Old Testament in Relation to Death

1. *Deliverance from Death*

The Yahweh revelation as seen in its central feature in the Old Testament tradition as revelation at Sinai is directed toward a collective, even "international" counterpart which bears the name "Israel" ("God is the Ruler"). It is the personal revelation of God to the collective entity Israel, or to its representative, Moses. As the personal revelation of God it is by nature exclusive. The exclusivity of God is also the exclusivity of Israel, because it is a revelation in the relationship of an "I" to a "Thou." Because this revelation of God is directed toward Israel as a collective entity, the individual participates in it, not as an individual, but as a member of Israel. This corresponds precisely to the individual's security in the collective whole in the thought structures of that time.

For this reason, the problem of death, which is always an individual problem, is not directly touched on in the Yahweh revelation. And yet a significant turning point has been reached; it has been called the desacralizing of the realm of death. It is a contradiction in the Yahweh revelation (which in the I-Thou relation of Yahweh to Israel takes place in the realm of human life and consciousness) that it directly includes the human condition of unconsciousness and death. Yahweh is not a God of the dead. Any confusion with the primeval power that is opposed to the cosmos and to life is excluded. Since God's revelation is exclusive and demands total commitment, any relationship to the powers of death and destruction is impossible.

This means that Israel was strictly forbidden to offer sacrifices to the dead or participate in ceremonies that expressed or enacted in any way recognition of or service to these powers. Surprisingly enough this did not lead to the disappearance of ceremonies of mourning for the dead. At the center of these ceremonies was the dead person, not the survivors. They were largely sympathetic ceremonies that expressed a becoming like the dead. Just as the dead person is returned to the earth, so the bereaved sat on the earth, placed dust on their heads or rolled in the dust. They fasted and mortified their body. They beat their breasts and tore their clothes, which represented the physical shell, because the body of the dead was now given up to decay. The funeral lament bewailed the painful solidarity with the dead. The grave was not just any trench, but the carefully prepared dwelling of the dead, whenever possible, of course, a family grave.

We should note, however, that in the course of history the drive toward individualism became stronger and finally culminated in the individual, permanent reburial of the undecomposed bones in an ossuary. Gifts placed in the grave are not to be explained in terms of fantastic concepts of a continuing physical life of the dead but as expressions of the full form of life led by the one who had died and of the desire to commit the dead person to the earth as unharmed as possible, clad in festive clothing and ornaments, that is to say, in his or her highest, most honored form. After the period of mourning, they would break the bread of comfort, would extend the cup of comfort to the especially grief-stricken immediate survivors, who were led in this manner back into life, and would exchange presents. All this is called "practicing *ḥesed*" (kindness). Not to observe these mourning customs is to deprive the people of peace and well-being (Jer. 16:5).

It is not at all a question of placing limits on the world of death and the dead. It would be a mistake to understand desacralization in modern terms. Its concern is rather to avoid any confusion of the relationship of Yahweh and Israel with the world of the dead, since it is characterized by life and consciousness, and also to avoid abandoning to mythological powers the world of the dead, separated as it is from the conscious relationship of Yahweh to Israel. Mythological religion divided the world into cosmos and chaos, into the realms of the living and the dead, and the anti-Zeus of Hades corresponded to the cosmic Zeus. The world of the dead also belongs to Yahweh, and he has power over the dead, but they are not involved in his revelation, because God is not a god of the underworld; wherever he is, there is life. The dead belong to Yahweh and cannot fall prey to ungodly, chthonic powers, but they are no longer in any relationship to God's revelation. Therefore the Psalmist can lament,

> Dost thou work wonders for the dead?
> Do the shades rise up to praise thee?
> Is thy steadfast love declared in the grave
> or the faithfulness in Abaddon?
> Are thy wonders known in the darkness,
> or thy saving help in the land of forgetfulness?
> (Ps. 88:10-12)

On the one hand this desacralization, this elimination of any independent power of death alongside God, and on the other, this exclusion from God's revelation must seem strange to us. Does this mean that death as a fundamental human problem fades into the background? People do not obtain total security in the collective community, and it is not only those who are old and tired of living who die. The experience of suffering and danger includes more than death, and there are situations in which the dead and the unborn are considered fortunate (Jer. 20:14ff.; Job 3; Eccles. 4:2f.). The Israelites knew that suicide was a human possibility, which is conceivable in certain situations, not only for a soldier like Saul or a prisoner like Samson, but also for a sage who knows in advance that he has forfeited his life, and now has only to put his house in order and be gathered to his ancestor's grave (2 Sam. 17:23). The Old Testament did not exclude this "stoic" aspect. But those are extreme cases. What of the normal threat of death that all must face? What is the relation of the dying person to God?

In the Old Testament we have a wealth of examples in the Psalter and elsewhere of prayers to God by those deathly sick and of laments of the individual, which bring clearly before our eyes situations of great danger. Ancient thought patterns were characterized by a very subjective concept of the boundary between life and death. The seriously ill person whose life force is severely diminished by disease regards himself realistically as being in the sphere of Hades. It is not that a person must die because of being sick; a person becomes sick because of being about to die, and thus has entered the realm of Hades.

> The cords of death encompassed me,
>   the torrents of perdition assailed me;
> the cords of Sheol entangled me,
>   the snares of death confronted me.
>
> (Ps. 18:4-5)

Or in another passage:

> I am reckoned among those who go down to the Pit;
>   I am a man who has no strength,
> like one forsaken among the dead,
>   like the slain that lie in the grave,
> like those whom thou dost remember no more,
>   for they are cut off from thy hand.
> Thou has put me in the depths of the Pit,
>   in the regions dark and deep.

> Thy wrath lies heavy upon me,
>> and thou dost overwhelm me with all thy waves.
>> (Ps. 88:4-7)

In a life-threatening situation the Israelite could turn only to the God of life. Resignation and surrender to death are apparently quite rare and seem in any case to be limited by the threatening consequence of separation from the revelation of Yahweh.

It is theologically important for us to see how in the Psalms of the individual, the individual becomes a symbol of Israel. Theological statements that are really applicable to Israel are applied to the individual. But the Israel that lives on is not concerned with the problem of individual death.

> The dead do not praise the Lord,
>> nor do any that go down into silence.
> But we will bless the Lord
>> from this time forth and for evermore.
>> (Ps. 115:17f.)

Yahweh is the God of life, and there is well-being or salvation only in the realm of life, in the realm of revelation and consciousness. For anyone who is critically ill, who is confronted by death, there is only one possibility for salvation—to be called back into this world of life, to share in Israel's existence, for there is no salvation in death.

Naturally there were many situations in which these prayers were not spoken in vain. In Hannah's song the one sick to death returned to health and experienced that

> The Lord kills and brings to life;
>> he brings down to Sheol and raises up.
>> (1 Sam. 2:6)

The deliverance from death which was experienced in the everyday life of Israel was not some fantastic exaggeration, but merely the obvious perception that the sickness left, because life returned, that creative powers flowed to the convalescent, that a genuine deliverance took place. In terms of individual experience then it was an accurate description of God when he was portrayed in Hannah's song as the one who kills and who makes alive.

> See now that I, even I, am he,
>   and there is no god beside me;
> I kill and I make alive;
>   I wound and I heal;
>   and there is none that can deliver out of my hand.
>
>   (Deut. 32:39)

Confessional statements such as this give expression to divine omnipotence. We can also understand how in the portrayal of God's saving acts through the "Servant of God" a special role is assigned to the miracle of raising from death. There are good reasons why such a miracle is reported as having been performed by the two prophets Elijah and Elisha. The totality of human life is brought by the "Servant" into the realm of God's transcendent activity. Each account takes pains to show how as an exception the sentence of death announced by God has been suspended.

But no matter how clearly the new life given to the sick was understood as God's radical action on behalf of an individual in Israel, we must regard it as highly unusual and specifically Israelite that humans in their experience of death, in their most extreme crisis of existence, relied on the God of life, the creator of all life, the founder and savior of Israel, who cannot be the God of the dead. As persons stand before the sacral vacuum of the realm of death they are kept from despair, from surrender to death, from entering the next life of mythological concepts. This results in a decisive ontological step forward in revelation. The Israelite is led to find true transcendence in the realm of his consciousness of belonging to Yahweh, the Lord of life, the life-giving spirit, that is, in a realm that exists independently of his physical existence and in which he can participate independently of that physical existence, because his "I" has entered into the relationship between God and Israel.

2. Eternal Life

In which realm of the Old Testament traditions do we first encounter this experience of transcendence through the participation of the self in a life beyond physical existence? It would have to be a realm in which the individual plays a vital role and in which an ontological spiritualization of this sort is possible. It begins in the area known as "Wisdom," and then moves on into the entire realm of personal piety, especially the Psalms.

We are to understand "Wisdom" as the early form of science. From a certain stage of culture onward this intellectual movement is found in every ancient civilization and was adopted as a matter of course in Israel also, specifically in the context of Israel's participation in the ancient Near Eastern culture at the time of Solomon. This early form of science took the entire world as its subject matter and explored its institutions, but in particular the study of humankind. In Wisdom sayings the results of life experiences are collected, and the order that is found in thousands of aspects of life defines the life of the wise man, who practices the discipline of submission to that order.

Although Wisdom was inevitably international in character and although this essentially rational control of the world was free from mythical and cultural religiosity (which always derives from natural traditions), it still took on a typically Israelite form. The Israelite experience, determined as it was by the experience with God, produced characteristic alterations. The Israelite transformation began in the late development of Wisdom, in theologizing. The early form of sciences, philosophy, of necessity led in Israel to a strong theological tradition, the significance of which has not yet been sufficiently evaluated. In the Book of Job, Israel confronted the ancient Near Eastern wisdom in a distinctive way, and here we can see the emergence of a new ontological structure, the discovery of a new, transcendental existence.

Job is confronted by his three friends. They represent the old way of thinking, the old experience of existence, that piety and well-being are directly related, that there is a connection between actions and consequences. Humans must submit in every respect to the divine order, and human suffering must be traceable to human sin, if not known sin, then unknown. Only confession of sin, that is, acceptance of the suffering as deserved can bring salvation and deliverance. However correct this old view may basically be, it does

not fit Job's case. From the outset he stands under Satan's accusation that he does not serve God for naught and his life should be
God's proof that the opposite is true, but his concern is not for
a happy life but for a right relationship with God. In his dire situation he cannot plead, as his friends urge, for a restoration of his
former good life, but rather he wishes for death. He has only one
request, a demand—that his relationship with God be recognized.
He does not want to be rejected by God. The new understanding of
piety is absolute, not tied up with human well-being. It is based on
a personal relationship to God that can bring the infinite God together with a worthless human by the concept of justification. In
the ultimate darkness of his experience of existence, Job knows that
he must have a *divine* advocate who can confront the *Deus abscondi-
tus* (Job 16:18-21). He struggles through to faith in his divine
"redeemer," who is there for him, even though the form of his
physical existence perishes.

> For I know that my Redeemer lives,
>   and at last he will stand upon the earth;
> and after my skin has been thus destroyed,
>   then from my flesh I shall see God,
> whom I shall see on my side,
>   and my eyes shall behold, and not another.
> My heart faints within me!

> (Job 19:25-27)

We cannot here consider subsequent developments: how in the
visions of God this anomaly in the concept of God is removed, how
Job experiences justification in his confession ("but now my eye
sees thee," 42:5 refers to the passage cited above), how God over
against Satan is shown to be in the right not only in what concerns
Job but also in reference to God's gracious, saving gifts, without
which human beings would not be able to survive. We can be sure
that in the theological wisdom of the Persian era, from which the
Book of Job comes, there was an experiencing of a transcendent
realm, the knowledge that a transcendence which goes far beyond
our physical existence corresponds to our personal relationship to
God.

The statements in Job 19:25-27, which mark this tremendous

transcendent advance, are found also in similar wording in Psalm
73, a Wisdom Psalm, which dates from the same period and also
deals with the so-called theodicy question. Here in vv. 23-26, after
the Psalmist has realized that his earlier dilemma and doubt were
stupid ("I was stupid and ignorant, I was like a beast toward thee"
v. 22), so that his new insight is experienced as a gift of a new
consciousness, we read,

> Nevertheless I am continually with thee;
>   thou dost hold my right hand;
> Thou dost guide me with thy counsel,
>   and afterward thou wilt receive me to glory.
> Whom have I in heaven but thee?
>   And there is nothing upon earth that I desire
>   besides thee.
> My flesh and my heart may fail,
>   but God is the strength of my heart
>   and my portion[1] for ever.

These are not isolated statements in the Old Testament, and
especially not in the Psalms. Here there has been a breakthrough that
is decisive for the history of revelations. It is the goal, the fruit of
the prayer of the one who is dying, as he struggles to find his portion
in Yahweh, the source of life. An entirely new mode of expression
grew out of the new theology, this new existence that transcends
ontology, expression that describes the transcendent fellowship of
the individual with God. Let us look at some examples.

In Psalm 73:24 we read "and afterward thou wilt receive me
to glory *(kabōd)*." Similarly, Psalm 49:15, after speaking of the
destruction of the human person in Sheol says, "But God will ransom my soul from the power of Sheol, for he will receive me." This
term "receive" (RSV "took") is used in Genesis 5:24 for the
translation of Enoch. But the primary passage where we encounter
it is the ascension of Elijah (2 Kings 2), where it is used in vv. 3,
5, 9, 10. The Elijah and Elisha traditions are distinguished by a

---

[1] Literally: "the rock of my heart and my portion of the land." "Rock" is
a metaphor for a permanent base, while "heart" designates the spiritual
center of the person. The assigned portion of the land as basis for the life
of the farmer can become a metaphor for one's share in life, one's destiny.

tendency to spiritualize. Israel is no longer identical with the nation, the state of Israel. One belongs to Israel only by a confession of Yahweh. God does not reveal himself in the elements of the old Sinai epiphany, but in an almost inaudible word. Neither is God limited to appearing at Sinai (or Horeb), or in one specific manner (cf. 1 Kings 19:9). Rather God's revelation is fully present in the word of his prophetic servant.

The numerous miracle stories are not intended to honor a widespread popular religious belief, but to express the transcendence of God in its "non-natural," supernatural expression in the struggle against the religion of Baal with its immanence in nature. In these accounts Elijah is portrayed as a second Moses who continues the Moses revelation in intensified form. This includes the story of the end of the prophet's life. The old accounts did not say anything about a transcendent existence of Moses after his death, but there is an attempt to move in that direction in the paradoxical observation that Moses was buried by God (Deut. 34:6). But of Elijah we are told that amid heavenly manifestations of fire and storm he was carried off by angelic hosts ("a chariot of fire and horses of fire" 2 Kings 2:11) into the realm of the transcendent. This tradition was adopted by Psalm 49:15 and 73:24 in order to formulate the expectation of eternal life in the transcendence of fellowship with God.

It should be mentioned in passing that the late traditions of Elijah brought together this seeing in him a basis for believing in eternal life and the hope of those near death for eternal life. The conclusion of the Song of Elijah in Sirach 48:1-11 says, "Blessed are those who see you (Elijah) and die (in love [?]; they will surely live" [Author's translation, based on the fragmentary Hebrew text and the ancient Greek; cf. also the Syriac]). This seems to indicate that seeing Elijah in the hour of death confers entrance to eternal life. Compare this with the condition for Elisha to be Elijah's successor, that he sees Elijah raised up in transcendence (2 Kings 2:10). This tenet of faith could result in the grotesque misunderstanding of those present at the crucifixion of Jesus, who did not recognize the fulfillment of Psalm 22, but thought he was calling in despair for Elijah (Mark 15:35), and in mockery offered him vinegar to drink (v. 36).

There are other illustrations of a new spiritual language. Psalm 25:14 says

> The close secret of Yahweh belongs to those who
> fear him,
> his covenant and also, to bring them knowledge.
> *(Jerusalem Bible)*

By "secret" (*sōd,* "secret counsel") we are to understand the highest prophetic inspiration, as it is described in Isaiah 6. In the Deuteronomic theology a true prophet is to be distinguished from a false one by the criterion of the inspiration of fellowship with the enthroned Lord (cf. Amos 3:7). Now any pious person in fellowship with God knows the mystery because this fellowship has become transcendent. Thus the old covenant can be understood in a new way. Its true knowledge brings this transcendent union with God.

The theme of Psalm 16 is safety in God. After it is stated that one's lot in life is determined by Yahweh himself and that an individual's life can be understood as a portion of land assigned by Yahweh, the course of life is subjected totally to the direction of Yahweh. The apodictic divine word has become God's counsel in terms of "Wisdom," because Yahweh's will is not only known but also understood. This insight in the Wisdom tradition brings with it a fellowship with God that goes beyond the limits of human life.

> I keep the Lord always before me;
> because he is at my right hand,
> I shall not be moved.
> Therefore my heart is glad and my soul *(kabōd)*[2]
> rejoices;
> my body also dwells secure.
> For thou dost not give me up to Sheol,
> or let thy godly one see Pit. (vv. 8-10).

---

[2] The soul can now be called *kabōd,* cf. Ps. 7:6; 30:13; 57:9; 108:2, but not Gen. 49:6 according to the consonantal text and the LXX. In the next to last line, "me" translates *nephesh* and means the individual life.

In Psalm 63 the worshiper thanks God for being permitted to see God's glory in the sanctuary. God's steadfast love is considered more than life itself (v. 3). For this reason God is to be praised in one's life and by one's life. Even in the night of misery (the profound, "poetic" understanding of night in the Psalter), the worshiper can be aware of fellowship with God and meditate on God in the watches of the night. Even here in this distress the worshiper is hidden under God's wings (which reminds us of the wings of the cherubim that protected the sanctuary). "My soul clings to thee; thy right hand upholds me" (v. 8).

Ps. 139 gives the strongest expression of fellowship with God as "being known by God." This transcends not only all the limits of space, including Sheol, but also the void when the worshiper is totally unconscious, an apparent reference to suicide.

> If I say, "Let only darkness cover me,
>   and the light about me be night,"
> even the darkness is not dark to thee,
>   the night is bright as the day;
>   for darkness is as light with thee. (vv. 11-12)

Similarly all limits of time are abolished. Even the spiritual nature of the worshiper was marvelously created though God's knowledge of the hidden world in the cosmic "beyond" known as "the depths." The future too is all determined by God. And the Psalm reaches a climax in the affirmation that there is no end to one's fellowship with God.

This theology, with its assurance of an eternal life with God found particular expression in a spiritualized concept of Zion. To be in this Zion, in God's sanctuary is to be with God.

> Even the sparrow finds a home,
>   and the swallow a nest for herself,
>   where she may lay her young,
> at thy altars, O Lord of hosts,
>   my King and my God.
> Blessed are those who dwell in thy house,
>   ever singing thy praise!
>
> (Ps. 84:3-4)

The comparison with birds has a deeper meaning than is indicated by the mere presence of birds in the sanctuary. Birds become a symbol of the soul, as in Psalm 11:1 or 102:6-7, where the soul of the dying is alluded to. The idea of a bird-soul is known in many cultures. It was an image ready at hand for designating the being that moves in the realm of the spiritual, and thus of the immaterial.

Jerusalem, the sanctuary of Zion, is the mother of all who believe. That is more than a metaphor; it is a spiritual reality. In the liturgy of the New Year festival entries are made in the spiritual register of births, God counts those who are his, and all national boundaries are eliminated.

> Among those who know me I mention Rahab
> 　and Babylon;
> behold, Philistia and Tyre, with Ethiopia—
> "This one was born there," they say.
> And of Zion it shall be said,
> "This one and that one were born in her."
> 　　　　　　　　　　　　(Ps. 87:4-5a)

Just as all souls are born from this mother, so here they are born for eternity. In place of collective security in the continuing life of the family, there is now eternal spiritual security in the sanctuary. Even to eunuchs God gives a memorial and a name in his Temple (Isa. 56:5).

These are of course theological statements that today are easily devalued, if not completely overlooked. In rejecting outmoded and abandoned idealist philosophy and adopting the modern negation of metaphysics, theology has let itself be led into neglecting this Old Testament spirituality in favor of investigating the "secular" character of the Old Testament. If on the contrary we acknowledge in the Old Testament this transcendent experience of existence in its immediacy as a stage in revelation, we will not pass over such vital biblical material in the name of alleged modernity. If so-called modern people are far removed from such experiences, they also seem to be doing their utmost to eliminate a priori through a variety of prejudgments the possibility of such experiences.

3. Resurrection

It would be a misunderstanding of the Old Testament to regard this spirituality centering on the individual as the end and goal of its theological development. The biblical revelation goes much further, attaining a universality that encompasses the world. The faith of the Bible, its hope and expectation, are not confined to the individual, or even to humanity as a whole, but they extend to the entire cosmos, culminating in the expectation of a new heaven and a new earth. Apocalyptic overcomes the final boundaries, and the goal of revelation is a new being in the new world of the kingdom of God, "the life of the world to come," the new creation of direct fellowship with God.

The origins of apocalyptic lie hidden in the period of the exile. In a magnificent vision Ezekiel saw the revivification of Israel in terms of a resurrection from death (37:1-14). This has been regarded as a metaphor for a new Israel after the political destruction of the old. What we find there, however, is not a random statement expressed in a secondary metaphor, but a vision, that is, the highest level of revelation. The content of the vision is a creation process. The "creative storm wind," blowing from the four cardinal directions, the *ruaḥ* of creation, brings about Israel's resurrection. This is not a mere restoration, but an act of creation, not creation out of the dead material of chaos, but out of the dead bones of the old Israel.

The new creation is not simply a second creation, even though greater or more perfect than the first, but it is much more, because it is creation out of the old. Here where the concept of a "new creation" is first mentioned, or better, presented to our eyes as a visionary occurrence, two possible misunderstandings are eliminated: first, that it is only a correction, repairing, or restoring of the old, and second that it is an absolutely different second creation. No, it is more, it is creation out of what was old and dead, so that it does not stand alongside the old creation but emerges through it and out of it in such a way that nothing is lost.

At the end of Old Testament apocalyptic there is a proclamation of the establishment of the kingdom on Zion as in Isaiah 25. After

the destruction of all heavenly and earthly foes of God, the glory
of God appears on Zion and fellowship with God at the great feast
includes even the physical world. Death and sorrow are destroyed
and the veil that represents distance from God in revelation, something that even Moses and Elijah experienced, is eliminated. This
is not some ideal scene, but the exact counterpart to Exodus 24.
Sinai has become the heavenly Zion, Israel has become all nations
of the world, and the sacrificial meal has become the offering of
thanksgiving, in which we can recognize the salvation history of
redemption. These are ultimate, pictorial realities that cannot be exceeded, and that fulfill the history of revelation. What does this
apocalyptic theology teach us about the death of the individual? How
does the individual participate in this goal of revelation? How is
the theology of revelation developed?

First we can call attention to a development within the exilic and
postexilic Isaiah tradition. In Second Isaiah (54:1ff.), following
on the statements of the last Suffering Servant song that the servant
(the true Israel, which is witness to Yahweh, passes through the
judgment) will see his descendants, a prophecy is given to Jerusalem, which is portrayed as a woman, that when the kingdom of God
is erected on Zion she will have many children and that her descendants will inherit the nations. This eschatological birth may be here
only a figure of speech, but it goes back to concepts of the individual finding refuge in "Mother Zion," as we saw them expressed in
Psalm 84 and 87.

The metaphor that when Yahweh comes as king, Zion will give
birth to the people of God was developed apocalyptically in Third
Isaiah (66:5ff.). All who belong to Yahweh are children of Mother
Jerusalem, and their birth takes place in the moment of the apocalyptic redemption.

This motif was employed in the Isaiah apocalypse. In the great
prayer at the time of the final judgment (Isa. 26:7ff.) the lament
is raised at the end that this birth cannot take place through human
strength:

> Like a woman with child
>   who writhes and cries out in her pangs,

> when she is near her time,
> so were we because of thee, O Lord;
> we were with child, we writhed,
> we have as it were brought forth wind.
> We have wrought no [eschatological] deliverance
> in the earth,
> and the inhabitants of the world have not fallen
> (i.e. been born in a miraculous manner). (vv. 17-18.)

An oracle of salvation replies to this lament. The crisis is interpreted in terms of the transcendent salvation that overcomes all earthly limits:

> Your dead will come to life,
> their corpses will rise;
> awake, exult,[3]
> all of you who lie in the dust,
> for your dew is a radiant dew
> and the land of ghosts will give birth.
> Go into your rooms (=graves), my people,
> shut your doors behind you (grave=Noah's ark,
>   cf. Gen. 7:16b)
> Hide yourselves in a little while
> until the wrath has passed.
> For, see, Yahweh will soon come out of his dwelling,
> to punish all the inhabitants of earth for their
>   crimes.
> The earth will reveal its blood
> and no longer hide its slain.
>   (Isa. 26:19-21 Jerusalem Bible)

The apocalyptic new birth is also the resurrection. It is the eschatological creation out of the depth of chaos, the eschatological birth that follows the judgment, just as at a later time baptism is the ritual representation of the new birth.

What the Isaiah apocalypse at the end of the fourth century B.C. still applies to the new Israel as a whole is regarded in subsequent apocalyptic in an increasingly individual manner. In the third century, Third Zechariah (12:10ff.) speaks mysteriously of the rites of mourning which are to be performed for the martyrs who fall in

---

[3] Following 1QIs^a and LXX the verbs are to be read as imperfects and translated as future tense.

the eschatological battle. The dirge is inspired by God and can be compared to the mourning for the dying and rising god Hadad-Rimmon at Megiddo. The reference to Megiddo can be explained as due to the equating of the martyrs and King Josiah, who was slain at Megiddo and for whom dirges were still sung in the time of the Chronicler (ca. 300 B.C.), and the mention of an Adonis-like deity is a hidden reference to the resurrection.

In the next century, belief in resurrection is found fully developed at the conclusion of the final vision of the Book of Daniel (12:1-4). Here there is, alongside the resurrection of the new Israel the concept of a general resurrection of all humans, some to eternal life and some to "shame and everlasting contempt." This supplements the last verse of the book of Isaiah (66:24).

To what extent is this concept of resurrection more than spiritual fellowship with God? To what extent does it represent a genuine advance in the history of revelation? Isn't it the case that the level of tradition designated above as the second stage is where the decisive step was taken, the advance to transcendence in the existence of the individual? Isn't that the reality of the completion of existence, while the apocalyptic expection is only a hope and not reality? The following observation must be made. It is not appropriate to set the factual and the futuristic in contrast to each other. The apocalyptic expectation is a promise from God, not some self-induced hope. It is the culmination of prophecy, and as we saw, it had a pronounced influence on individual piety.

In a corresponding manner the spirituality of the second stage was largely in the nature of promise. For an example of how the apocalyptic hope influenced the course of a life and in so doing marked a genuine advance beyond the second stage we can turn to Psalm 22. In this individual lament, with a supplementary song of thanks, the rescue of the individual from death becomes a comprehensive eschatological experience of salvation. The repentance of the world, the share that the dead have in God through worship, and the confession of loyalty to Yahweh for all time to come (vv. 27-31) are brought together with this deliverance from death. There is good reason for Psalm 22 to be the final words of Jesus on earth, and this means more than a cry of dereliction by one forsaken by God.[4]

But where then, in terms of the history of revelation, is the step forward from transcendence in spirituality to the apocalyptic promise. Transcendence is not a spiritual meta-space in which an individual can continue to exist after the end of his physical life, but one's proper existence, in contrast to which the existence experienced in this life seems derivative. This proper existence then must become one's total existence, that is to say, the new existence must be a new creation. If we see the Old Testament in terms of this theme as developing in three stages, we must at least glance at the conclusion and the goal, the *telos* of the process of revelation in the events of the New Testament.

The New Testament Event

The life of Jesus brought about the messianic establishment of the kingdom of God. The preaching of the gospel, the healing of the sick, the forgiving of sin, the establishing of peace, and the fulfillment of the Torah ushered in the new aeon. The boundary between Israel and the Gentiles was abolished, and the twelve apostles became the representatives of the new Israel. The sentence of death came as the response to this action in the adoption of the divine promises and in the exercise of direct authority. Only as a response to the messianic activity can this total negation be understood, this sentence of death that is pronounced on all humanity, symbolized there by the religious representative of Israel, the high priest Caiaphas, and by the political representative of the worldwide Roman empire, the Prefect Pontius Pilate.

In this most dreadful, shameful, painful death of the true Messiah, in this primeval suffering, the great turning point was reached. The death of Christ is the culmination of the final depths of human existence, the uniting of the holy One with the most extreme suffer-

---

[4] To correct what I said in my book *Vom Sinai zum Zion,* p. 194, I want to note that *palin* (Matt. 27:50) signifies, as does the Heb. ᶜod, "continuously," the continuation of the cry and not a new, second cry (cf. also Mark 15:13; John 18:40).

ings of death. And the light of the new creation breaks forth through the death of the Son of God. Thus the resurrection does not occur only when the Son of man comes to judge the world; victory over death took place here. Here we move forward from an analogy to transcendence at the end of time to true transcendence here and now. The resurrection has occurred, the breakthrough to transcendence is complete, being has swallowed up non-being, and life, death. Through his Son, God has undergone for us our death, our mortal suffering. The immeasurable gap between the infinite holiness and greatness of God on the one hand and our human depths of guilt and sin, weakness, fear, and distress, our human suffering and dying on the other, is abolished by God's coming in the one who was crucified, in the image of the deepest human shame, our own deepest shame. The Easter light of the new creation streams into our darkness, the light of the new Godlike existence.

The Christian, who in baptism has died together with his Lord, and thereby become a partaker in the new being and awaits the resurrection, lives in this world, but lives by the power of the other, new world. He suffers and dies in this world, but that is only the death of his old being. For this reason he can commit himself to the world, sacrifice himself for it. He does not need to flee from the world and neither can he be defeated by it. He can truly love, because he serves and yet seeks to win those he loves. He lives in faith and waits for the time when he will be able to see, when the day will dawn and the light of God appear.

III

The Law

I T IS CUSTOMARY TO REGARD BIBLICAL THEOLOGY as a complex
system characterized by two polar concepts. Old and New
Testaments, as the names seem to indicate, are contrasted to
each other as old and new covenant, and by their content, as law and
gospel. To be sure, a contrast between old and new covenant is valid,
but only in terms of the realization of salvation history, and it should
not be overlooked that the Old Testament talks about this new covenant that was expected, and that in the Old Testament the concept of
a new covenant is established and its content developed. Neither can
the contrast of law and gospel separate the two Testaments from
each other.

Although the concept of law is central in the Old Testament and
shaped the Old Testament as a whole, shades of difference must
be recognized in its theological significance. Even Paul, whose theology seems to draw the strongest polar contrast to law, can use
the concept of law in a positive sense. When in Romans 8:2 he
says that "the law of the Spirit of life in Christ Jesus" brings
freedom "from the law of sin and death," the ambivalence of the
concept of law may be largely a rhetorical device. But in Romans
13:8-10 he speaks of fulfilling the law through love and cites the
decalogue (Lev. 19:18; Exod. 20:13-17, or Deut. 5:17-21), indicating that it is possible for him—at least when he employs older traditions—to use "law" in a positive sense. The Letter to the Hebrews

contrasts the law with "the word of the oath" (7:28), but at the same time brings in the Old Testament covenant terminology (cf. Ezek. 17:18f.), which is also a part of the concept of law.

"Law" can thus not only have various shades of meaning, but it can also influence significantly that which is regarded as its opposite. The more keenly we feel the problem of the relationship of the New Testament to the Old, the more necessary it is to understand correctly what is meant by "law," since this seems to be decisive for the contrast between the two Testaments. In particular, the theology of Paul can be fully understood only when the meaning of law is seen with full clarity. The deeper our understanding of law in the Old Testament, the more clearly we can see the relationship of the Testaments to each other. Moreover, we must not fall into the practice of many Christian exegetes of the Old Testament who leave the concept of law in the background in their evaluation of the Old Testament.

The Foundations of the Old Testament Concept of Law

What is Torah? The first place where we find the concept of law in the sense of a collection of revealed statements of God's will is in Deuteronomy, for example 4:44, "This is the law which Moses set before the children of Israel." Deuteronomy is the first collection of traditional material representing God's revealed will that was presented in a comprehensive way and from particular points of view. The material is, to be sure, much older, and even the attempts to arrange and systematize it reach far back into the past.

Without going into Deuteronomy in greater detail here, we can at the outset observe that the traditional material of God's revealed will is not something partial, but it includes the entire revelation insofar as it can be described. Only in this way can we understand why it was cast in the form of Moses' farewell address, that is as the summation of his "tradition," his teachings that go back to the revelation. According to its form this teaching consists of "commands" (*mitzvoth*), for example, Deuteronomy 6:1, "Now this is the commandment, the statutes, and the ordinances which the Lord your God commanded me to teach you, that you may do them in the land to which you are going over, to possess it." That the teaching is in the form of commands is not an indication that it is limited, but rather it is intimately connected to the nature of the revelation of Yahweh on Sinai.

Revelation is first of all speech, because it is devoted to the human consciousness; second it is communication, because it challenges the hearer, the "thou"; third it is command, because the "I" who is revealing himself has absolute authority. The content is related to the gift of life in the promised land, as a part of salvation history. In this new possibility of life that is opening up, the commands are to be put into practice, indeed they portray this new possibility of life. Finally, the content of the commands is marked by the exclusive relationship of God's "I" to the "thou" of Israel in well-being and peace (*shalom*), which can exist only in this relationship established by revelation. In the deuteronomic sense law is thus not some partial ordinance, nor an entity in itself, but it is the opening up of a life of peace in relation to God, it is the salvation that God brings.

Did this concept of Torah as the content of revelation begin with Deuteronomy? Hosea, who can be called a precursor of the deuteronomic theology, had used the concept of Torah in the singular as a designation of the whole of the teaching transmitted by the priestly circles. The condemnation and threat in 4:6 is especially instructive:

> My people are destroyed for lack of knowledge;
> because you have rejected knowledge,
> I reject you from being a priest to me.
> And since you have forgotten the law of your God,
> I also will forget your children.

The priest whom God is addressing here is accused of having refused to use "knowledge" in the proper manner, and of not preserving it and teaching it. He has even forgotten God's Torah, for which he was responsible. Therefore, he cannot serve as priest any longer, and the hereditary office of priest is taken from him and his sons.

The concept of knowledge, which as "knowledge of God" plays so decisive a role in Hosea's theology, is stressed even more here by the concept of God's Torah, and it is also assumed that the priests were to teach this "knowledge" to the people, so that the priests are responsible for the inner decay of the people. That "knowledge" and "Torah" are parallel here shows that Torah in the comprehensive sense can denote the total content of revelation. The use of "Torah" in the singular is appropriate to this total and not partial meaning. More must be meant than specialized knowledge, important to the priests, when it is taken for granted that it is to be taught to the people. From the explication of his knowledge in Hos. 4:1-2 by listing the commands of the Decalogue, we can recognize what Hosea meant by "knowledge," and the deuteronomic compilation of the Torah can be seen as an outgrowth of this Torah concept found in Hosea.

In any case, Torah in Hos. 4:6 is clearly the concern of the priests, and behind the formulation there we can still see the original meaning of Torah as an individual priestly oracle. Torah in this original sense is used in an especially clear manner in the context of the classic description of the priestly office in the oracle to Levi in the blessing of Moses. Here the chief function of the priest is given as

> They shall teach Jacob thy ordinances,
> and Israel thy law. (Deut. 33:10a)

On the one hand, the content of such priestly instruction was concerned with conditions under sacral law, such as cultic purity and impurity, qualifications for admission to worship and for taking part in the cult, as we can find in the ancient declaratory formulas of the Torah. On the other hand, it was concerned with questions of the ordinances of sacral law and thus with legal traditions including requirements for entering the sanctuary, which describe the basic legal integrity which is presupposed for access to the sanctuary (e.g. Ps. 15; 24:3-6). Thus from the first the purpose of Torah was the definition of the state of well-being. Through the application of Torah to the ordinances of sacral law the entire realm of law is included, because "normal," secular law of the community is embedded in sacral law and finds its basis there. This does not mean that a judge had to occupy the priestly office, but rather that the judge has to know *how* he is to judge, and the priest *what* is right and proper. The basing of secular law in sacral law is especially clear in certain borderline cases, e.g. capital offenses, unsolved crimes where some atonement is necessary, or insoluble crimes, where an ordeal is called for. Injustice disrupts the condition of *shalom,* but that condition must be based on and maintained by observance of the sacral law. Thus Torah establishes order, which because it is a state of salvation, is sacral in nature.

Order becomes possible only because of the sacral nature of that order acknowledged by the priest. The details of the priestly Torah seem quite specific, but we must bear in mind that it constitutes a complex whole that embraces "knowledge" as the acknowledgement of order. Only secondarily do such specialized areas of early science as medicine and law develop out of the traditional priestly lore, and only secondarily does the empirical knowledge of those called "wise" become a part of that lore. Even the prophetic oracle is rooted in priestly lore, since knowledge gained charismatically had not yet been distinguished from the general acquisition of knowledge.

In Israel priestly knowledge is based on revelation, handed on in terms of the Sinai revelation, and the Sinai tradition constitutes the framework for the transmission of Torah. It is here that we find the core of Old Testament tradition history.[1] Torah was not isolated from the mainstream of salvation history, but was central to it; indeed it comprised the content of revelation. It is not accidental that despite the variety of developments of the Sinai tradition in later times, there are very ancient references to the participation of the priesthood in the events at Sinai. The Levitical priests were mentioned as present at Massa and Meribah in the oasis of Kadesh, the starting point for the Sinai wanderings, and because of the events there, a distinction was drawn in favor of those who committed themselves to Yahweh (Deut. 33:8-11). Later this event was transferred directly to Sinai (Exod. 32:25-29). This indicates how we are to understand the conspicuous role of Aaron alongside Moses, and the remarkable choice of the early priests Nadab and Abihu (who were later rejected) in the old traditions in Exodus 24:9.

---

[1] Cf. my *Vom Sinai zum Zion,* pp. 31ff.

Moreover, in one of the oldest accounts, the Sinai revelation is designated by an oracular term meaning "to answer" (Exod. 19:19).[2]

The relation which the revelation at Sinai has to Torah is to be
seen in the content of the revelation itself. The statement, "I am
Yahweh," is the self-revelation of God to Israel in an exclusive
relationship which precludes all other relationships. In it the divine
"I" enters into partnership with a human counterpart, who gains
identity through this relationship. Thus the revelation of Yahweh's
being which is given here cannot be separated from the revelation
of Yahweh's will. God's self-disclosure in this relationship places
God's nature at the center of the revelation; it is a new nature that
results from this revelation. Israel comes into being in the revelation
as a people that stands before God, and to whom God is bound:
"I am Yahweh your God."

It is thus appropriate that this statement which summarizes God's
revelation to Israel forms the introduction to the Decalogue. It is not
a mere prologue but represents the total content of the revelation,
from which the commands of the Decalogue then specify the regulations for well-being in the new life that follows. The Ten Commandments are a summary of the Torah, and commands relating to
the nature of God stand alongside others that regulate the relationships of the people to one another. This shows that the Torah com-
bines revelation of God's nature and of God's will, and that any
separation of the two would be artificial. The Decalogue is concerned with a new life which this revelation shows to be a new life
under God.

The Decalogue not only illustrates that the revelation of God's
nature and his will belong together in the Torah, but it also shows
how the tradition brings the two together to represent the whole of
Torah and revelations.[3] The so-called ethical decalogue (Exod.
20:2-17)[4] describes for the Elohist the entire Sinai revelation, inso-

---

[2]Cf. the passage Exod. 34:29-35, which represents less a prophetic oracle
than a priestly one.

[3]Compare the detailed presentation in "Der Decalog als Ganzheit be-
trachtet," *Vom Sinai zum Zion*, pp. 63ff., esp. 73ff.

[4]Exod. 20:2-17 is of course an older, pre-Deuteronomic form, and vv 18-
21 were additions to adapt it to the Deuteronomic concepts.

far as it consists of commands, and for Deuteronomic tradition it is the main part of the revelation, given to Israel itself (Deut. 5:6-21), while all the rest is mediated through Moses. This makes it clear that a summation of the Torah is intended, which was to correspond to the entire revelation.

How does the Decalogue accomplish this? It is a collection of apodictic statements which originally had the structure found in all other comparable collections: double sentences dealing with two aspects of an issue. Just as Hebrew (and other ancient Near Eastern) poetry was similarly constructed in a parallelism of members, so here one issue is always dealt with in two aspects. According to the original numbering of the commands, the first two relate to God, the first dealing with the exclusive nature of the relation to God and the second with the impossibility of any image of God, which would violate the personal relationship of Yahweh to Israel. These aspects of God's revelation as exclusive and personal are so closely bound up together in the tradition that not only are they preserved as separate commands (Exod. 34:14-17), but in the explanation they are treated as one command (cf. Exod. 20:4-6).

Just as the first pair of commands relates to God himself, the second pair deals with holiness, reverence for the name of God, which is basic to any act of worship and observance of the sabbath, with its regularly recurring holiness in the realm of time and for the inviolability of the world of creation.[5] That is, it deals with the integrity of God's relation to Israel and to his creation.

Moving from this two-fold aspect of holiness to human relationships, the realm of the sexual, which is basic to humanity, the next two commands in the original numbering deal with reverence for parents and the prohibition of violating the marriage of another. The protection of one's own family and the family of others is the two-fold aspect of this third realm, which leads in turn to a fourth, dealing with humanity in general, the prohibition of murder and of slavery (stealing persons). Here protection is provided for all humans, not merely for members of one's own society. The latter is pro-

---

[5]See below, pp. 86ff.

vided for in the final pair of commands, which speak of one's neighbor. Testimony about him must be true, and his household must be protected from intrigues. Thus in concrete commands the rights and possessions for our neighbors as a whole are protected in the community.

Thus we can find in the Decalogue a universal system of five areas that are concerned with God, with what is holy, with the family, with humanity in general, and with one's neighbor. Here Torah is describing the condition of well-being which Israel attains through the revelation that makes a new life before God possible. The entire Torah, which corresponds to the entire revelation, must be kept in mind as the determinative point of view when we look at the many detailed regulations that came to be included in the Torah tradition. A Torah scholarship concerned with the ordering of all of life could easily develop an interest in such detail. We are not justified in taking the opposite course of moving from individual regulations to a Torah tradition consisting of a more or less unstructured mass of regulations that deal with purely practical problems and only incidentally and in retrospect seeks its authority through a relationship with revelation. Torah was always concerned with a whole; the order that can be seen in the details is only a part of the order of the whole.

We must also bear in mind that the transmission of the Torah did not take place in total isolation from the rest of the tradition. Salvation history belongs together with the priestly tradition. Originally it too was not isolated, nor did it constitute the sole substance of the Yahwist tradition. Modern theologians in their interest in the Old Testament for its transmission of salvation history, often give the impression of such isolation. But note that during the celebration of Passover the story of the Exodus is recounted, and in the Old Testament there is no Passover tradition without an Exodus tradition. Or we might look at the numerous traditions from the Patriarchal and Wilderness periods, with their cultic etiologies. In all these cases we find the content includes these two streams of tradition. Even though the Torah tradition uses a distinctive form, in its content it presupposes salvation history. This explains why it is that Torah traditions can be found in the context of historical accounts.[6] This is not only true of the later Priestly document, but it was already the case with J and E, and even though J and E arose outside priestly circles, they do not constitute something alien when incorporated into the P corpus, with its greater dependence on priestly lore and thought.

To sum up, the early history of the concept of Torah is deeply rooted in the Old Testament's core of tradition history, and the Old Testament as a whole is basically determined by the concept of Torah. This core is God's revelation of himself to Israel, his self-disclosure in an exclusive personal relationship of God and Israel, which institutes a new state of *shalom,* and consequently Torah is that which can be handed on concerning this relationship. It is the tradition in respect to the new life created by this revelation, that is, the order and arrangement of the new life. The apparent one-sidedness of the concept of revelation that results is bound up with the nature of revelation. It is not the revelation of a transcendental world of myth, not an independent secular commandment, not an independent order of things, but well-being in the life that God gives in relationship to himself. The Torah begins with the combined first and second commandments of God's revelation and includes all the areas of well-being under God. It sums up the formula "I am Yahweh," the Lord who reveals himself. That it is formulated as a commandment grows out of the structure of the revelation of the diviine "I" to the human "Thou" as the basis of the responsible life under God— *coram Deo.*

Two Major Compilations of Torah: Deuteronomy and the Priestly Code

In the Bible we find law transmitted primarily in two quite different expressions, in the Deuteronomic corpus and in the Priestly document. In Deuteronomy, as we saw, it first took its form as "Torah"

---

[6]The possible inner connection between a historical account and the description of an ordinance can be seen in a different way in the primeval history, Gen. 1-11. These traditions demonstrate from pre-Israelite times an interest in the derivation of the world order out of primeval events, without exhausting this basic etiological character in an explanation in terms of history.

in the sense of a comprehensive tradition. It is appropriate to look at the background for this compilation of Torah and also to recognize that the tradition was not continued simply by an editorial expansion of Deuteronomy, but that it produced a new, very different compilation. This new compilation, however, did not replace Deuteronomy, with the result that there are two formulations that express the whole of Torah.

DEUTERONOMY arose in Judah during the time of its total subjugation as a vassal of Assyria in the seventh century B.C. It was the outgrowth of the great crises produced by the Assyrian conquests in the last third of the eighth century, which are no less significant than the catastrophies at the beginning of the sixth century. The Assyrian conquest led to the destruction of the northern kingdom of Israel and to the loss of Judah's independence. It brought into doubt the existence of Yahweh's Israel, not only politically, but also in the comprehensive sense of salvation history. The establishment of an Assyrian world empire represented not only the victory of a nationalism that was subjugating other peoples, but the triumph of a universal idea of a supranational human order which could include nations, peoples, cultures, and religions under Assyrian hegemony.

That the so-called classical prophecy of the eighth century could see Yahweh's judgment on Israel in the Assyrian conquest, presupposes more than only a continuation of the old tradition of Israel's privileged position. Amos revitalized the original event of deliverance in the Exodus. Hosea described salvation history from their forefather Jacob on as a history of apostasy. Isaiah foretold the decline of the Davidic dynasty, and Micah the total destruction of Zion. Consequently some profound change must have taken place if this did not mean the revelation had come to an end. It had to mean that Israel was something that was not to be absorbed into the system of nationalities, the civil order of world history; that true salvation history consists in the consciously established relationship of love for God in total personal commitment.

So history led to a profound transformation. Beyond the outward institutions of nations and governments, the true inner being was to come forth. Customary verdicts and traditional cultic practices were no longer adequate in the light of the standard of true right and genuine piety. It was necessary that there emerge out of the nation a community of those who in this time of judgment saw themselves as Yahweh's Israel. Instead of the king and his might, they fixed their hope on the Messiah, who listens to God. In prophecy an ontological transformation took place: present reality became merely background, and reality stood revealed as a newly perceived transcendence. Israel consciously took its stand before God. This new consciousness demanded by the prophets found its expression in the content of Deuteronomy. Deuteronomy is the direct result of this transformation.

In the years after the storm, north Israelite traditions were brought to the south and their study led to a bringing together of the threads of the tradition that constitutes the basis of the Old Testament: the Yahwist as combination of J and E in interpretations similar to Deuteronomy, the complex collection of historical traditions in the special Deuteronomic layer, and above all the Torah compilation of Deuteronomy. This collection known as the Torah is the "knowledge of God" that the prophets expected of the individual Israelite. Law could become an objective entity, because its subject, the individual, was challenged in these crises and rose to the challenge. When the objective nature of the law is judged negatively and its demands on the individual criticized as inadequate in contrast to the old basis of right in the collective life of the people, the critic is ignoring the fact that this subjective consciousness grew out of the messages of the prophets and in turn forms the basis for the objective character of Deuteronomy. At the beginning of the earliest core of Deuteronomy we read, "And you shall love the Lord your God, with all your heart, and with all your soul, and with all your might" (6:5). It is prophecy that leads to law.

The original core of Deuteronomy presents a distinctive picture of the early history of Israel.[7] Israel was born in the Exodus and through a forty-year initiation in the desert was brought up to be God's son. Prior to crossing over from the wilderness beyond Jordan,

---

[7] I am referring to the so-called "discovery tradition."

the people received the revelation of the commands for life in Moses' farewell address. (In terms of the presentation in a pluralist framework of the traditions in the form in which they had been handed down as revelation at Sinai/Horeb, and definitively after Deuteronomy was added to the Tetrateuch, it took the form of a second repeated law, as "Deuteronomy.")

Three conclusions can be drawn from the framework of Deuteronomy:

1) In the transcendental realm of early history revelation took place as a personal commitment in great depth, in a way that customary history cannot fathom. The primeval history is conceived of in metahistorical terms.

2) The gift of salvation history is the land that makes life in history possible. But this is not all; it is only the outward condition of life. Something inward must be added, the keeping of the law.[8] The law is therefore not merely a guideline of significance in special cases in life, but as a positive ordering of life itself it is continuously to be worked out in life situations. The concept of Torah includes the idea that law has its counterpart in the revealed nature of human life in relation to God. Human salvation consists in the fulfillment of a revealed order. We should not reject the basic idea of this active nature of the commandments, because it represents accurately the consciousness of the Israelites who received the revelation, as this consciousness is assumed in Deuteronomy.

3. This consciousness is seen most clearly in that the commandments are to be learned, and thus also to be taught.[9] God reveals the law by teaching it, and the law becomes *doctrina*. It is the responsibility of the head of every family to teach his sons, just as Moses taught the Israelites. Indeed a literary category of "the son's questions" with the father's answers was developed in the form of a catechism. Teaching the law became the basic task of the religious life. The nature of the law in objectified form led to the collecting

---

[8]Note how frequently the verb "to do" is used with the revealed laws in Deuteronomy.

[9]Note the frequent use of the verb *lmd* in Deuteronomy.

of the traditional materials. We might say that Deuteronomy was the beginning of the Bible.

Deuteronomy arose out of the experience of living under a threat; and the PRIESTLY DOCUMENT arose out of the experience of being protected through the catastrophe. Deuteronomy arose in the collecting of the tradition in Judah; the Priestly Document in the new assembling of the tradition during the exile. Deuteronomy was assembled by the Levitical priests throughout the land; the Priestly Document by the Zadokite priests in Jerusalem. In addition to these profound historical distinctions there are also differences in content that can be seen because the Old Testament placed the two complexes side by side without attempting any harmonizing or any continuation of either tradition. Indeed, the Priestly law code can be regarded as the antithesis to that of Deuteronomy.

In spite of all its legal details, the P tradition bears, much more than does D, the stamp of a tradition of salvation history, thanks to the basic role played by the priestly view of history. Consistent with this, P's view of history is outwardly more conservative, but what internal changes have been made! The course of history goes from the creation account, to the flood, to the realm of natural humanity, living by the covenant with Noah, then through Abraham's separation from the heathen world to salvation history in the covenant with Abraham, and to Israel. Just as the sign of the covenant with Noah is in the cosmic realm—the rainbow, the sign of the covenant with Abraham is in the human realm—circumcision. The goal is reached in the revelation, which transcends the category of covenant.

This self-revelation of God is essential to the revelation of the cult, through which Israel comes to share in holiness. If the goal of the Deuteronomic law is keeping of the law, the goal of the Priestly law is being holy. This holiness, made possible by the revealed cult, enables the people to lead a holy life, and formulates for the first time the saving relation of God to Israel that is contained in the revelation, "You shall therefore be holy, for I am holy" (Lev. 11:45). Such a law can only be kept; it cannot be fulfilled.

It would be a basic mistake to regard this law, determined as it is by cult, as a slipping back into the cultic religion of pre-prophetic times. The prophet Ezekiel can be called as a witness against that view because he was closely related to the Priestly tradition. In his overview of history in Chapter 20 he shows how Israel's perversity had led to worship that was not good. "Moreover I (God) gave them statutes that were not good and ordinances by which they could not have life; and I defiled them through their first-born, that I might horrify them" (vv 25-26). Ezekiel saw a fundamental difference between the old cultic practices and the new worship that was appropriate to the revelation at Sinai. Ezekiel 20:25-26 makes it clear that the transmission of the law can represent a revelation of punishment, or better, a revelation that educates toward maturity. Above all it shows that the law that corresponds to revelation is not something that is given once for all, inalterable, static, but it gives expression to the relationship of God to Israel, to the content of revelation, and this relationship involves growth, a dynamic development in salvation history.

On the other hand, Ezekiel cites the sabbath commandment as an example of the primary, basic revelation at Sinai, with the words, "Moreover I (God) gave them my sabbaths, as a sign *('ot)* between me and them, that they might know that I the Lord sanctify them" (20:12). In doing so he is describing the cultic concept of P (cf. Exod. 31:13 P). We can summarize it in the following statements.

1) Cult corresponds to a transcendental reality. Just as the sabbaths are God's sabbaths, that is days of rest that correspond to the structure of creation (cf. Gen. 2:1-3 P)—the basis for the sabbath in the P tradition refers to this (Exod. 31:17 P, cf. 20:11)—so the entire cult reflects the transcendental primeval pictures (*tabnit* Exod. 25:9, 40; 26:30 P).

2) The law is therefore more than the command establishing a human order of life—it is the transcendental basing of life in symbolic actions. Transcendental reality can be portrayed in human reality. The concept of symbol is expressed in ontological terms, as for example in representing the ceremony of sealing the covenant in a symbolic act (Gen. 9:12-17), and the symbol represents the relationship to transcendence. Reality can only be alluded to; it is the

"wholly other" of revelation, not what is confined to doctrine. It is for this reason and not as a slipping back into something "primitive" that cultic symbolism has a distinctive meaning.

3) The goal of Torah is holiness, which can be symbolically achieved in the cult. This occurs properly through atonement. The act of dedication to God, by which the distance from what is holy is symbolically bridged by the substitutionary offering of blood, is so central for the cult of the Priestly Document, that not only is the great day of atonement the highest holy day, but also every sacrifice takes on the nature of atonement, for it is only atonement, not offering a gift, that can express the meaning of the cult.

It is clear that an increase in theological depth was necessary for the development of P, and this was provided, at least in part, by the prophets. Just as Jeremiah is connected with Deuteronomy, so Ezekiel and the development of the priestly tradition cannot be separated from one another. The mentality which has grown tired of metaphysics and has become unreceptive to symbols is most likely to belittle the priestly tradition. We are fond of stressing the humanitarian spirit of Deuteronomy, but we should not forget that famous statement, "You shall love your neighbor as yourself" (Lev. 19:18) comes from the P tradition and constitutes the high point of the so-called "singular decalogue" (vv 13-18). The great cosmological depth and breadth, the metaphysical sublimity of symbolic ontology, by no means preclude the deepening of humanitarianism. On the contrary, it is in this tradition that for the first time compassion and sympathy for the poor are transformed into a loving commitment to others. In this respect too the Priestly Document rightly stands beside Deuteronomy.

In the New Testament the question is raised, what is the greatest commandment (Mark 12:28-31 and parallels). Is it by chance that the two-part answer brings together the beginning of the earliest form of Deuteronomy (6:4-5) and the high point of the singular decalogue of Leviticus 19? That alongside the *Shema* of Deuteronomy this distinctive statement from P is cited? Of course there are reasons of content involved here, but anyone who is familiar with the structure of the Torah knows that this also gives expression to the two sides of the Torah tradition.

The Influence of Wisdom Literature and Eschatology on the Torah

The concept of Torah in the priestly tradition is not far from the ideas of world order found in the later theology of wisdom literature. As we have seen, this law was not solely or primarily concerned with human actions but with being. It portrayed transcendental reality, used symbols to point to the being of God, and thus mediated and gave reality to the truth as God's order. Consequently, an analogy to the order of creation and the order of human life is derived from it, and we are then close to the wisdom tradition. According to the priestly conception, for example, the sabbaths that Israel observes place Israel in an intimate relation to the cosmic order, and it would be inconceivable in this theological tradition to think there might be an order of the world and of creation independent of and parallel to the law. Rather both are related, in fact they are different stages of one revelation.

This agrees with the presentation given in the priestly history. The creation is not presented as an introduction, providing as wide a background as possible for the real presentation of history, but it is an initial account, in which the basis for existence is established. It moves through the accounts of the world after the flood and the patriarchal world to the fullness of revelation in God's self-disclosure. P has a concept of law in which law is finally also the revealed order of the universe. This pattern of theological thought was essentially formed and preserved by the Jerusalem priesthood, but it exerted wide influence beyond the priestly circles. Now another theological tradition was brought together with it, the wisdom tradition.

Israel naturally was a participant in the ancient wisdom tradition, the earliest form of a scientific understanding of the world, especially since this international intellectual movement was not dependent on national religious traditions. It was a profoundly human undertaking that endeavored to express the experiences of life and the world in the scholarly form of a description of a basic order, which then was valid as a rule for life; a guide for those who accepted its discipline and lived in accordance with the acknowledged order. In contrast to many forms of modern theological thought, however, revelation and experiential knowledge could not be separated in Israel, but rather they had to be intimately related to each other, because revelation was revelation to human persons.

So in Israel, wisdom became a form of theology. Its secular, purely human, and empirical character could not be absorbed by the heathen religions, so permeated by mythical concepts, but in the development of philosophy as a special tradition of religious persons, it could be more or less adapted, though it frequently constituted a crass counterpart to the religious tradition. In Israel, however, wisdom thought and Torah traditions were merged to form theology. From the heathen point of view, Torah in Israel was regarded as wisdom. "Keep them and do them; for that will be your wisdom and your understanding in the sight of the peoples, who, when they hear all these statutes, will say, 'Surely this great nation is wise and understanding people' " (Deut. 4:6).

It is obvious that in the description of creation in the Priestly Torah (Gen. 1), the early knowledge of natural science about the structure of the world was not brought in superficially, but was incorporated into the structure of the passage. Outside Israel, the wisdom of natural science brought with it the transformation of myth into natural philosophy, as for example in Phoenician natural philosophy with the god Taautos, and its distinctive transformation of the tradition of a god of weather. This then had great influence on the cosmogony of Anaximander and the limited world order of Democritus.[10] Here the way led to philosophy. In Israel, however, revelation, in the form of an ongoing Torah tradition, could be the center of a scientific view of the world. In the Priestly account of creation, the sabbath is the goal of the creation process (Gen. 2:1-3), proof of the close relationship of cultic Torah and the knowledge of natural science.

---

[10]Cf. *Die Religionen der Menschheit,* ed. by Ch. M. Schröder, 1961ff., vol. X2, pp. 33, 203.

Psalm 19, which attained its present form no later than the fourth century B.C.,[11] contains in part one (vv 1-6), praise of the inaudible word of creation in the form of wisdom riddles. It gives as an example of this creation logos a sun doctrine, whose mythological origins are obvious. This concept of creation in wisdom categories is followed in the second part of the psalm (vv 7-14) by praise in wisdom terminology of the Torah of Yahweh. The purpose of this is to identify the Torah doctrine with the divine command. The new subject matter in 7-14 is certainly not a later "false" interpretation of the first part of the psalm, but develops naturally out of the scientific and theological understanding of the doctrine of creation as a doctrine of Torah.

A similar identification of wisdom and Torah in the realm of human existence, which is the primary concern of wisdom teachings with its decisive human characteristics, can be demonstrated. The ethos of a wise life consisted in subjecting oneself to the order identified by wisdom. This inevitably came to be identified with submitting to Torah. The wise person is the one who lives according to the law. Psalm 1 takes up the metaphor of a tree and water that was already well-known in Egyptian wisdom and that occurs also in a wisdom setting in Jeremiah 17:7-8, and uses it to describe the wise person, who is none other than the one who longs for and studies Torah.

This is not an accommodation made by Torah piety to something essentially alien; in Israel, wisdom of necessity consisted in the fear of Yahweh. Human attitudes can be explained in terms of this fear in the same categories as are appropriate in terms of Torah and of prophetic warnings.[12] Differences in nuances can be explained by the difference in form between the divine command and wisdom warnings, and by the corresponding difference in *Sitz im Leben*, but not by a discrepancy in content. Even in their formal elements Torah and wisdom came closer and closer together. The prophets of eighth century encouraged human awareness and responsible knowledge of God's commands. Wisdom, on the authority of Yahweh, called for

[11]Cf. *Vom Sinai zum Zion,* 147ff. and 159ff.

[12]Cf. the appearance of Wisdom as a prophet in Prov. 1:24-28.

persons to decide between life and death (e.g. Prov. 8:32-36), using prophetic and deuteronomic vocabulary.

Of special importance for the understanding of Torah that developed through the influence of wisdom literature is the formation of a normative doctrine of the nature of wisdom *(hochma)*. From the start, knowledge in the wisdom tradition was knowledge of the order of the world, and thus, *hochma* could be regarded as the order of creation, occupying an intermediate position between God and creation, and, as the principle of creation, it could be given precedence over all that was created, though it was by no means to be identified with God. The poem on wisdom in Job 28 illustrates this transcendance of wisdom, whose proper place in neither the realm of nature (vv 1-11), not even in the depths of the earth, nor the realm of human affairs (vv 12-19), however far human trade and commerce might reach, and of whom Abbadon and Death have heard only a rumor (v 22). Its proper place is with God (v 23-28). At the creation,

> Then he saw it and declared it;[13]
> he established it and searched it out (v. 27).

As that which was prior to creation and thus transcends the world, wisdom was founded by God, to serve him as the measure of creation. Through it God imparts himself to the world. Directly following this statement and at the conclusion of the praise of wisdom, we read,

> Behold, the fear of the Lord, that is wisdom;
> and to depart from evil is understanding (v. 28).

This is not some inappropriate addition, but the answer to the thematic question of the whole passage: wisdom, as the highest and ultimate goal of human knowledge is identical with God's command.

This text, which perhaps dates from the fifth century, has its sequel in the song in praise of wisdom (Prov. 8:22-36), dating from the fourth century. The world-transcending pre-existence of wisdom found here its clearest expression at the same time that its function as mediator was being worked out.

---

[13]Read Qal as "count," i.e., use it as a unit of measure.

When he (God) marked out the foundations of the
    earth;
    then I was beside him, like a master workman;[14]
and I was daily his [15] delight,
    rejoicing before him always,
rejoicing in his inhabited world
    and delighting in the sons of men.
    (Gese: "the sons of men delighted in me.")

Humans participated in God's joy over the world through their rejoicing in the knowledge of the order of the world. For the biblical way of thinking it is significant that this mediating of God to people who have knowledge can be expressed only in a personal relationship. Hypostatized wisdom, seen by God as the measure of his being, is God's beloved child, who shares God's throne; and whom the person who has knowledge encounters. The widespread view of wisdom as a woman is not based on this passage, but it can give clear expression to the deep inner relationship of a man to wisdom and it accords precisely with the personal categories relating to revelation. There might be influences here from the history of religions, but they would require more than a mere external point of contact, that is, such influences would have to correspond to the data.

Quite apart from the fact that in a text like Proverbs 8:22-36 the identity, or at least the essential correspondence, of wisdom and Torah is portrayed, it would be inconceivable in the Israelite tradition to praise wisdom in this extreme way, without also thinking of Torah, or to speak of the creation without seeing revelation as the center of that created order. In the song in praise of Wisdom in Sir. 24 (ca. 200 B.C.) we find the conclusion of this development in tradition history which brought wisdom and Torah together and greatly enriched the concept of Torah through sapiential theology. In the framework of the Priestly tradition's understanding of Torah, it was possible to accomplish the identification of wisdom with Torah by the consistent adoption of the Zion tradition with its teachings of God's dwelling on Mount Zion as the goal of revela-

---

[14]So RSV. Gese translates, "on his lap." See below, p. 195.
[15]Cf. LXX.

tion. Wisdom, as the divine logos of creation, not only permeates
the world from without, but it takes up its dwelling in the innermost parts of the world, and, as the Zion tradition describes, the
result of this is that God's revelation to Israel is intensified to the
point of his condescending to dwell on Zion.

This can be understood as Wisdom dwelling with Israel in the
tabernacle and on Mount Zion. Wisdom was seeking, as did the
Ark, a place in the world, an "inheritance" where it could live forever. So it became the *shekinah* on Zion, where it provided the "liturgy" of the worship of God that centered in the Ark, as described by
P, and is therefore identical with the Torah that God revealed to
Israel (cf. v. 23). God mediates himself to the world as the ground
of all being by revealing himself in the glory of his dwelling in
Zion. Wisdom and Torah, the word of creation and of revelation,
transcendence and immanence become one. The structure of the
transcendent logos Christology is thus the logical outcome of the
development of the concept of revelation in the Old Testament.

The merging of Torah with cosmic law which took place under
the influence of wisdom literature was accompanied by an apparently
quite different development, in which the law was placed in an eschatological setting. The one development did not exclude the other,
as can be illustrated by the Priestly concept of Torah. Just as there
the closeness to cosmic law is clearly seen, so also the symbolic aspect
of the law points to a transcendence that does not permit the law
to be fulfilled in a self-contained *opus operatum.* The postexilic
cultic observances on Zion, which had to be carried out without their
central feature, the Ark of the Covenant, must have been regarded
in the light of the cultic regulations in P as something merely provisional. Thus an objective deepening of the concept of law to an
all-embracing system does not a priori exclude an eschatological element, whose nature would be determined by the subjective experience of human inadequacy, of *hamartia,* the knowledge of separation from the holy. Under the influence of a fully developed concept
of covenant, there arose relatively early a doctrine of a new covenant,
under which men and women, in contrast to the first covenant, are

fully drawn into the holiness of God's self-disclosure, and the *hamartia* that causes separation is overcome.

Aside from late allusions in Second and Third Isaiah, the teaching of the new covenant is found in two forms. One of these (Jer. 31:31-34), shows the influence of the Deuteronomic tradition and the other (Ezek. 36:25-27), shows that of the tradition which led to the Priestly document. According to Jeremiah, through the forgiveness of sins it will be possible to overcome completely the separation of subject and object. Everyone will "know" God, because the Torah will be written directly on every heart. Torah will be regarded as knowledge of God, and God himself will place this knowledge in the human heart. According to Ezekiel, the forgiveness of sins occurs in terms of a cultic cleansing. Hearts will be created anew and quickened with a new spirit *(ruaḥ),* so that there will be total obedience to the Torah. Because Torah is transcendent in nature, nothing in its form needs to be altered. In both Jeremiah and Ezekiel we have an eschatological revelation of God and an ultimate, fully valid covenant, which, unlike the old covenant, cannot be broken.

Has the Torah, at least insofar as it can be described in human terms, been changed in this eschatological revelation? It should be obvious that this revelation, as God's self-discolsure, is identical with the "I am Yahweh" of the Sinai covanant. But how is it to be defined as Torah? From the large number of relevant texts, let us look at two. Psalm 46 describes how God, after overcoming the chaos of nature and of history, reveals himself on Zion to all peoples. The Psalm uses the basic formula of Sinai, "Know that I am Yahweh" (RSV. God, v 11), and gives a negative basis for the eternal state of well-being *(shalom)* in the destruction of all implements of war, and a positive basis in the revealing of Yahweh's kingship, his *basileia,* over the world.

According to Isaiah 2:2-4 and Micah 4:1-4 the peoples will of their own accord flow to Zion, which has become the center of the cosmos, and from which there issues forth the Torah that will bring eternal peace. In contrast to the old Sinai revelation, the new, eschatological revelation is addressed to all peoples, and they will become aware of the kingship of God. The Torah therefore describes the state of *shalom* in a more comprehensive manner, and this revelation is given, not at Sinai, but on Mount Zion. We can state it briefly by saying the Sinai revelation has become the eschatological Zion revelation, and the Torah of Sinai and that of Zion are different.

In the light of the dynamic development of Torah which we have observed, it is not surprising that the Zion Torah is more than just a quantitative expansion of the Sinai Torah. The Old Testament provides illustrations of a qualitative change in Torah. Psalm 50 is an example of Zion revelation. Yahweh appears on Zion amid fire and wind and reveals himself to the covenant people, "I am Yahweh your God" (v. 7; RSV "God, your God"). The following Torah discourse is not a decalogue or something else from the Sinai tradition, rather, in contrast to that tradition, it is a rejection of the normal forms of blood sacrifice. Only one sacrifice will be accepted by God— the *todah,* or thank offering. This is the sacrifice that unites the presentation of the sacrifice with the proclamation of salvation and not only gives expression to a state of well-being, but celebrates salvation as redemption from ill-being and portrays it as an act of redemption. In addition to the new sacrifice Torah, the last part of the Psalm announces a more profound Torah for human life. In an argument similar to that in the Epistle to the Romans, Israel's purely outward fulfillment of the law is rejected. Those who do only this are really hating discipline and casting God's word aside. Finally, to those who rely on this purely external fulfilling of the law but really are forgetting God, God calls out

> He who brings thanksgiving as his sacrifice
>   honors me;
> to him who orders his way aright
> I will show the salvation of God! (v. 23).

The entire understanding of law is thus involved in this thanking God and acknowledging him as the redeemer from death and misery.[16]

Accordingly we can distinguish in the Old Testament between Zion Torah and Sinai Torah. We have found evidence for an es-

---

[16]Cf. the discussion in the Käsemann *Festschrift,* 1976, pp. 57-77.

chatological revelation at Zion, and we see that even Torah is drawn into the eschatological dimension. At the conclusion of the process there is a new Torah. Isaiah 25, the center of the Isaiah apocalypse, shows by analogy to the Sinai revelation in Exodus 24 that at the end of time, the *telos,* the Zion revelation will be there, just as the Sinai revelation was there at the beginning. As Sinai has been replaced by Mount Zion, the world mountain, so Israel has been replaced by all the peoples. The covering with which Moses and Elijah covered themselves[17] in order to be able to endure the transcendence of the revelation, is now removed from everyone, and all see God face to face. Death is abolished, the pain and suffering of life is done away with, and all tears are wiped away. The great sacrificial meal that takes place here corresponds to the *zebah* of Exodus 24, when the Israelites saw God and ate and drank (v. 11), but it now has become a thank offering. The quotation of the great songs of thanksgiving from the Psalms identifies the offering as *todah.* The new Israel—all mankind—finds its voice, praises God, and thanks him, and by so doing transforms the simple sacrificial ritual of physical communion with God into the act of acknowledging God in the deepest spiritual communion.

We have reached the end of the Old Testament and in conclusion we may ask how the distinction between Sinai Torah and Zion Torah and the expectation of an eschatological Torah revelation affected Israel's existence in late Old Testament times. We can express the answer in the well-known words of Third Isaiah:

> Keep justice, and do righteousness *(ṣedaqa)*
>   for soon my salvation will come,
>   and my deliverance *(ṣedaqa)* be revealed (56:1)

This statement has a structure that corresponds exactly to that of the well-known words of John the Baptist (Matt. 3:2) and Jesus (Matt. 4:17, Mark 1:15): comprehensive exhortation based on the approach of the eschaton. It uses the term *ṣedaqa* in two senses, the first of

---

[17]That this is the meaning of *loṭ* (vs. 7) is clear from the technical term *luṭ* in 1 Kings 19:13, together with the many mentions of a covering during the Sinai theophany (Exod. 3:6; 33:20; 34:29ff., etc.).

which refers to the human "fulfilling of the law," and the second, in analogy to the first, but differing from it, to the revelation of God's eschatological saving deeds. The precise usage here highlights something that would be lost in a less precise statement, and the truth of the statement would be obscured. In the context of the increasing de-eschatologizing at the end of the Old Testament, this "righteous" action of men and women can result in a representation of the awaited redemption, in that the life lived here anticipates that which is awaited as eschatological salvation, as a gift from God.

In the context of the unfortunate experience of the Hasmonean monarchy with its total orientation to this present world after the great eschatological tensions of the Maccabean struggle, a new group emerged. It was concerned, in contrast to the strong expectation of revelation in the end-time, with emphasizing the realization of that fulfillment in our life in the here and now. This was done by expanding the contents of the Torah tradition in a ceremonial life, by quantitatively increasing to a tremendous degree the Torah requirements. For example, the Levitical laws for worship in the Temple were brought over into everyday life, in an analogy here and now to the circumstances at the time of the end. A group was formed of those who separated themselves from the world, *perushim,* and in this sense performed the works of the law. This Pharisaic party, from the middle of the second century B.C. onward, held to an eschatological expectation, but they let it be obscured by the great work of the human fulfillment of the law. Rather than hold to a hope for the end, a hope that became tense to the breaking point, it was thought to be more effective to create in their own lives a model of the consummation for which they waited. But we must not auomatically project back onto the Old Testament something that appeared in the mid-second century as a de-eschatological tendency and in so doing ignore the essentially eschatological components of the concept of the law found in the Zion Torah.[18]

---

[18]On the other hand we should not simply identify the attitude of the Pharisees we encounter in the New Testament with the Pharisaism of late Judaism, which developed out of the catastrophe of A.D. 70 and with completely new presuppositions carried out the reconstitution of Judaism.

In addition to Pharisaism there were other attempts at the end of the Old Testament period to eliminate eschatology. We might mention the Zealots who wanted to use the sword to make way for the kingdom and to force it to come by human political means. Then there were "spiritual" circles which projected the many-sided apocalyptic expectations and speculation onto an inward spiritual kingdom and attempted to transport themselves into the transcendental realm of revelation by meditating on its contents. As a result eschatological apocalyptic was transformed into a gnosticism free of eschatological aspects. Thus in terms of history of religion, the end of the history of revelation was reflected negatively in these anti-eschatological tendencies, in contrast to the positive way in which we can see it in the Old Testament tradition history as it moved toward its culmination. The fullness of time had come. Jesus of Nazareth entered into the existence for which the history of revelation had prepared the way.

The New Testament Concept of Law

1. *Jesus and the Law*

In the life of Jesus the messianic establishment of God's kingdom was accomplished. The proclamation of the good news, the healing of the sick and the forgiving of sins, the selection of the Twelve as representatives of the true Israel and the crossing the boundary that kept the Gentiles out, fellowship with sinners and the establishing of peace and reconciliation, the revelation of what was hidden and the final proclamation of the Torah—all this ushered in the new aeon. What kind of Torah is this? It is the Torah of peace—of *shalom,* which recognizes no more boundaries and divisions; it is the Torah of the one who welcomes sinners, who shows love to his enemies, who overcomes curses by blessing, because he gives himself in service to the world (Mark 10:45). In this self-sacrifice the holy no longer consists in separateness, but it permeates the secular. The old holiness, such as that of the priest who serves his God in Levitical purity, can no longer be of help to the one who has fallen among thieves and is under the threat of death, because he is under the power of all that is impure and unholy (Luke 10:30-37). Through

Jesus, however, God's eschatological holiness takes control of secular unholiness. Yes, God's holiness makes its appearance in the midst of the greatest shame and disgrace, in the greatest human suffering.

This meant the rejection of the specific pharisaic exegesis of the Torah, as seen, for example, in the extending of the rules for tithing to include herbs (". . . for you tithe mint and dill and cummin . . ." Matt. 23:23), while the essential nature of Torah is ignored. The result of such exegesis of the Torah is an externalizing of the law: ". . . you cleanse the outside of the cup and of the plate, but inside you are full of extortion and rapacity" (Matt. 23:25). And the greatest danger of such a life, regulated externally but not inwardly, is hypocrisy. "So you also outwardly appear righteous to men, but within you are full of hypocrisy and iniquity" (Matt. 23:28).

The New Testament, however, does not make the Torah more stringent, nor does it merely spiritualize it. It gives us a Zion Torah in the sense of God's taking total possession of the world in a final revelation and penetration, in which he commits himself to the world by drawing all that is secular into the holy. This does not by any means mean a dissolution or destruction of the Torah. This can be demonstrated by an obvious example, Jesus' attitude toward the sabbath.

In addition to accounts of healings performed by Jesus on the sabbath, the synoptic gospels contain other material dealing with the theme of the sabbath, the account of the disciples threshing the heads of grain on the sabbath (Mark 2:23-28; Matt. 12:1-8; Luke 6:1-5). The usual interpretation of this account is that it intends to show that Jesus regards human needs, here the satisfying of hunger, as taking precedence over the sabbath. Such an illustrative account seems to make this attitude toward the sabbath all the more understandable, since only an exaggerated interpretation of the prohibition of work on the sabbath could forbid such a trifle as an occasional threshing of grain in one's hands. Thus it is held that Jesus was here defending human freedom against an exaggerated legalism.

From the point of view of the Old Testament, however, this incident takes on an entirely different character. For we know that the primary concern of the sabbath was not human rest from labor, but the prevention of human violation of the environment, the restoration of the integrity of the created world. The earliest sabbath commands are the prohibition of plowing and harvesting (Exod. 34:21), and of kindling a fire indoors (Exod. 35:3), and these can hardly be explained in terms of rest from labor.

Down to the last working out of the sabbath regulations in the Mishnah *Tractate Sabbath,* we can trace the criterion of whether a human action involves an invasion of "nature," of the environment, or whether it remains in the purely human realm. It is only because the concept of work *(melaka)* is oriented to farmers and craftsmen that the sabbath commandment can be understood as a comprehensive prohibition of work. In principle, however, it is concerned with the inviolability of the created world, which humans must respect at least symbolically every seventh day. The environmental catastrophes of our own generation seem to have opened our eyes for the first time to the significance of the idea of a sabbath for a world undisturbed by humans, and which is preserved holy and entire. Every seventh day Israel encounters the holiness of the sabbath, is made aware of the integrity of the created world, experiences how alien mankind is to the world of nature, and so gains an openness to the experience of transcendence.

A correct understanding of the holiness of the sabbath gives this synoptic account of threshing the grain its proper and very great significance. Jesus' disciples have not violated some exaggerated detail of sabbath legislation, but they have overstepped the boundary which the sabbath has drawn, and this becomes a model of human intervention in the sphere of the sabbath. What is at issue here, a violation of the sabbath, or the performing of a messianic work? In this account, Jesus' refutation of the Pharisees' criticism deals with David's legitimacy in matters of sacral law. Although he was fleeing from Saul he was already the hidden king and the high priest of Israel, and so he could make use of the holy "bread of the presence." Just as there can be no scruples about the sabbath in the temple, so also the Son of Man is Lord of the sabbath because he abolishes the boundary between humankind and nature. In an eschatological manner representative humans, in the midst of their most typical concerns and activities (here represented by eating), enter into the holiness of the sabbath. They no longer are violating the integrity of the created world; the essence of the sabbath becomes theirs, and the transcendence of the previous sabbath relationship is abolished in the all-pervasive holiness, into which Jesus' disciples have now entered.

The Torah of Jesus is more than a simple and questionable freedom from Torah; it is the foundation of complete and perfect *shalom,* in which God's holiness penetrates the furthest depths of the world. Matthew portrays Jesus' proclamation of Torah as the "Sermon on the Mount," in continuity with the tradition of revelation on Sinai, and on Mount Zion. By the references to the decalogue of the original Torah ("You have heard that it was said to the men of old . . ., but I say to you . . ." Matt. 5:21-22, etc.) the complete Torah of the New Covenant is shown to be the completion of the history of revelation. The statement in the preface of the presentation of this new righteousness says that the Torah is not to be abolished but to be "fulfilled," and this is absolutely correct. Only by ignoring the powerful dynamic of the ongoing history of revelation and being content with a totally static, unhistorical concept of law is it possible to fail to understand that in this final Torah every "iota" and every "dot" has been preserved, indeed, has been brought to its final truth.

The synoptic gospels contain another account which gives a basic answer to the question of Torah, the story of Jesus' Transfiguration (Mark 9:2-8; Matt: 17:1-8; Luke 9:28-36). It gains great importance through its position in the composition of the gospels and cannot be explained as a "misplaced Easter story." We should read this account too through the eyes of the Old Testament. Jesus ascends a mysterious "high mountain" that is not further identified. The text says "after six days" without giving any starting point for this period of time. But we know that after six days during which a cloud covered Mount Sinai Moses went up the mountain into the light of God's glory (Exod. 24:16). He was accompanied by Aaron the high priest and the original pair of brother priests, Nadab and Abihu (Exod. 24:1). Here Jesus is accompanied by Peter and the brothers James and John, sons of Zebedee.[19] Just as Moses entered the cloud and the divine light (Exod. 24:18) with the result that his face shone (Exod. 34:29-35), so Jesus was transformed by a light not of this world. Beside him appeared Moses and Elijah, the only ones in the Old Testament who received a revelation on the "mountain," and they converse with him. Peter naturally thought that this was the place where the tents should be erected for the three recipients of revelation, the tents which the Old Testament describes (Exod. 33:7-11) for use in the ritual observance of the Sinai event. But Peter did not know what he was saying. The Old Testament says, "Then the cloud covered the tent of meeting, and the glory of the Lord filled the tabernacle. And Moses was not able to enter the tent of meeting, because the cloud abode *(shakan;* Gk: *hoti epeskiazen ep autēn hē nephelē)* and the glory of the Lord filled the tabernacle" (Exod. 40:34-35). Here they themselves were covered by the divine *doxa,* and they heard the revelation of the new covenant. In the ancient event at Sinai God revealed himself in the formula of self-introduction, "I am Yahweh," and then he gave the Decalogue. Here, however, God introduces his son, "This is my beloved Son," and then he continues, "listen to him." Jesus himself has become the revealed Word. The gospel writers could not present it more powerfully: Jesus himself is the Torah.

2. Paul's Understanding of the Law

How does Paul's understanding of the law relate to all this? Is it something totally different, in opposition to the tradition, or did it develop out of the tradition? If the latter, why did his developmen occur? Does it provide a further development and a more profound understanding of the law on the basis of the course of revelation history? The fact is that while the above presentation of the concept of Torah in the synoptic tradition sees Torah in terms of the proclamation and life of Jesus, Paul, with his theology of the cross, understands the law in terms of salvation history's goal—the death and resurrection of Jesus.

---

[19]Note the placing of the definite article in the account in Mark. 9:2 *ton Petron kai ton Iakōbon kai Ioannēn.*

Paul clearly begins with the final Old Testament view of law as found in apocalyptic literature, that is, he takes for granted the contrast of the old and the new aeon, and accordingly, the contrast between Sinai Torah and Zion revelation. He knows that in the old aeon there is only a shadow of the truth, a reflection of the light, and not the light itself, and that in the old aeon no one is adequate to the truth. In continuity with Jeremiah 31:31-34 he sees the contrast between old and new covenant in all its sharpness. For Paul, "law" is the Torah of Sinai.[20]

From this point of view Paul can completely reject the pharisaic Torah piety. The pharisaic "imitation" of the heavenly Torah of necessity remains a deception. The world of Adam is a world of *hamartia*, an existence in opposition to God. To be sure, the world order, which is identical with Torah, is through wisdom indirectly accessible to the Gentiles as the universal law which is the basis of the created world (Rom. 1:18-23), and as the *logia tou theou* it is directly accessible to Jews (Rom. 2:17-24), but in this era everyone, Jews and Gentiles alike, are far from the glory of God (Rom. 3:23). This is true in reference not only to what we do but to what we are, a factor that is often overlooked. In his discussion in Romans 7:7-25 of "You shall not covet," Paul shows how the power of *hamartia* has a profound effect on the physical aspects of human life, producing unholiness and even death. In this aeon of the "flesh" no one can attain to the glory of God, because "the law is spiritual," but we are "carnal" (Rom. 7:14).

The anthropological arguments in Romans have their counterpart in cosmological arguments in Galatians. Humans are subject to the "elemental spirits of the universe" (Gal. 4:3-10). The inability to become righteous, the *hamartia* in Romans has its counterpart in Galatians in slavery to those elemental spirits.

Even in the details of his presentation Paul stands firmly in the Old Testament tradition. He borrows the scheme of Sinai and the eschatological Zion and relates it to the polarity between Hagar and

---

[20]Only occasionally does he use *nomos* in the meaning of Zion Torah, e.g. *nomos pisteōs*. (Rom. 3:27), and "the law of the Spirit of life in Christ Jesus" (Rom. 8:2); the latter is more than a rhetorical embellishment.

Sarah (Gal. 4:21-31); Sinai, located near Hegra, Hagar's place of origin, and the apocalyptic Jerusalem, "mother of us all" (Isa. 54:1-17; 66:5-14; Ps. 87). Already in the Deuteronomic tradition there was a distinction between the revelation in the Decalogue as a direct revelation from God and the revelation of the "details" of the law, meditated through Moses (Deut. 5; cf. Exod. 20:18-21). This corresponds to the mediation through "angels" in Galatians 3:19-20 (cf. Acts 7:53; Heb. 2:2). The Priestly code, however, presents the revealed cult as only the shadowy representation of the heavenly original. Paul's reasoning does not falsify the Old Testament, but it refutes Pharisaism on the basis of the development of the Old Testament tradition.

What then is the positive significance of the Sinai law? What was the role of the law in the old aeon? Paul firmly rejected any identification of the law with sin (Rom. 7:7). As world law and world order, the *nomos* is God's will, and it is because of human inability to keep the law that slavery and guilt arise. Thus Torah serves to make *hamartia* obvious, subjectively, since it results in the knowledge of sin (Rom. 3:20), and objectively in that it increases the sin (Rom. 5:20). Galatians expresses this in terms of wisdom and salvation history. Law is *musar*, "discipline," confinement, restriction, a "custodian" (*paidagōgos*) to bring us to Christ (Gal. 3:23-24). To put it differently, the Sinai law reveals how far humans are from God's *doxa*; it permits "transcendence" to arise. That which in terms of salvation history functions in the history of Israel as judgment is, viewed in the history of revelation, the experiencing of the law of that order which is the basis of our existence and the experience of our distance from that order; it is the experience of holiness in the recognition of sin. By means of the law, transcendence as such is revealed.

If this is the meaning of the law, then its end, its goal, its *telos* is the revelation of Christ here in our human existence of *hamartia* (Rom. 10:4). It is the disclosure of the transcendence in our own immeasurable distance from the holiness of God, in the greatest shame, in the deepest grief. In the person of his son, God enters into our mortal existence, overcoming the transcendence and binding us to himself (Rom. 8:3-4; Gal. 4:4). Atonement takes place not merely metaphorically in symbolic cultic actions of human commitment. God himself appears in the one who was crucified, in our deepest unholiness (Rom. 3:25) in the realm where we are under the curse (Gal. 3:13). Jesus fulfills the law, gives himself over to the elemental spirits of this world for us, and so bears in our stead our death, Adam's death. In the cross of Christ the dichotomy between our human aeon and God's being is overcome. God is with *us*. That is atonement through Christ's blood.

Law has therefore the greatest positive significance for Paul's theology. Here law truly becomes important (Rom. 3:31). It is law that leads to the cross and to the event that took place there. The law was basically designed for our existence in tension with God. For human beings, law becomes the lack of holiness that leads to the cross. If we encounter the law in our sinful existence, then all of us fundamentally encounter the cross (1 Cor. 15:56). In the fullness of time, God went to the cross, and the crucified one is the fulfilled law. Here in "our" death we meet God. Here there is life and blessedness.

The law is the form in which redemption takes place. It is not gospel and law that are contrasts to each other, but gospel and the human attempt to become ourselves the law. The gospel is the fulfilled law, the end and goal of the law. So we find in Paul the apostle the fulfillment of the Old Testament understanding of law.

IV

The Atonement

THE NEW TESTAMENT SPEAKS in a variety of ways of Jesus' death as a comprehensive atonement, atonement for our sins and for the sins of the whole cosmos, as universal reconciliation. This concept rightly constitutes the center of Christian dogmatics. Christology in all its nuances is related to this event of atonement, and the Christain doctrine of justification follows directly from the doctrine of atonement.

It is thus all the more disquieting to note that in the various forms of modern theology the specific doctrine of the atonement recedes more and more into the background, and that today it is difficult to give clear expression to what the Bible calls atonement. It is incorrect to replace the biblical idea of atonement with a doctrine of satisfaction for sin. More and more frequently we encounter the view that the idea of atonement, especially when expressed concretely as cultic atonement through blood, is simply inconceivable to a modern man or woman. This can be seen in those modern translations of the New Testament which are intended as literal translations but simply render the phrase *haima Christou,* "blood of Christ," as "death of Christ" or something similar.

On the other hand an attempt is made to avoid the offense of the doctrine of atonement by seeing it as only one of the many possible interpretations of Jesus' death on the cross and by disputing its importance for soteriology. Widespread cultic concepts from biblical times have been adduced which do not necessarily relate to Christian soteriology. Indeed, the central message of the theology of the cross can be formulated without reference to concepts of atonement. The demand is sometimes made that "outmoded" conceptions should be abandoned. Behind the efforts to portray atonement as a peripheral concept there appears to be a desire to control anything that we cannot identify with.

For the present we can pass over such questions of evaluation, since our primary concern is to gain a precise understanding of the meaning of atonement in the Bible. Even the practical question of how a modern person can accept the biblical concept of atonement is not to be decided a priori by the alleged modern lack of feeling for transcendence but in terms of the truth as it is known. To be sure, we have lost the ability to incorporate directly into our thought world such statements of the New Testament as those concerning the atoning death of Jesus on the cross. We perceive the strange cultic presuppositions as something alien. Whether we are historians or not we are aware of the fact of historical distance. But this means we must employ a historical understanding and not rest content with only that which we can directly apply.

It is certainly "modern" to say that the traditional doctrine of atonement is incomprehensible, but it is not an appropriate contemporary attitude to be content with only that which is immediately understandable. If the sense of history has made us aware of distance, then we must accept the demands of historical investigation. The goal of historical research is to understand that which has come to us from the past. We can no longer accept tradition absolutely and directly and determine its relevance on the basis of our thought world, but we must determine its relevance by means of that which we encounter historically. If the Christ event was understood as atonement, we must take this tradition seriously and make every effort to learn to understand it.

The Concept of Atonement

One of the basic human experiences is finding oneself in a situation where one's life is forfeit. He or she has committed homicide or murder, or, even though not in the eyes of the law, in a moral or religious or other light he or she has "merited" death. The person stands in an irreparable plight, irreparable because it encompasses the limits of existence itself. Nothing can any longer be made good. A people (not a "society," but a collective unit in which all are responsible for one another) can find itself in a situation where the limits of its legal, moral, and religious capability of existence have been transgressed, as, for example, when it recognizes its guilt for the bloodshed of war or has brought on itself responsibility for some dreadful disaster. Also a land (not a geological area but a human habitat that is a quasi-anthropological entity) can be totally corrupted by the occurrence of some disaster, so that it can no longer support life. Is there any possibility of release from this plight for a person who is so guilty as to reach the limit of existence, or for a nation in a similar situation? Is there any possibility for a new life beyond an irreparable event? Is there any atonement?

Our modern concept of atonement does not adequately represent the biblical concept. The old high German *suona* means verdict, judgment in the sense of a "substitute" restitution, and in this sense *suonen* means judge. It is the reconciliation of parties to a fight, or opponents whose conflicts or disagreements are settled through some symbolic action, frequently something non-material, such as kneeling in submission. Our concept of atonement is basically limited to the legal realm of transactions between persons, and its content to restitution through some symbolic action.

The biblical concept, expressed in the Hebrew root *kpr,* usually presupposes the disruption of one's relation to God in the widest sense, sinfulness, the loss of cosmic integrity, and expressly an offense that from the human side is irreparable. It involves guilt that encompasses life itself, a situation where one's existence is forfeit. It involves one's very being. Atonement makes possible a restitution that affects one's own being, a final reparation in which a substitution is made or atonement accomplished symbolically. Thus *kopher,* atoning, becomes a sort of ransom, always understood as a substitution for one's existence. It is *pidyon nephesh,* the redemption of an individual life (Exod. 21:30). Atonement thus occurs through a (substitutionary) total commitment and is as such a saving of a life, for which the person strives and which God accomplishes. God does not command atonement, the individual requests it. The order of the universe requires an exchange, especially in ultimate issues, but atonement allows humans to continue to exist. It is a restoration of those who have fallen, a healing of the terminally ill.

Let us consider some examples. After Israel sinned by worshiping the golden calf, Moses said to the people, "You have sinned a great sin. And now I will go up to the Lord; perhaps I can make atonement *(akappera)* for your sin" (Exod. 32:30). The account continues, "So Moses returned to the Lord and said, 'Alas, this people have sinned a great sin; they have made for themselves gods of gold. But now, if thou wilt forgive their sin—but if not, blot me I pray thee, out of thy book which thou has written" (32:31-32). Moses wants to atone. He offers himself a *kopher,* that is, he offers his existence which is recorded in the book of life. It is a substitution of life for life through a total surrender of self.

In 2 Samuel 21:1-14 we read that Saul's blood guilt toward the Gibeonites had brought a three-year famine on the land. King David is in the position of responsibility. How can he atone *(kpr,* v. 3)? The Gibeonites demand the life of seven members of Saul's family, whom they then hanged "on the mountain before the Lord" (v. 9). Once again sin is removed by the sacrifice of a life, in this case in an old Canaanite manner. The distinctive feature of this text, however, is the emphasis that the land was restored to a state of wholeness only after the corpses, which had been guarded by Rizpah, were buried in the tomb of Saul's family. Rizpah's heroic action surpassed that of the men of Jabesh who rescued the corpses of Saul and Jonathan (cf. v. 12). "And after that God heeded supplications for the land" (v. 14b). To atonement, piety is added, but the decisive factor is God's compassion.

The land can be defiled not only by Israel's sin, but also by violence done to Israel. The essential feature is the state of unwholeness, the violation of the cosmic order. Thus God's restoration of Israel can be said to take place by means of God's "wrath" on Israel's enemies, which through atonement avenges the loss of life. Through the offering of life the wholeness of the cosmic equilibrium, of order-liness, can be restored. The hymn at the conclusion of the Song of Moses says

> Rejoice, O heavens, with him (God),
>   pray to him all you gods!
> For he avenges the blood of his servants,
>   takes vengeance on his enemies;
> He repays all who oppose him
>   and makes expiation *(wekipper)* for
>   the land of his people.
>   (Deut. 32:43 according to 4Q)

Isaiah 6:7 illustrates how the performing of atonement does not involve an actual total sacrifice but can be performed symbolically in a quasi-cultic act. Isaiah sees God, and he knows that because he is "unclean" this means he must die. A seraph takes a burning coal from the altar where incense is offered to God, and through contact with the all-consuming heavenly fire, atonement *(kpr)* is made for Isaiah, that is, for his sin. We do not need to consider here the reasons why his uncleanness is viewed as uncleanness of his lips. (The glowing coal is touched to his lips.) Of course this would have burned Isaiah fatally, but the act of atonement is symbolized as a cleansing burning by the cultic fire.

It is not surprising that symbolic rituals of atonement arose, which under special circumstances portray the substitutionary sacrifice of life. Deuteronomy 21:1-9 describes how the blood guilt for a murder committed by an unknown person is atoned for by the killing of a heifer which has never been worked, that is, has not yet been re-moved from the original state of nature. Beside a perennially flow-ing stream where the land is in its natural state, the heifer's neck is broken. The representatives of the communities responsible for the area where the murder was committed wash their hands over the heifer and testify, "Our hands did not shed this blood, neither did our eyes see it shed. Forgive *(kapper)*, O Lord, thy people Israel, whom thou has redeemed, and set not the guilt of innocent blood in the midst of thy people Israel" (vv. 7-8). In this way the guilt of innocent blood is purged *(wenikkapper,* v. 8b). The land that

was profaned by innocent blood, received blood given in substitution. The land and the shed blood are, through this ritual to restore
the cosmic order, returned to their natural state, and the flowing
water belonging to this land symbolically washes away the blood
guilt and balances it by the blood taken up from the life given in
substitution. Note that in this ritual of slaying an animal, no sacrifice is offered in the biblical sense. This is not an act of presenting
an offering but of taking life, for which the breaking of the neck
is typical (cf. Exod. 13:13; 34:20).[1] In addition, for Deuteronomy,
sacrifice was legitimate only when offered on Mt. Zion. Neither is
there any need to assume the concept of sacrifice in terms of history
of religion as a presupposition for this ritual, since it can be fully
explained in terms of atonement as a substitutionary offering of life.

The institution of the sin offering was intended to transfer the
ritualizing of the act of atonement into the realm of sacrifice. This
presupposed a complicated system of concepts. Atonement is something other than merely making God gracious, which in appropriate
circumstances could be thought of as possible by means of a quantitative increase in the offering, and it is striking that the late atonement
offerings were always limited in number. In pre-exilic times there
is no evidence at all for the existence of a sin offering. It says in
1 Samuel 3:14 that the iniquity of Eli's house could not be ex-
piated by sacrifice or whole burnt offering,[2] but this does not mean
sin offering. Rather the two basic types of sacrifice are mentioned
in order to encompass the entire priestly sacrificial system, which
would never be able to wipe away the guilt of this priestly house.
An atoning function is not adduced here for the sacrifice as such
but for the regularly specified priestly worship. The passage means
that the guilt cannot be made good, that life is forfeit. Only 2 Kings
12:16 could be cited for the existence of sin offerings in the pre-
exilic period. It says that the money used by King Jehoash at the
end of the ninth century for renovating the temple did not represent
sin offerings. This is probably a gloss that presupposes the limits of

---

[1] Also no female animal could be offered in sacrifice, in the sense expressed
in the later expiatory sacrifice.

[2] *minha* is used here in this sense.

the realm of holiness prescribed in the Priestly Document and was intended to show that no use was made of the offerings given for atonement, because such misuses would have profaned the temple.

We must therefore make a clear distinction between the many possibilities of actual acts of atonement, with the ritualizing of such acts from time to time on the one hand, and on the other, atonement as an element of sacrifice, which is not found before the post-exilic period. Here atonement takes on special meaning as an element in biblical theology. We must, however, first determine what special character it took on in the context of this system of sacrifices.

We can summarize as follows what can be said in general concerning atonement. As the Lord of creation, in majestic omnipotence, God frees humans from sin, but, for those humans, atonement means a readiness to die. Moses interceded for Israel, Saul's sons had to lose their lives, and Isaiah experienced a burning in his heart. *Kopher,* "ransom," is that which pays the price of a life, which can substitute for my life. *Kipper* means to find such a *kopher,* to pay the penalty of death, and from the human side that can be accomplished only by total surrender. Atonement does not mean forgiveness of sins and errors that can be made good. Everyone should look out for themselves in such cases. Restitution, where it is possible, must obviously be made. To atone does not mean to bring reconciliation, to accept forgiveness for what can be made good again. It means to snatch one away from a death that is deserved.[3]

---

[3]Etymologically the basic meaning of the root *kpr* is to "wipe away" or "cut away," as in Akkadian in the intensive stem, and then "root out," "cleanse" in a cultic sense. The latter is the basis for the Hebrew meaning "atone," also in the intensive stem. Apparently the fact that it was used only in a technical sense indicates that the development in Akkadian can be presupposed for the Hebrew. It also passed into Arabic in the intensive stem. From the root meaning "wipe away" we can explain the Aramaic "wipe away," "deny" (Arabic, "hide," "conceal," "cover"), "renounce" (Arabic "deny," "be an unbeliever"). It is not possible to assume a root meaning "conceal," even though by chance *kipper* in Jer. 18:23 corresponds to *kissa* ("close up") in Neh. 3:37. For the following discussion it is important to note that the Hebrew noun *kapporet* formed from the intensive stem, which is used to designate the symbol of atonement on the Ark of the Covenant, does not mean "lid" (this does not fit the data, since the Ark was a closed chest) but rather "implement for atonement," "symbol for atonement,"

Atonement and Cult

In the collapse of the nation and cult of Israel-Judah as a result of the Assyrian and Babylonian conquests, there arose in Judah under the influence of prophetic theology, a new understanding of cult and of atonement. In the Priestly theology, atonement is regarded as the basis of cult. It was recognized that cult is possible only as an act of atonement, and therefore atonement must determine the nature of the cultic realm. The recognition of the cult of atonement and the deeper understanding of atonement that resulted from it produced a new orientation of cult. It is hard for us to understand this and to properly evaluate it because the cultic dimension has become so foreign to our sense of reality.

Cult is worship in ritual procedures. These function as symbols, because human cult can represent our relation to transcendence only through symbols. It is this representative character of cult, this making the intangible accessible to our senses that constitutes our particular difficulty. Either we look on cult as something unreal, a kind of serious "theater" that really has nothing at all to do with God because the human acts are not commensurate with the divine realm, or we take the other extreme and regard it as magic, a kind of theurgy. The ancients, however, were aware of the inadequacies of cult —in general we regard them as much too naive, but they could not see anything absurd in its symbolic nature. Wasn't every relation to the transcendental mere symbol? Wasn't every human statement about the truth we aim for only a representation of it, and isn't our language and our prayer also only symbol? Isn't there the deepest connection between word and symbol? When they face the absolute, humans do not renounce speech and sign. Cult goes back to the primeval history of mankind and has accompanied the most varied stages of human consciousness. It encompasses not only speech but all human physical existence. It is "present" to us, and the ceremonies unfold in the realm of the senses where humans exist.

Just as the biblical revelation is revelation to humans, so also Israel is inconceivable without cult. The difference between pagan cult and biblical cult is as great as that between pagan religion and biblical revelation. We might mention the absence of any image of God, and the one focal point of revelation. It is obvious that in the meaning of cult, Israel experienced its own historical, comprehensive, cultic development, because the spiritual and theological development went hand in hand with that of the cult. The essential stages—development of the state, new orientation through the classical prophets, and reestablishment after the exile—found expression in basic segments of the cult history, which can be labeled as Zion, Deuteronomy, and the Priestly conception of cult. Cult thus became an essential part of Israel's life. Israel's worship stands in the closest possible relationship to the revelation which God gave to Israel.

How are we to understand that in the post-exilic cult, as interpreted by the Priestly code, atonement came to be regarded as the basis of cult? How did it come about that the exceptional procedure for atonement, which basically had nothing at all to do with worship, was taken up into the regular cultic practices? Why was this quite extraordinary feature, this escape by total surrender from the guilt that deserved death, this complete renewal from total corruption, accepted as the basic occurrence in the cult? In order to answer these questions and to clarify the special characteristics which the concept of atonement acquired in this form of the cult, we must turn to concrete details of this cult. Only in this way can we draw a total picture and grasp its meaning and significance.

Among the sacrifices, those which involve the shedding of blood occupy a special place. In Israel they involve only those domestic animals raised for human consumption, and so no prey from the hunt, and specifically no "inedible" animals (compare the regulations for ceremonial cleanness). These sacrifices fall into two categories: burnt offerings (*ᶜolah*) that after slaughter are wholly offered to God by burning (transfer by fire into the sphere of *pneuma*, which was conceived as immaterial[4]), and the "meal offerings" (*zebah*) which after slaughter were for human consumption, and of which only specific pieces of fat were to be burned on the altar. According to the cultic situation and the rise of supplementary cultic customs, special sacrifices came to be offered, especially varia-

---

[4] The concept of matter is oriented to measurable extension in space; matter is thus solid or liquid.

tions of the meal sacrifices, which could vary from a normal feast after the slaughter of an animal to the great liturgical feasts of the community (*shelamim,* sacrificial meals to express the condition of *shalom*).

In pre-deuteronomic times these could be celebrated without any particular occasion merely because of the slaughter of an animal, or, for example, in special forms as the cultic new beginning of a person's life after surviving a life-threatening crisis *(todah,* "thank offering"). The two categories of *°olah* and *zebah* correspond to the two categories of human control over "life" [5]: at conception (animal husbandry) and at slaughter human interference demands a sacrifice that acknowledges the Lord of life. It is easy to understand that an *°olah* can involve only a male animal and takes precedence over the *zebah.* The highest rank is naturally occupied by the sacrifice of the first-born male.

When in the Priestly document new sacrifices for atonement are added to this simple and yet comprehensive system, they do not seem to fit well. In fact in P sacrifices for atonement are clearly distinguished from this inherited system. It is only as a supplement that the sacrifices are presented in the great rituals of consecration in Exodus 29 and Leviticus 8-9, with the clear distinction that only in connection with atonement sacrifices are the quantity and type of animals designated precisely. Nonetheless the sacrifices seem at first glance to constitute categories that correspond to *°olah* and *zebah.* There is a "sin offering" *(ḥattat)* and a "guilt offering *(asham).* The latter is only a negative "meal offering." The one who brings a guilt offering, brings in one sense a meal offering, but it is eaten by the holy priests and not by one bringing the sacrifice.

This is also true for a sin offering when an individual brings it on his own behalf, but a special blood rite is involved. Some blood is sprinkled on the horns of the altar of burnt sacrifice, and the rest is poured out at the foot of the altar. This may be called the minor blood rite, because the sin offering can also involve a major blood rite when it is a sacrifice for all Israel or for its cultic representative, the high priest. In this case the blood is applied to the temple itself.

---

[5] The concept of life is based on animal life.

The curtain in front of the holy of holies is sprinkled with blood, some is sprinkled on the horns of the incense altar in front of the holy of holies, and the rest is again poured out at the foot of the altar of burnt offering. In this case the sacrifice cannot be eaten as it was in the "negative meal offering," but it is burned, destroyed outside the sanctuary.

In addition to the major blood ritual there is another greater ritual, when on Yom Kippur the blood is sprinkled on the place where God appears over the ark of the covenant, on the so-called "mercy seat." It is clear that behind this variety of atoning sacrificial rites, with their similarities and differences there is a definite system, but because of certain borrowings and adaptations that can be understood in terms of a historical development, the system is not immediately obvious. Let us first look for explanation in the process through which and in which atonement *(kpr)* takes place.

The first striking fact is that in P not only do the sin offerings bring atonement, but all sacrifices do. The whole sacrificial system serves to atone and finds its meaning in the atoning function of sacrifice itself. This is true for the earliest form of P, Ezekiel's draft for the constitution of the community. In Ezekiel 43:18-27 we find enumerated not only atonement sacrifices for the dedication of the altar but various burnt offerings, and they all bring atonement (v 26). After the list of the gifts for the sacrifices (Ezek. 45:13-17) the purpose of all the offerings is stated as "to make atonement (v 17). So also in P in the description of the bringing of the first sacrifices at the inauguration of the priests (Lev. 9:7), it says that all sacrifices—those of the consecrated priests, or those of the people —are for atonement.

In the laws governing sacrifices we read in connection with the first kind of sacrifice, the *°olah,* "he (the offerer) shall lay his hand on the head of the burnt offering, and it shall be accepted for him to make atonement for him" (Lev. 1:4). The entire sacrificial cult after Ezekiel's time finds its meaning in atonement. In looking at this new conception of the nature of sacrifice, it is difficult to avoid the judgment that Ezekiel pronounces on the previous conception. God gave Israel "statutes that were not good" (Ezek. 20:25)—a second revelation after the first, true revelation at Sinai—and "defiled them through their very gifts in making them offer by fire all their first-born" (v 26). And this had been the noblest sacrifice of the whole cultic system, and even for Deuteronomy it was the sacrifice that was not to be profaned. This was done, however, because Israel did not keep the command that makes holy, that is observance of the sabbath (v 21).[6] This new Torah for sacrifice, which unites sacrifice with atonement, puts an end to all falsified, half-true sacrifices. The further development of Torah is thus dependent on the power of the prophetic movement.

How then is atonement accomplished ritually in all types of sacrifices? Two procedures are essential to the cultic process of atonement—the laying on of hands and the blood ritual. In Leviticus 1:4 we saw that atonement is made possible for the one offering the sacrifice in that he places his hands on the animal. In the rededication of the Jerusalem sanctuary after it was cleansed by Hezekiah (in the Chronicler's account), the various animals for burnt offerings were first sacrificed and then the sin offerings were brought, for which it was necessary that the king and the worshiping community should lay their hands on the animals (2 Chron. 29:23). Thus we see that the laying on of hands is a characteristic of the atonement ritual in offering the *hattat,* and that from there is crept into the other sacrifices as they took on the nature of an atonement.

What does this ritual gesture of laying on hands *(semikah)* in the atonement process signify? Unfortunately there are quite contradictory answers to this question about a detail that is decisive for our understanding of atonement.[7] Some see the laying on of hands as the ex-

---

[6]Cf. H. Gese, "Ex. 20:25f. und die Erstgeburtsopfer" in *Festschrift* for W. Zimmerli, 1977, pp. 140-151.

[7]For explanations as a rite of transference see P. Volz, "Die Handauflegung beim Opfer" *(Zeitschrift für die alttestamentliche Wissenschaft* 21, 1901, pp. 93-100; K. Koch, "Sühne und Sündenvergebung um die Wende zur nachexilischen Zeit" *Evangelische Theologie* 26, 1966, pp. 217-239); R. Rendtorff, *Studien zur Geschichte des Opfers im alten Israel,* 1967, pp. 214-126. For interpretations as a sign of involvement, see R. deVaux, *Institutions of the Old Testament,* 1961, p. 416; B. J. van der Merwe, "The Laying on of Hands in the Old Testament," *Die Ou Testamentiese Werkgemeenskap in Suid-Afrika Pretoria* 5, 1962, pp. 33-43. K. Elliger (Handbuch zum Alten

pression of the transfer of sins to the animal, and others see it as expression of the involvement of the one bringing the sacrifice in the atonement accomplished by the sacrifice. Supporters of the transference theory take as their starting point the unequivocal passage Leviticus 16:21-22, but we should endeavor to look at all the many examples of such a laying on of hands. By laying on hands, a person can appoint someone as his successor (Num. 27:18, 23; Deut. 34:9), and Levites can be consecrated (Num. 8:10).[8] Thus we do not have here a transferal of sins, but a continuation of the subject in a delegated succession.

The role of the subject in collective acts is especially stressed in that it is not an individual representative but a collective group that lay on their hands (Lev. 4:15; 2 Chron. 29:23). However, an individual can accomplish a transferal of sins with an appropriate confession, as Leviticus 16:21 shows. The hands are not placed on the shoulders or back which are used for bearing burdens, but on the head, which is the expression par excellence of individuality. This too speaks against transferal and for identification.

The transference theory would hardly play any role over against the identification theory if there were not an actual account of transference in Leviticus 16:21-22. And yet even this passage speaks against that theory. Here first of all it says that the high priest performs the *semikah* on the scapegoat, and second, he speaks the confession of sin and "gives" *(ntn)* these sins to the goat, who carries them away. Thus in this ritual of elimination there is in addition to the *semikah* and connected with it a transferal which is primarily expressed ritually as a confession that is spoken and a "giving." We have here therefore a special case in which a transferal of sins is explicitly added to the *semikah,* that is, the two are to be seen as sepa-

Testament I 4 (1966) p. 34 adopts the identification of the offerer with the sacrifice, but thinks that for P this meaning is limited to the substance of sin, so that a transfer of sin is also in the picture.

[8]This late passage in the P material is decisive against any later limitation in P to sinful substance (see the preceding note). There is a borderline case when the laying on of hands expresses a succession in a state of unholiness, a negative delegation, cf. Lev. 24:14; but here a succession to the subject is intended, not an objective transferal.

rate procedures, and the *semikah* takes place here only in parallel to the atonement ritual of the first goat. We will have to come back to the question of how the elimination ritual of Leviticus 16:21-22 is related to the atonement ritual proper, but we can with assurance decide the question of the laying on of hands by saying that it expresses an identification in the sense of a delegated succession, a serving in the place of, and not a transferal of mere "sinful material." This gesture expresses a transference of the subject but not of any object.

The significance of all this for the understanding of atonement is that atonement takes place through the sacrifice of the life of an animal which, by a laying on of hands, is identified with the one bringing the sacrifice. This is in agreement with our earlier definition of atonement as a total substitutionary commitment of a life. The act of atonement is not to be thought of as a transfer of sins wih the subsequent execution of the one bearing the sins, the sacrificial animal. In that case there would be only a substitution that excludes one party; instead, in cultic atonement the sacrifice of the victim's life is a substitution that includes the one bringing the sacrifice. Moreover the giving up of life is not simply an act of destruction. The animal is not killed in order to bring about a destruction of the sinful object or to achieve appropriate punishment of the one who is guilty of the sin, but rather a holy ritual of blood is performed. The animal is taken to the sanctuary of God, where it comes into contact with what is holy. Cultic atonement thus is not accomplished merely by the death of the sacrifice, but in the commitment of life to what is holy, in contact with holiness. In the inclusive substitution by means of atoning sacrifice, this ritual brings Israel into contact with God. The new, positive aspect of atonement finds its expression in the blood rites.

We are inclined to see magic practices in blood ceremonies, manipulations that seek to achieve with blood, (a material erroneously conceived of in dynamic terms) that which cannot be achieved in any other way. Blood ceremonies are known from abundant material from the field of history of religion. The drinking of blood, or smearing the body with blood is done in order to gain strength, to take into oneself particular powers. But there is a fundamental distinction between this type of blood practice and the uses of blood in Israel, where blood is treated with the greatest respect. Any consuming of blood is excluded, and it is fundamental that blood must be given back to the earth. The special significance of blood does not consist in its being a dynamized, and thus dynamizing material, but in its appearing at a sacrifice, a ritual killing.

Under normal circumstances, human interference with life, the life of animals, is possible only in sacrifice.[9] Ritual slaughter, a cultically legitimate killing, is a shedding of blood by means of the implements of slaughter. As the life here disappears in a ritual death, the blood becomes free. Blood thus appears in a normal and legitimate manner only in a ritual slaying. As a consequence, there arose a concept of blood that is relevant to blood's cultic function, that is, the ritual release of blood is the release of (individual) life, of the *nephesh,* and in a cultic sense, blood is the life substance that has been set free. The "legitimate" presence of blood in the normal daily sacrifice is decisive for the concept of blood, especially in the cultic realm. Here blood was thought of not as a neutral bodily substance in a medical sense, nor as a source of power in a magical sense, but as that which it ordinarily seems to be when an animal is sacrificed, the substance of life.

In this light it is possible to understand the statement, "For the life (*nephesh,* individual life, soul) of the flesh (the bodily animal being) is in the blood; and I (God) have given it for you upon the altar to make atonement for your souls (plural of *nephesh*), for it is the blood that makes atonement by reason of the life *(nephesh)*" (Lev. 17:11). The identification of the *nephesh* of the one making the offering with the sacrificial animal is presupposed (we saw that it is effected by the laying on of hands), and through the shedding of the animal's blood the life of the person who brings the sacrifice is symbolically offered up. The decisive factor for the cultic act of atonement is that this sacrifice of life is not a mere killing, a sending of life into nothingness, but it is a surrender of life to what is holy, and at the same time an incorporation into the holy, given expression

---

[9]It is to be understood that the post-Deuteronomic, secular slaughter, which is only a substitute for ritual slaughter, is not under consideration here.

throughout contact with blood. By means of the atoning rites in which blood is applied, the *nephesh* is dedicated to and "incorporated into" the holy.

The passage Exodus 24:1-11—vv 3-8 (E² strand)—gives a new interpretation of the sealing of the covenant between God and Israel as a blood ritual. In the light of vv 9-11 the meaning of the ceremony is clear—there is now a community with God. The ceremony presents this in terms of sprinkling half the blood on the altar and the other half on the covenant people. This produces a final binding together of God and Israel. In P, the consecration of the priests takes place in a similar manner. "And you shall kill the ram, and take part of its blood and put it upon the tip of the right ear of Aaron and upon the tips of the right ears of his sons, and upon the thumbs of their right hands, and upon the great toes of their right feet (the points that mark the extreme limits of the body and are here symbols for the whole, cf. the ritual significance of the horns of the altar), and throw the rest of the blood against the altar around about" (Exod. 29:20). The *nephesh* substance, the blood, can thus effect a consecration to the holy, an integrating, permanent contact of life with life.

In this sense cultic atonement has the greatest positive meaning. Here sins are not simply wiped away or capital punishment inflicted, but in a comprehensive substitution the *nephesh* is dedicated to the sanctuary and bound up with the holy. According to P, atonement occurs in every sacrifice, in that by the laying on of hands there is a substitution (Lev. 1:4) and the blood is sprinkled around the altar (e.g. Lev. 1:5). This occurs especially in the sin offering in the minor blood rite (consecration at the altar of burnt sacrifice) and in the major blood rite (consecration at the limits of the Holy of Holies: curtain and altar of incense), but in its highest form on the great Day of Atonement. The basic idea behind the post-exilic cult is that Israel is brought to the holy. Cult is symbolic atonement, because it is the way to the holy that of necessity leads through our death.

The prophet Zechariah, a member of the priestly tribe, recounts a vision of the inauguration of the post-exilic cult (Zech. 3:1-7) in

which the high priest is assured at his investiture, "If you will walk
in my ways and keep my charge, then you shall rule my house and
have charge of my courts, and I will give you the right of access
(read *mahalakim*) among those who are standing here" (v 7). The
highest goal and consummation of priestly activity is thus access to
the divine majesty, entrance into the heavenly gathering of the
angelic beings who serve God, access to God's throne. The goal of
cult in post-exilic time is access to God. The community of God with
Israel, the ties between Yahweh and Israel, which constituted the
original meaning of Old Testament revelation was to have its fulfillment in cult as specified in the Priestly Document, following on
Israel's already having been understood as a holy people (Exod.
19:6 D). This means that Israel was to share in the divine sphere of
holiness: "You shall be holy; for I the Lord your God am holy"
(Lev. 19:2 etc.). This view of full community with God corresponds
significantly to the belief that humans can come before God only as
those whose lives are forfeit. The encounter with the holy destroys
all that is unholy. The logical outcome of the idea of full community with God is atonement, that is, atonement in the new, positive
sense of surrender to the holy. For P, the cult in which one encounters God can be only atoning cult. Thus this final, highest
understanding of cult in Israel, that worship is community with
God in the fullest sense, participation in God's *doxa,* his glory that
fills the "Tent of Meeting," God's "dwelling" (Exod. 40:34) leads
to the most profound understanding of sin: humans, as such, in their
distance from God, are, in the light of God's *doxa,* worthy of death.
But God opens a way to himself through symbolic atonement, which
takes place in the cult that God has revealed to us.

This post-exilic cult includes a highest and final ceremony, in which
we see the full original meaning of cult—the atonement on Yom
Kippur. Before discussing it we will attempt to understand the
striking differentiation between it and the sin offering as we described it at the outset. First what is the difference between the function of the sin offering and that of the guilt offering? The guilt offering *(asham)* includes only the simple rite of sprinkling the blood
on the altar, which was added secondarily to all sacrifices in P. Ori-

ginally therefore the blood rite cannot at all have constituted the essence of this sacrifice. The guilt offering was used in cases of negligent offenses committed by an individual, and wherever possible, that is, when material damages can be made good, involves restitution and a penalty of a fifth of the damages. The essential form of the sacrifice consists in the already described "negative meal offering," in being excluded from the shared meal that celebrates the state of *shalom*. The guilt offering is thus, aside from its secondary character as atonement which accrued to all sacrifices, not at all a ritual for atonement, but a ritual for repentance, which developed out of the sacrificial meal.

The sin offering *(ḥattat)* was used for cases where sins had been committed and also for ceremonies of consecration (Exod. 29; Lev. 8, 9; Ezek. 43:18ff.; 45:18ff.). Our understanding of cultic atonement makes this at once comprehensible, but the atonement occurring here is basically a ritual of consecration, because it is a matter of access to the holy. Quite independently of any specific human offense and solely because of the human distance from God, the rite of consecration has this positive atoning character as a bringing into contact with the holy. If the sacrifice of atonement was used in cases of sin, it was never used to deal with guilty acts (for that the guilt offering was available, and that was originally concerned not with atonement, but with repentance) but it was to deal with the depraved *being* of humans, into which they came without any conscious act *(shegagah)*. Leviticus 5:1-13 lists such cases: violation of the rules governing ceremonial uncleanness, the human failing of uttering a rash oath, the passive failure to bear testimony, that is, anything that is understood as not bringing guilt. By means of the sacrifice for atonement, the damaged being is reconsecrated and healed.

The blood ritual which follows the laying on of hands is the constitutive element in atonement. What is the purpose of the "negative meal offering" that comes in addition to the sin offering? (In the minor blood ritual, the meal is eaten by the priests, but in the major ritual the emphasis is on the holiness of the entire community, including the priests, understandably without eating the offering). In

Ezekiel 43:19-21, a text that antedates the Priestly Document, the ritual for the sin offering is described without any mention of burning the fat, therefore without a "negative meal offering." In the description of Aaron's consecration in Leviticus 8:15 atonement also occurs without any meal offering, except for the obvious addition in v. 16. Finally, the burning of the fat is missing in the preparation of the ashes of the red heifer, which is explicitly called a ritual for a sin offering (Num. 19:9). It is only with the later development in which the sin and guilt offerings are brought closer together (Lev. 4-5) that the atonement ritual for the individual is expanded by the addition of the penance ritual of the "negative guilt offering," and this led finally to the introduction of the burning of the fat even in the observance of the general sin offering.[10]

Another late development is the differentiation between the blood rites. The major rite, which placed the blood on the boundary of the Holy of Holies and thus also on the altar of incense, serves as atonement for the sanctuary (Lev. 6:23). Originally, however, this was true of the atonement sacrifice in all instances. As Ezekiel 43 shows, consecration of the sanctuary is really consecration of the altar of burnt offering. This can be seen also in Exodus 29:10-14 and 2 Chronicles 29:18-24. The altar for burnt offerings stood in the middle of the sanctuary, and it is natural for blood to be used on it. The original use of blood for atonement was therefore to apply it to this altar. The major blood rite was derived by an intensification of this observance, and the final step was the Yom Kippur ceremony, to which we must now turn.[11]

The most important service of atonement was assigned a special

---

[10]The development reached its climax in the systematic paralleling of fat and blood (cf. Lev. 3:17).

[11]The above portrayal of cultic history differs from that of R. Rendtorff (cf. *Studien zur Geschichte des Opfers im alten Israel*, 1967, esp. pp. 233f., 239-241.) He regarded the original *ḥattat* as also the sacrifice for consecrating sanctuary and temple, but he separated it from atonement for persons, which originally was accomplished for the community by the ʿolah and for individuals by the *asham*. The two forms then were combined in the *ḥattat*. But then why did the *asham* ritual continue to be observed? It remains unexplained how the burning of the fat was introduced from the *zebah* rite as a ritual element.

day in the New Year festivities, Yom Kippur. The atonement accomplished here is the highest cultic act in Israel, and for it the high priest enters the Holy of Holies for the only time during the year. Only on this day was the name Yahweh pronounced. Sirach 50:5ff. describes the entrance of the high priest in connection with the act of atonement as the culmination of all cultic activity. The account of the ritual in Leviticus 16 is concerned only with the progress of the ritual events and therefore lists essentials and non-essentials together. We can however readily recognize that the central act of atonement is to be separated from the ritual of the goat for Azazel, which does not represent cultic atonement in the sense of the Priestly Document, but a removal of sin. It is a rite of elimination belonging to popular culture, similar to rituals in Leviticus 14:1-9 for cleansing lepers, in which a bird symbolically carries the leprosy away (v. 7).

In the strict, cultic sense atonement takes place by means of the sprinkling of blood in the Holy of Holies. We have seen that out of the minor blood rite, in which blood is sprinkled on the horns of the altar of burnt offering there developed the major blood rite as an intensification of the lesser rite, and it reached to the edge of the Holy of Holies. There the blood was sprinkled on the curtain and on the horns of the altar of incense, which by its nature was to stand in front of the place where the divine presence was localized. This intensification reached its culmination in the atoning rites of Yom Kippur, when the high priest entered the Holy of Holies, the place of the divine presence itself.

In the Holy of Holies there was nothing but the Ark of the Covenant, which symbolized that this was where God dwelt. When God was regarded as king, as Yahweh Sabaoth, the people thought of him as enthroned invisibly above the Ark. Thus in the temple of Solomon the wings of the creatures supporting the throne, the cherubim, were outspread over the Ark. The Priestly Document states concerning this most holy part of the sanctuary, that on the Ark was located the "mercy seat" (*kapporet*), a sheet of pure gold, of the same dimensions as the ark. Two cherubim were placed symmetrically above it as bearers of the invisible One enthroned there. "There I (God) will meet (*weno ᶜadti*) with you (the sanctuary is called in P *'ohel mo^eed* "tent of meeting") and from above the mercy seat, from between the two cherubim that are upon the ark of the testimony, I will speak with you of all that I will give you in commandment for the people of Israel" (Exod. 25:22).

The central place in the sanctuary is the place where the revelatory theophany take place. Following the cultic, symbolic thought patterns of P, it is represented by a simple plane on top of the ark.[12] Beyond this plane are the cherubim that represent the place where God appears. One of the oldest texts dealing with the Sinai revelation reads, "And they (the seventy elders of Israel) saw the God of Israel; and there was under his feet as it were a pavement of sapphire stone, like the very heaven (firmanent) for clearness" (Exod. 24:10). Here we find this "plate" again, which is compared so mysteriously to the firmament. It is the boundary where transcendence begins, and in the firmament it becomes perceptible to us. Above this "plate" of transcendence, the One seated on his throne meets with humans.

The high priest, who only once in the year goes beyond the curtain into the Holy of Holies, performs the highest and most comprehensive atonement when he sprinkles some of the blood of the sacrifice on the mercy seat—and sprinkles it seven times before the mercy seat (perhaps a secondary expansion of the ritual). Meanwhile the cloud of incense is covering the mercy seat, or else the priest would die in front of the place where the divine *doxa* appears (Lev. 16: 13-15). In reference to the priests and the people and the two animals for sacrifice, the bull and the goat, the rite is described as performed twice. The doubling of rites actually reflects only the completeness of the one rite. The less important rites of atonement are added here for the sake of completeness (vv 16b-19).

The meaning of the central Yom Kippur rite is clear. By a substitutionary sacrifice of life, Israel is brought into contact with God himself. In a ceremony that enacts the approach to God's presence even to the point of ultimate physical contact and still preserves the outward sublimity of that contact in the sprinkling of the drops of blood, the primeval phenomenon of the saving encounter with God

---

[12]It is noteworthy that while P is not sparing in listing measurements, the thickness of the gold plate is not indicated.

is carried out. This is the contact between the God who reveals himself and humans who completely surrender themselves. We see the scene at Sinai reenacted cultically. The cloud of revelation covers the divine *doxa* and the representative of Israel who approaches God.

Cultic, sanctifying atonement is in no sense a negative procedure of removing sin or of penance. It is coming to God by passing through the sentence of death. The post-exilic cult of Israel, oriented to the concept of atonement, correctly portrays the final stage in the history of revelation of the development of Israelite cult in general. It is a fundamental error in theological judgment concerning such cultic practice to ascribe to the Priestly Document and the late Israelite priesthood a simple ritualism that deceives men and women with the security provided by a cultic *opus operatum* and that necessarily lacks the eschatological aspect, with the result that only a self-sufficient, self-assured theocracy is to be seen there.

Quite apart from the fact that such a judgment ignores the symbolic character of all cult, especially such a rite as this, it also underestimates the inner earnestness, the intense inner involvement that the performance of this cultic act requires of the priests and the laity (cf. Lev. 16:29, 31). We may assume that all areas of life were deeply influenced by such cultic thinking. In this light we can compare the tractate from the first half of the first century A.D., the so-called book of Fourth Maccabees, with its concept of martyr death, with the substitutionary (i.e., with blood) atonement for Israel (6:29; 17:22).[13]

---

[13]Of course the general concept of atonement, of substitutionary total self-surrender, could also be used outside a cultic context as an important metaphor in theological statements. According to Isa. 43:3-4 God gives as a ransom *(kopher)* for the life of Israel the pagan nations that come to Yahweh, so that their idolatrous worship ceases (cf. 45:14-17). Thus finally through the judgment Israel emerges alive and justified. In Isa. 53:10 on the other hand, the statement that the life of the servant of Yahweh is an "offering for sin" *(asham)* does not involve the concept of atonement, but of penance. Israel gives herself as a penitential sacrifice for the heathen. The late passage Isa. 27:7-9 is indirect evidence that Israel's sufferings were often understood as atonement. That passage, however, exhorts Israel not to rely on her suffering, but to seek atonement only in the rejection of idolatry. It is uncertain whether 2 Maccabees 7:37f. sees martyrdom as atoning or only as moving God to be gracious and conciliatory.

Above all a negative evaluation overlooks the quite "provisional" nature of this cult. The Ark was lost when the Solomonic temple was destroyed, and the crucial mercy seat, the *kapporet,* never existed. The high priest entered the Holy of Holies *as if* the Ark were there (cf. the description in Yoma V 3f.), and he sprinkled the blood upwards *as if* the mercy seat existed. This provisional nature of cult *as if* must have been deeply disquieting to Israel, and there was no lack of eschatological hope for the rediscovery of the Ark (cf 2 Macc. 2:4-8), and even for the divine throne itself to appear (cf Jer. 3:16-17; Ezek. 43:7).

In Romans 3:25 Paul quotes a confessional statement of the early church, "(Jesus) whom God put forward as an expiation *(hilastērion = kapporet)* by his blood, to be received by faith. This was to show God's righteousness." This eschatological confession means, that now God has revealed and activated his "mercy seat," and he applies this to us by dedicating us through his blood. The crucified one represents God enthroned, and unites us with him through the sacrifice of life by the shedding of human blood. God appears to us and becomes accessible to us in the one who was crucified. Atonement is not instituted by humans in the rite of substitutionary shedding of blood, the sacrifice of life, but it is instituted by God. God establishes this unity with us. Union with God becomes possible, because God appears to us in our present plight, in our suffering, in our existence in *hamartia.* The curtain in front of the Holy of Holies has been rent in two. God is near to us, present with us in death, in suffering, in our dying.

"Christ died for our sins in accordance with the scriptures" (1 Cor. 15:3b). Atonement is the sacrifice of life for the sake of making life whole. It brings the abyss of human life into union with the highest divine *doxa.* Human life that has given over to death is consecrated by God's glory, and God's *doxa* shines forth in our mortal existence. Atonement means a corporate life, it is always the whole that is atoned for, and so it is not only that the individual comes to partake of the holy through God's atonement; the atoning death of Jesus is sufficient for us all, it has reconciled the world with God.

The saving nature of Jesus' death can be grasped only in terms of atonement. This is what it means to talk about the blood of Jesus. His blood means that it was not for himself that Jesus died, however innocent his death, but that atonement was achieved. Here the Son gave himself for the world, shedding the life substance, his blood, instituting the new covenant, sanctifying the new Israel, yes, the entire world. Through his blood we gain a share in the new reality of salvation. To speak of atonement means death and resurrection together. In Jesus' death, his cross, we have life. This death, by breaking through to life, by reconciling us to God, has atoned for the entire cosmos.

As the starting point for our interpretation of post-exilic cult, we chose Zechariah 3. In a supplement to the great vision of the re-establishment of the cult after the exile the new priesthood is explained as a symbol: "Hear now, O Joshua the high priest, you and your friends who sit before you (the new group of priests), for they are men of good omen: behold, I will bring my servant the Branch" (3:8). The new Davidic king (the "Branch") will be the fulfillment of this cult. The New Testament shows us the one who gives us "access" (v 7) to God once and for all, for us and for all creation. By his death we have union with God. And so his death is the victory over death, the dawn of a new creation.

V

The Origin of the Lord's Supper

TO UNDERSTAND SOMETHING HISTORICALLY means to understand its essence. It means that we come to a knowledge of
the matter through its development, in a manner appropriate
to our consciousness. The question of the origin of the Lord's Supper
leads us into the essence of this sacred meal. Historical knowledge
includes an understanding of the roots, the presuppositions of a
phenomenon. Even if we hold that the Lord's Supper had its origin
in a specific situation in the life of Jesus, we cannot ignore the as-
sumptions and the traditions that lie behind it. Deriving an observance from a situation is not an alternative to understanding it
in terms of a tradition. Neither is it the purpose of a historical investigation to ignore what is specific and distinctive. By investigating
the origin of the Lord's Supper in the pre-Christian tradition, we are
not overlooking what is distinctive; we are seeking to understand
it correctly.

Two factors increase the difficulty of a historical understanding
of the Lord's Supper:

1. The texts and sources are limited in extent. This may be explained by the fact that those for whom the New Testament texts

---

[1]In this lecture I develop further the thesis concerning the origin of the
Lord's Supper which I proposed in the essay "Psalm 22 und das Neue Testa-
ment" (*Zeitschrift für Theologie und Kirche* NF 65, 1968, pp. 1-22 = *Vom
Sinai zum Zion* pp. 180-201) and deal with possible objections to it.

were written knew how this worship service was observed, and thus there was no need to be exhaustive. We should not therefore assume on the basis of the scarcity of texts that the Lord's Supper was of minor importance or that there was wide diversity and great freedom in its observance. Rather we must assume that the central significance of the Lord's Supper for worship was not the result of a late development, but on the contrary already in the time of Paul (Acts 20:7) the regular Sunday worship had been decisively influenced by the Lord's Supper. We should also proceed from the assumption that there were no appreciable regional differences in the form of the Lord's Supper, since because of its significance, tradition must have largely determined its form, and it was the common possession of all Christian communities. In any case the burden of proof lies on those hypotheses that assume there were important differences in observance.

2. We must, however, reckon with *historical* differences, with developments in the Lord's Supper. This is the case with the question of its relationship to an ordinary meal. In 1 Corinthians 11:17-22 Paul was confronting a pronounced separation of the sacramental meal from an ordinary meal. At Corinth an ordinary meal preceded the sacramental meal, and this seems also to have been the case in *Didache* 9f. In the sources themselves we can detect the development that led to the isolation of the sacramental meal, a development that is easy to understand. This may have involved nothing more than external features of usage, or at most a question of congregational order which Paul could regulate himself in distinction to essentials which were firmly fixed by tradition. There is thus no reason to cite possible historical developments as indications that the early church observed two completely different types of the Lord's Supper.

By holding that the form of a sacramental meal was "Hellenistic" and could not have already existed in the "Jewish" church in Jerusalem, some have felt it necessary to postulate two types—an original fellowship meal of the disciples and later of the Jerusalem church as a continuation of the fellowship at table with Jesus, and in the Hellenistic churches a sacramental meal, at which the body of the Lord was eaten. Lietzmann assumed that Paul used the formula,

"For I receive *(parelaben)* from the Lord what I also delivered *(paredōka)* to you" (1 Cor. 11:23) in reference to his Damascus experience,[2] but the opposite could be true, that Paul is handing on with his apostolic authority a tradition that was not to be altered. We must distinguish between a firm tradition and the understanding of that tradition, which can be quite different in Hellenistic circles from what it was in Jerusalem.

But we cannot start with the assumption that in a single decade (Paul met with Peter no later than A.D. 39, and perhaps as early as 37-38, cf. the visit with Peter and James, Gal. 1:18-19 and Acts 9:25-26, and the escape from Damascus, 2 Cor. 11:32-33) the understanding of the Lord's Supper was totally transformed from a non-sacramental meal into a sacramental meal (and the two forms then continued side by side) without any support in the texts for such a hypothesis. The basis for that hypothesis is the question of origins. It is assumed that the sacramental interpretation cannot be derived from the Jewish concept of a meal, so that reference must be made to the analogy of the Hellenistic cultic meal in order to clarify the difference between the Pauline and the pre-Pauline understanding. This brings us to the first major part of our investigation.

Possible Derivations

We can begin by setting aside the Hellenistic cultic meals of the mystery religions, because such practices could have influenced only secondarily the existing, fixed institution of the Lord's Supper by affecting the interpretation which individuals, or perhaps congregations adopted, and could have influenced the church's understanding of the Lord's Supper only through the formation of theology in post-Apostolic times. In addition, because of the arcane discipline that was enforced, we know next to nothing about these Hellenistic meals that could cast light on specific features of the Lord's Supper. Whatever verdict might be rendered on the explanation in Hellenistic terms, it must take second place to the explanation in terms of

---

[2]H. Lietzmann, *An die Korinther* I, II (Handbuch zum Neuen Testament 9) 4th ed., 1949, p. 57.

Jewish presuppositions, and come into consideration only as a possible supplement.

1. The Jewish Meal

The Jewish meal has certain basic characteristics, because a ceremonial meal in ancient times grew out of a basic form of sacrifice, the *zebah,* or meal offering. In pre-deuteronomic times animals could be slaughtered only at an altar. The eating of meat presupposed a meal offering, during which the specified fat pieces were burned on the altar, while the celebrant partook of a sacral meal, which could of course be prepared in a variety of ways. In any case, the basic elements were bread and wine, although these blood-free substances did not themselves require the presence of an altar.

The nature of this meal as a sacrifice had a double meaning. In the meal there was fellowship with God, through participating in his sacrifice, and fellowship among the participants, expressing a state of well-being. There was *shalom* among those taking part in the meal, and therefore the meal offerings, which were celebrated as public liturgical feasts, were called *shelamim.* The meal thus always was joyful, whatever the occasion it celebrated, and the great festivals always included such a meal. There were however no funeral meals. Mourning means fasting, and only at the end of a period of fasting could the "bread of consolation" and the "cup of consolation" be extended to the nearest of kin, who were in this way called back into life.

Bread and wine are the basic solid and liquid elements of a meal, aside from the meat of the animal slain at the altar. Melchizedek the ancient priest-king of Jerusalem gave bread and wine to Abraham (Gen. 14:18) and thus Abraham participated in the sacral meal of the Jerusalem cult, without the killing of an animal or the presence of an altar for burnt offerings; blood sacrifices achieved their full legitimacy only after the revelation at Sinai. Even today a Jewish meal begins with the *beracha,* the blessing over bread and wine. In a ceremonial meal, wine plays a special role. As the cup is raised a sacral declaration, a blessing, a sanctification or something similar can be spoken, and thus "celebrated" in this meal. That is, in this meal something comes into being and is blessed or consecrated in the declaration. Thus the wedding feast inaugurates the new state of marriage, through the sacral declaration as the wine cup is raised. As the coming of the sabbath is celebrated in the home, the raising of the wine cup sanctifies *(qiddush)* the sabbath, that is now in force in the house. The ancient sacral meal thus inaugurates a state of *shalom,* which can be proclaimed in all special cases by raising the cup.[3]

The meal offering takes on special meaning from the particular occasion that is being celebrated. In Exodus 24:11 the meal inaugurates the covenant made on Sinai between Yahweh and Israel, and in Isaiah 25:1-10a the new covenant on Zion is concluded by a meal, here in the form of an offering of thanksgiving. Indeed a great variety of types of meal can be pictured. Consequently we must pose the question, what is the particular sacral meal from which the Lord's Supper is derived and by which it can be understood? On the basis of the synoptic account of the institution of the Lord's Supper, we think first of all of the Passover, which, in keeping with the system of sacrifice, is naturally to be understood as a special from the *zebah.*

2. Passover

At the time of the spring equinox when the full moon in its declining path crosses the rising path of the sun, on this spring night, Israel celebrates the Passover, the feast of the Exodus from Egypt. It goes back to an ancient festival of semi-nomads, who, before they broke camp to go to their summer pastures, killed a meal offering and performed the apotropaic rite of symbolic anticipation of protection. The outside world, the threatening world, was to become a protected world; correspondingly the inside world of the tent was not to be touched by danger, and the blood of the sacrifice, the utmost limit in the material realm, is a symbol of the last boundary, marking the threshhold at the tent's entrance, which cannot be crossed.

For the night of the Exodus Israel slays the Passover sacrifice.

---

[3]The cup of wrath and judgment is to be understood as a terrifying inversion of this rite, which institutes a state of unwholeness.

(Originally the year-old lamb was probably killed by dislocating and breaking [*phs*] its backbone.) Then in ancient times the house entrance was marked with blood, producing a protected interior realm, while the "Egyptian" world outside sank into chaos and the Angel of Death (*mashhit*) slew the first-born. They ate the Passover sacrifice with the unleavened bread of the nomads and the bitter herbs of the wilderness, ready and dressed to depart, and thus the beginning of Israel's salvation history was commemorated. Passover is the festival of Israel's birth out of an Egypt that was in decline, the rising of a new cosmos out of a night of chaos. With the centralization of Passover in Deuteronomy, the slaying was performed at the Temple as a normal *zebah*. The sacrifice was eaten in the houses of Jerusalem, which constituted the only realm of wholeness and safety from the *mashhit* and all that was unwhole.[4] According to the synoptic account Jesus went out of Jerusalem at night[5] to Gethsemane and the Mount of Olives and gave himself up.

Was the Last Supper a Passover celebration? Joachim Jeremias defended this often-discussed question.[6] The account in the synoptics is the only support for the view that it was. The Gospel of John reports the identification of the betrayer and Jesus' Last Supper (Chap. 13), but says nothing about the institution of the Lord's Supper or the Passover meal. Indeed we have there a different dating alto-

---

[4]In the later Jewish Seder, the door is opened during the Passover celebration and the imprecations of Ps. 79:6; 69:25; Lam. 3:66 called down on the world of godlessness.

[5]According to Strack-Billerbeck, II p. 838 (cf. I p. 839f.) this is not a violation of the *halacha* against leaving Jerusalem during the night of Passover, since Bethphage and the Mount of Olives were considered a part of Jerusalem and Bethphage marked the outer boundary of the city's territory. But interestingly enough this is not the case in all the rabbinic material, as Billerbeck has to admit. In the Old Testament the Brook Kidron was the city boundary. (2 Sam. 15:23; 1 Kings 2:37; cf. the pagan shrines on the Mount of Olives, 1 Kings 11:7f.; 2 Kings 23:13, and the role of the Mount in the apocalyptic passage, Zech. 14:4; the Mount of Olives is the site of the ascension because it is the site of the parousia, Acts 1:11, cf. Mt. 24:3; Mark 13:3). The boundary must have been extended at a later time. Even though the rabbinic material is not unanimous, for the New Testament we should assume the older concept; only so can Mark 11:1 and the parallels be understood.

[6]*The Eucharistic Words of Jesus*, Oxford, 1955.

gether. The death of Jesus took place at the time of the killing of the Passover sacrifice on the day of preparation (19:14, 31, 36, 42). This dating has been explained as the result of the tendency to portray Jesus as the Passover lamb (cf. 1:29), and consequently an account of the Last Supper as a Passover meal would be impossible. We should note that the Johannine placing of Good Friday on the 14th of Nisan makes it possible to date the death of Jesus in A.D. 30 or 33. But the synoptic chronology, according to which the night from Thursday to Good Friday is the night of Passover, and Good Friday falls on the 15th of Nisan, excludes the period after A.D. 27 and before A.D. 34, the *termini a quo* and *ante quem*.[7]

To this must be added the fact that interrogation and judgment by the council during the night of Passover and crucifixion on the first day of Passover, which was a sabbath-like *yom tov*, would conflict with all Jewish regulations. Nor is it any help to assume that the calendar used by the Qumran community and attested in the books of Jubilees and Ethiopian Enoch 72-86 was observed by Jesus for a private celebration of Passover. In that calendar the 14th of Nisan always falls on a Tuesday, which contradicts Mark 14:1-2, not to mention other difficulties created by this hypothesis. Though it is certain that Jesus' death was closely connected with the time of Passover, we cannot decide between the synoptics and John by means of a precise historical reconstruction. But there would be no point in here pursuing these historical details further. They can yield us no decisive arguments for or against the derivation of the Lord's Supper from Passover. We merely learn that we cannot base our arguments on the historic date of Passover, but must concentrate on the Synoptic view of Jesus' Last Supper as a Passover meal, and this view is of even greater weight theologically, if it is more than just a historical datum.

If the Lord's Supper is compared to Passover, it becomes clear that all specific features to the Passover meal are missing, and there

---

[7]At best one might assume that the new moon crescent of the first month was discovered one day too late, which in view of the importance of this phenomenon for the calendar and the meteorological conditions of Palestine is practically excluded.

are correspondences only where the basic characteristics of an Old Testament meal ceremony are involved. Aside from the wine, the three essentials of the Passover meal are the lamb, the unleavened bread, and the bitter herbs. In ancient times the bread used in the Lord's Supper was never unleavened. In the Eastern Church this is still the case, as it was in the West until the excluding of the people's oblation between the ninth and eleventh centuries. Bitter herbs have never even been considered. More important than these elements is the time, the night of the spring full moon. Passover is first of all a point of time, and despite all the historicizing of the festival in Israel the natural time is so decisive that removing it from this fixed place in the course of the year would be totally senseless. The controversy over the date of Easter shows that the early church had similar feelings.

The words of institution of the Lord's Supper cannot be connected with Passover. It is inappropriate to introduce this celebration of Passover with a parabolic interpretation. By his reference to the broken pieces of bread and the "blood" of the grapes, Jesus identified himself as the true Passover sacrifice. The "breaking," that is the breaking of the bread, is the act of dividing, concretely understood, with which the idea of death can be joined only allegorically, and clearly the words over the cup were in contrast to the blessing of the wine. In the interpretation in terms of a parable, it is impossible to understand why no mention is made of the Passover lamb. This is where we would expect the application of the parable to begin. And finally, in this interpretation we confront the major difficulty that the parabolic interpretation disappeared so soon and the Lord's Supper was reinterpreted as a sacramental meal.

Is then the understanding of the person of Jesus as a Passover sacrifice an argument for finding the origin of the Lord's Supper in the Passover meal? Not only is the shape and content of the passion narrative determined by Passover and its theology, but Jesus is regarded elsewhere as the Passover sacrifice. This is especially true of 1 Corinthians 5:7-8. "Cleanse out the old leaven that you may be a new lump, as you really are unleavened. For Christ, our paschal lamb, has been sacrified. Let us, therefore, celebrate the festival, not

with the old leaven, the leaven of malice and evil, but with the unleavened bread of sincerity and truth." That the death of Jesus can
be understood as the saving event of Passover, as liberation and new
birth out of the chaos of the old world is one thing, but understanding the Lord's Supper as the Passover meal is another, and we
should not confuse the two. Paul is not speaking here of the Lord's
Supper but of the new way of life of Christians who have been
liberated by the Christ event. He makes not the slightest allusion
to the Lord's Supper. He does speak of *heortazein,* "celebrate a festival," but this means the new existence, not the Lord's Supper. Thus
1 Corinthians 5:7-8 cannot serve as an argument for interpreting the
Lord's Supper in terms of Passover. Quite the opposite. If Paul had
interpreted the Lord's Supper as Passover he would not have formulated it in this way.

In contrast to the conspicuous absence of the main features of
Passover, the synoptic account refers to Jesus' Last Supper as a Passover meal. How are we to understand this account? From the point
of view of literary development Mark 14:12-25 is a larger complex,
but there is no need to examine here the early stages of its components. Its basic outline is as follows: 14:12-16 describe the preparation for the Passover meal, and v 17 adds the statement that
Jesus came with the Twelve, which must mean that the Passover
which they had prepared was celebrated. Verse 18 begins, "And
as they were at the table eating," but goes on to introduce the section
in which the betrayer is identified. Only after this does v 22 begin
again with "and as they were eating," and report the institution of
the Lord's Supper.

Therefore this composition is speaking of the Passover and in the
framework of this Passover or in addition to it, first, vv 18-21 recount the identification of the traitor, which cannot be an element
in the celebration of Passover, and second, vv 22-25 recount the
institution of the Lord's Supper, which also is not and cannot be a
feature of Passover, unless it marks its conclusion. Thus the Lord's
Supper is mentioned only in the framework of Passover or as an
addition to it. Two question must be raised. How was the unusual
position of the Lord's Supper at the conclusion of Passover under-

stood? And what is the meaning of the total composition, Mark 14:17-25?

The placing of the Lord's Supper at the conclusion of Passover shows that this meal, which is shown by the words of institution to be clearly sacramental, could have constituted the conclusion of a larger meal. In 1 Corinthians 11:20-34 we learn that in Corinth the Lord's Supper was preceded by an agape meal, and that it did not come until the end of a congregational gathering. And in *Didache* 10 the prayers for the Lord's Supper presuppose this same order. This cannot be accidental. As to the time of celebration, the agape meal corresponds to the Passover. This is entirely understandable, and in reference to the suffering and death of Jesus it is of great theological significance. But the Lord's Supper is clearly distinguished from Passover, even though it follows it immediately, and it is to be interpreted in its position after the agape meal. This well-known sequence from the life of the early church is thus presupposed.

Passover meal and Lord's Supper are also separated from one another in Mark 14:17-25 by the identification of the traitor in vv 18-21. This section shows that Jesus not only knew that he was to die but he knew who would betray him. Jesus could therefore have escaped betrayal, but he let it happen. In a passive manner he sets it in motion by identifying the traitor. This "designation" is a prophetic proclamation of disaster, which is set in motion by its pronouncement. If this is the background for the institution of the Lord's Supper, it was not by accident that this was Jesus' last supper, but it was essential that it should already lie beyond that boundary between Jesus' life and his death; his death has already been set in motion and Jesus has entered the sphere of death.

Paul also was aware of this point of reference in time, as seen in his words of institution "on the night when he was betrayed" (1 Cor. 11:23). The night of betrayal is the starting point, and this gives the tradition an anticipatory quality, which is also found in the theology of the Lord's Supper: the supper is the proclamation of Jesus' death (1 Cor. 11:26). This placement at the final point in the life of Jesus is underlined by his concluding words, "Truly, I say to you, I shall not drink again of the fruit of the vine until that day when I drink it new in the kingdom of God" (Mark 14:25). The Lord's Supper was Jesus' last meal on earth and was observed in anticipation of the heavenly meal. It thus forms an analogy to this heavenly meal of the risen One.

The composition of Matthew follows that of Mark, but Luke, who often composed freely, has a different structure. He uses the designation of the traitor to introduce a larger unit about discipleship. We can recognize this as a special secondary formulation which does not need to be considered here. The question of whether the Lord's Supper is derived from Passover must be answered in the negative. Moreover, we have seen that the basic synoptic account does not identify the two but presents Passover as the meal that precedes the sacramental Lord's Supper and that is to be clearly distinguished from it. The decisive factor for the institution of the Lord's Supper is the approaching death of Jesus.

3. Further Possible Sources

The Qumran community held sacral meals and had regulations for meals in the messianic age, in which the Messiah, like the "prince" in Ezekiel 40ff. is clearly a layman subordinate to the high priest (1QSa II, 11ff.). The meal itself corresponds to the *zebah*, even though interestingly enough there is only a blessing over bread and grape juice *(tirosh)*. Here we can see the influence of a polemic against sacrifice, which we will consider later. As is the case with all special forms of the normal *zebah*, we cannot find any particular similarity to the Lord's Supper, because there is no reference to the death or the saving activity of a person.

Attempts have been made to derive the Lord's Supper from other New Testament accounts of Jesus' meals, such as the miracles of feeding the crowds or the meals at the Easter appearances. But the miraculous multiplications of bread do not include any direct reference to Jesus in the meal itself. They reflect the manna typology and present Jesus as the one who performs the miracle. Only secondarily is the meal itself related to the person of Jesus, as, for example in John 6:35, 48 etc. ("I am the bread of life"), where we can clearly detect the influence of the Lord's Supper (John 6:53).

We probably should assume that there was a similar influence of the Lord's Supper on the accounts of the miraculous feedings at the stage of transmission reflected in the synoptics. But it is precisely because of this relation that the Lord's Supper cannot be derived from these accounts. They are to be understood in the light of the Lord's Supper, but the Lord's Supper did not arise out of the memories of the miraculous meals.

The meals at Jesus' appearances in the Easter stories play a special role. Can the origin of the Lord's Supper be found there? The meals have quite different functions and do not constitute the center of the accounts but are secondary, though important, features. The meals can be explained as due to anti-docetic tendencies (Luke 24:41-43), and they specify as the center of the worship of the early church the presence of the risen One (Mark 16:14) or the recognition of him (Luke 24:30-35). Only John 21:9-14 deals primarily with a meal instituted by the risen Lord, but this is a meal of fish, so that the relation to the Lord's Supper can be only indirect. In any case, in these accounts the meal is subordinate to the resurrection appearances. The accounts seem to presuppose the practice of the Lord's Supper (and the fellowship of the disciples at the table) rather than being a possible source for it.

The *Todah*

In our search for origins we have examined the most significant scholarly explanations thus far advanced and have reached a negative conclusion. Remarkably enough the scholars have overlooked a specific form of sacral meal that has deep roots in the Old Testament and also played a prominent role in Judaism at the time of Jesus (as reflected in the Mishna[8]). This is the *todah*, the thank offering. This sacrifice is a part of the *zebah*, the meal offering in the wider sense, but differs from it in the ritual "life setting" and its meaning in relation to the general meal offering. Here we find the relationship we have been searching for in connection with the death and salvation of the one bringing the offering.

---

[8] See *Vom Sinai zum Zion,* p. 196, Note 30.

The thank offering presupposes a specific situation. When someone is rescued from death, from an illness, or from persecution that poses a threat of death, then the divine deliverance is celebrated by a worship service built on a thank offering as a new foundation for the person's existence. Here he confesses (*jd*[*h*] hiph) God as deliverer in a thank offering *(todah)*. He invites those who belong to his immediate community, contributes an animal for this particular *zebah* of thanksgiving, and in the meal offering celebrates with those invited the start of his new being. The essential element is that the thankful acknowledgement of God is expressed in a so-called song of thanks of the individual, which refers back to the time of troubles and "thinks on" *(zkr)* the deliverance and the experience of death and salvation.

This remembering can assume special importance through recitation of the song of lament which the individual sang when in trouble and which when possible concluded with the vow of a thank offering, which has now been brought. In the Psalter the individual songs of thanks even contain partial quotations from laments, or a song of thanks follow immediately on a lament, thus showing their common cultic "life setting" in the *todah* meal. The explanation of the striking perspective in many laments of the one already rescued and the thankful conclusion at the end of many laments is that they are formulated with reference to the situation in which the thank offering is presented. One commemorates God's deliverance and gives thanks for it only by commemorating the passage through troubles and the event of deliverance.

In the thank offering the focus is not on a general state of well-being, *shalom,* as it is in a normal meal offering but on the bringing of well-being out of a state of trouble. It is not ordinary sacrificial worship, but a service of worship in which by a sacrifice Yahweh is praised and acknowledged as the deliverer. Worship through word and meal and praise and sacrifice here constitute a unity. In this the sacrifice cannot be misunderstood as a "gift" to God, but it is rather the "honoring" of the deliverer, and it is God's gift that the one rescued can begin his life anew in the sacred meal.

In many respects the outward form of the *todah* differs from that of the usual meal offering. Psalm 116 is a psalm of thanks that brings the raising of "the cup of salvation" and the sacral declaration and proclamation that follow it (vv. 13-14) into a parallel with the sacrifice itself (vv. 17-19). We can understand how the rite of the sacral declaration when the cup is raised gained special significance for the thank offering, as it here deals with the confessional proclamation of God's saving deeds. If the acknowledgement of divine deliverance was an essential component of the sacrifice, then this rite could be seen as a pendant to the sacrifice itself. The cup corresponds to the proclamation and the sacrifice to the meal of the thank offering.

But in addition the meal is characterized by a remarkable feature. Leviticus 7:12-14[9] specifies for the thank offering that four different bread and wafer offerings are necessary, including everyday leavened bread. One portion of each of the four types is allotted to the Temple and the other serves as the sacred bread for the *todah* meal. Such bread and wafer offerings are known as "food offering" *(minha)* and normally accompany the burnt offering but not the meal offering. What does the special bread offering mean in this setting? Moreover, leavened bread is also required, something that is inadmissible for a *minha* (Lev. 2:11). Leavened bread contains old dough, already used and therefore profane. Amos 4:5 is evidence that the thank offering was distinguished by the burning of leavened bread (later this was modified to have it as a sacrificial gift to the priests). When the leavened bread, the normal bread of daily life, plays such a role, the meaning of the bread offering cannot be a mere quantitative expansion of the thank offering in contrast to the general meal offering. Rather it represents through the sacrifice the basic human nourishment for the life of the one who has been rescued.

Thus this "daily bread" could even be offered on the altar, where nothing leavened was to be placed. In contrast to the meal offering the thank offering includes not only a bloody offering of meat, but a bloodless offering of bread, and it is the only sacrifice that includes

---

[9]Note the interesting requirement that the meat must be eaten the same day it is sacrificed, that is, it is tied to the thank offering.

leavened bread. Thus in the thank offering bread and wine gain special meaning. The one becomes a part of the sacrifice itself and the other takes on meaning as a constituent part of the proclamation.

The Psalter shows that in post-exilic worship the thank offering played a role that can hardly be overestimated. The laments and song of thanks of the individual have their life setting here, and along with them and in the context of the thank offering the shapes of individual piety developed. (Note the songs of confidence that developed out of the individual laments.) It can be said that the thank offering constituted the cultic basis for the main bulk of the Psalms. It not only represents the high point of human life, but in it life itself can be seen as overcoming the basic issue of death by God's deliverance into life. The official post-exilic cult, with its sharp separation between priests and laity on the basis of a far-reaching concept of holiness, become more and more the concern of the priests, while private worship was largely determined by the thank offering. In connection with this offering, therefore, basic theological developments took place.

1. Psalm 69, an individual lament with a concluding hymn of thanks exalts the praise of God in the thanksgiving sacrifice above the virtues of the sacrificial animal.

> I will praise the name of God with a song;
> I will magnify him with thanksgiving.
> This will please the Lord more than an ox
> or a bull with horns and hoofs[10] (vv. 30-31).

In place of the old concept of sacrifice as a gift to God, Psalm 50 understands it as thanksgiving *(todah)* in which human deliverance from death and the praise of God are intimately connected with sacrifice. This new understanding of sacrifice (vv. 7-15), together with a new understanding of human conduct and the law (vv. 16-23), is portrayed as God's revelation on Zion, which is a continuation of the Sinai revelation (vv. 1-6).[11]

---

[10]The expression refers to animals that completely satisfy the requirements of ceremonial cleanliness.

[11]On Ps. 50 see H. Gese, "Psalm 50 und das alttestamentliche Gesetzesverständnis," *Festschrift* for E. Käsemann, 1976, pp. 57-77.

2. In the context of this type of piety, in which life expereince is brought into a basic relationship with God's saving acts, and in which life is experienced as judgment and grace, there developed a new, inward understanding of suffering, as Psalm 51 illustrates. This lament does not plead for the removal of external troubles but for the forgiveness of sin (vv. 1-2), and the human being knows that one's being in its basic relationship to God is under the dominance of sin (vv. 3-5). The deliverance that God is asked to grant is the forgiveness of sin (vv. 7-9), and a new spiritual relationship to God (vv. 10-12), and in addition the external sacrifice of thanksgiving is transformed into an inward sacrifice of one's own life:

> For thou hast no delight in sacrifice;
>   were I to give a burnt offering
>   thou wouldst not be pleased.
> The sacrifice acceptable to God is a broken spirit;
>   a broken and contrite heart, O God, thou
>   wilt not despise (vv. 16-17).

These statements are found in the place in the Psalm that otherwise would contain a vow of praise. Even the praise of God that accompanies the thank offering is internalized in a striking manner and is transformed into instruction similar to wisdom teachings, that sinners are to turn to God (vv. 13-15). To be sure, Psalm 51, with its consistent spiritualization of all the elements of the traditional lament of the individual, is a special case, but it still shows how through the spirituality of the *todah* the understanding of sacrifice and of life could mutually influence each other.

Related to Psalm 51 is Psalm 40:1-12, a Psalm of thanks, where obedience to the law is stressed as essential in contrast to sacrifice (vv. 7-9). With allusions to the terminology of the new covenant (Jer. 31:33; Ezek. 36:27) the complete internalization of the thank offering is presented as the goal. In these psalms we do not have the expression of an enlightened critique of sacrifice, but rather the total involvement of the person in the essence of sacrifice, as that involvement grew out of a deeply rooted spiritual understanding of the thank offering. This may, of course, be regarded as the starting point for a rejection of blood sacrifice, but this is a development that took place outside the Old Testament.

3. Although this spirituality was primarily a private matter, its vision was not confined to the individual, because each time a group gathered for a thank offering it represented all Israel (cf. e.g. Ps. 22:23; 69:32). The *todah* spirituality could, like the apocalyptic theology, open itself to the eschatological dimension. In a discussion of Psalm 22 [12] I have shown how the deadly suffering of the individual could be seen as expanded to the dimensions of universal, primal suffering, and how, in a similar manner, deliverance could escape all historical limits of the saving events and become a symbol of the eschatological dawning of the kingdom. In apocalyptic perspective the basic experience of death and deliverance in the *todah* spirituality could be made into an absolute, and deliverance from death led to the conversion of the world, to enabling the dead to participate in life, and to the eternal proclamation of salvation (Ps. 22:27-28).

Just as Psalms of thanks can express the spirit of apocalypticism, so the apocalyptic texts can display the spirituality of the thanksgiving sacrifice. At the eschatological feast of the kingdom, Isaiah 25:1-10a, which corresponds to the feast of the Sinai covenant, Exodus 24 (cf. Isa. 24:23c and Exod. 24:9-11) but is celebrated on Mount Zion with all the nations, the song of thanksgiving is sung (vv. 1-4) and this transforms the feast into the thank offering of the entire spiritual community of God. In the thank offering we see not merely another special type of sacrifice but an institution that supports human life in Israel and that in ever increasing measure influenced the entire Old Testament. We can understand the verdict of the ancient rabbis, "In the coming (messianic) age all sacrifices will cease, but the thank offering will never cease; all (religious) songs will cease, but the songs of thanks will never cease." [13]

---

[12]See *Vom Sinai zum Zion,* pp. 182-192.

[13]*Pesiqta* ed. S. Buber, 1868, p. 79a; ed. B. Mandelbaum, 1962, I, p. 159.

The Lord's Supper

The Lord's Supper is the thank offering *(todah)* of the One who is risen. When we approach the death and resurrection of Jesus in the light of our understanding of the institution of *todah,* we would expect to find the *todah* as the worship appropriate to the event of the resurrection, the deliverance of Jesus from death. Biblical thinking would indicate that the new beginning of Jesus' life from death, the Easter event of deliverance, would take the form of a thanksgiving meal. Here Easter occurs for the followers of Jesus as fellowship with Jesus in a meal and participation in Jesus' sacrifice—participation in the one delivered and in the deliverance. For this reason the Lord's Supper is the proclamation of the death of Jesus (1 Cor. 11:26), and at the same time it is praise of God, rejoicing over the salvation God has wrought (cf. Acts 2:46-47). The Lord's Supper is celebrated in remembrance of the saving death of Jesus.

The proclamation of salvation is made when the cup is raised. This is stated in the words consecrating the cup as preserved by Paul and Luke, and this is the older form of the tradition.[14] "This cup is the new covenant in my blood" (1 Cor. 11:25; Luke 22:20). The cup is the "cup of salvation" which is lifted up during the *todah* (Ps. 116:13), and which in praise of God declares, proclaims, "blesses" his saving deeds ("the cup of blessing," 1 Cor. 10:16).

---

[14]The words, "This is my blood of the covenant, which is poured out for many" (Mark 14:24; Matt. 26:28) are to be understood as an exact parallel to the words over the bread, and the difficulty of this formulation can be traced back to this secondary parallelism, which beyond the equating of wine with blood is intended to express the idea of covenant, and the no longer necessary attribute of "new" is thus missing here. A shift in meaning occurred then to a limited extent and was expressed in the change from the words over the cup—drinking from the cup is to share in the covenant sealed by blood; and in the words over the wine—drinking the wine is to share in the blood of the covenant (cf. Paul's words, 1 Cor. 10:16). Only outside the Jewish thought world could wine and blood come to be equated and the concept arise of a sacramental drinking of the blood. In the words over the bread, however, the use of *sōma* indicates clearly that in speaking of bread and wine there was no thought of equating "flesh" *(sarx)* with blood, but that *sōma* means the whole body. In spite of all attempts at making them parallel, the words over the bread and those over the wine exist on different levels: wine and cup relate to the event of proclamation in the *todah,* but the bread relates to the sacrifice itself.

Salvation is described as the new covenant which has been established through the atoning death of Jesus on Golgotha. As the old Covenant was instituted through a blood ceremony that united those who were parties to it (Exod. 24:3-8), so the new was instituted by the atoning sacrifice of a life at Golgotha. To drink from the cup is to become a party to this covenant of blood. In form, the words over the cup correspond to the old *todah,* but in content this *todah* of the new covenant goes far beyond the old one. This incomparable new *todah* of necessity had to take on new fundamental forms.

In the old *todah* the one who had been rescued brought an animal as a sacrifice for himself and the community. The risen One, however, gave himself; the sacrifice is his sacrifice, his earthly, bodily existence that is being offered up. In Psalm 40 the true sacrifice was obedience, in Psalm 51 it was "a broken spirit," "a broken and contrite heart," and here there is no longer any sacrifice of some animal. The true, proper sacrifice is the body of Jesus himself, his own physical life. This is the meaning of the words over the bread, "This is my body" (Mark 14:22; Matt. 26:26; cf. 1 Cor. 11:24; Luke 22:19, which add "which is given for you.").

The bread of the thank offering has as elsewhere in Jewish meals, the function of representing solid food. It also takes on the function of the blood sacrifice, which is the sacrifice of Jesus, of his physical life *(sōma),* his earthly life. The food of the sacral meal, represented by the bread of the sacrifice, is, in respect to its sacral nature as a sacrifice, the body of Jesus. The bread does not thereby lose its true earthly character as the basic human food, but in the holy meal, through participation in the saving event of the one who offers himself, it is the body of Jesus. The bread is not a metaphor for the body of Jesus, but, in its own way as the substance of the meal, in the meal of the thank offering it *is* the sacrifice of Jesus.

In the old sacral meal of the *todah* the new being of the one saved was established by eating the sacrifice. By this even the physical realm was involved in the life given by God the deliverer and savior, and the community of the one who brought the sacrifice participated in the new life and in the power of salvation and life as fellowship with the one who had been saved. In the new "sacramental" meal of the *todah* of the risen One, participation in the saving event of Jesus' death and resurrection comes about through partaking of the food, which the bringer of the sacrifice identifies with his own sacrifice: he gives himself as sacrifice. His body which is sacrificed takes the place of the slain sacrificial victim, and in that sacrifice we participate by eating the bread as the shared food which constitutes the basis for human life, even in all its physical aspects.

The omission of a special sacrificial animal has already been prepared for in the development of the Old Testament tradition, but only with the true, ultimate sacrifice is the possibility of any substitution of an animal eliminated. In the Lord's Supper, the one bringing the offering offers himself as sacrifice, sacrifice and deliverer are identical, and the fellowship around the table becomes fellowship in the "body of Christ." The bread which we break (i.e. distribute), is it not a participation in the body of Christ? Because there is one bread, we who are many are one body, for we all partake of the one bread" (1 Cor. 10:16b-17).

The old *todah* was a sacral meal, but in practice it had been largely separated from the Temple, where only the slaughter of the sacrificial animal took place. The meat was prepared in various ways for the communal celebration which was observed the same day in the houses of Jerusalem (*Zebahim* V, 6). In later times bread was offered as the gift of the tithe to the priests, without the necessity of the bread being present in the Temple at the time the animal was slaughtered. The killing of the sacrifice automatically sanctified the bread (*Menahot* VII, 3). Thus private worship had in practice been so divorced from the Temple that only the killing of the animal still took place there, and the sanctifying of the bread took place of itself through the shedding of the blood of the sacrifice.

When the new *todah* meal was connected with the wholly different sacrifice of the new covenant, it was freed from any connection to the Temple, and yet even so, following old sacral concepts, a holy meal could be celebrated. The sacral *todah* meal had been a full meal for the satisfying of hunger, even, according to the circumstances, a sumptuous meal, with the meat of the sacrificed animals and all the offerings of bread. The identification of the holy *todah* bread with Jesus' sacrifice eliminated any specifications for a quantity of bread, as had been the case when bread was an independent element in the offering, and with the reduction to bread and wine the holy meal was limited to the basic ritual observance of the meal. Adding this liturgical *todah* to a ceremonial community meal made it possible to begin with a meal. But by the nature of the occasion, the sacramental observance was from the outset clearly distinguished from an ordinary meal for nourishment. Paul stressed this distinction, and it became more marked with the passage of time, until finally the agape was completely separated from the eucharist.

In conclusion let us turn once more to the synoptic account of the institution of the Lord's Supper. In the old *todah* the one saved presents the animal for sacrifice, and invites his community to participate. That is, he himself institutes the feast of thanksgiving. We have seen that according to Mark the Lord's Supper was instituted at the end of Jesus' life, after the events of his death had been set in motion by his identifying the one who was to betray him. Paul speaks of the night of betrayal *(paradosis)*, indicating this border point. This makes it clear that the content of the Lord's Supper brings together death and resurrection as a unit. This anticipation should not be a cause of offense, because it corresponds exactly to the rest of the presentation of Jesus' passion (cf. the "prophetic" identification of the betrayer, the quoting of Zech. 13:7 in Mark 14:27, the accusation based on the statement about the destruction of the Temple and its being rebuilt after three days, Mark 14:57-59; 15:29b etc.). It was impossible for Jesus' last meal not to have reference to the totality of the events of Good Friday through Easter.

Thus this instituting of the Lord's Supper at this final boundary according to the synoptic account does not conflict with the nature of the Lord's Supper as a meal at a thank offering. The institution of the Lord's Supper is to be understood as the dedication of Jesus as the sacrifice, prior to his death. It is not just a case of martyrdom, but the sacrifice that marks the turning point of the aeons and that anticipates Easter, just as Psalm 22 anticipates out of a prototypical suffering the dawning of God's eschatological kingdom. Jesus himself sets his death in motion by identifying the traitor and then

consecrates himself as the sacrifice, which he permits his followers
to share. So by this celebration he brings about the breakthrough to
the new being, to the kingdom.

The *todah*-eucharist is the worship in which the community experiences the saving event of Jesus' death and resurrection in its
profoundest depths. In this *todah* we find the fulfillment of the
meaningful development of the human experience of death and redemption, the development of the sacred meal, of the fellowship
with the Savior and of the human basis of life, the development of
sacrifice. The eucharist is the end and goal of the biblical development of worship. It brings together manifold elements, and bears
testimony to the unique, final saving event of Christ.

We have reached the end of our investigation. It would be interesting to follow the course of liturgical history as traversed by the
Lord's Supper in the early church, and to ask how this development
is related to its origins. But this cannot be done concisely. Instead I
shall in conclusion make certain practical observations.

1. The celebration of the Lord's Supper is the Easter celebration
of the Lord's Day, and not an occasion of penitence. Confession must
be clearly distinct from the celebration itself, and should not be
placed in the foreground. In the sacred meal the Lord's death is
proclaimed, but this is what gives the celebration its Easter character.
Even atonement can be understood only in terms of Easter. And
the anchoring of the Lord's Supper in the night of betrayal opens
the final, eschatological dimension and does not move our attention
away from Easter.

2. The development of the liturgy brought about a close unity
of the word and the Lord's Supper in worship. It makes no sense
to try to isolate the Lord's Supper in such a way as to make it an
appendage to worship through the proclamation of the word. Christian worship is centered in the celebration of the Lord's Supper, and
prayer, word, and meal of necessity constitute an indissoluble unity.

3. There are inadequacies in the observance of the Lord's Supper in the Reformation church. It was necessary to remove from the Mass of the late middle ages all elements which, at least as they functioned and were interpreted at that time, interfered with a biblically-based understanding of the Lord's Supper. There was no positive example of the original tradition that could be followed. Today, however, we can no longer proceed as if the early Christian form of the Lord's Supper were unknown to us. If the Lord's Supper is a thank offering, a *todah,* then the saving act of Christ's sacrifice and the dawning of the kingdom of God at Easter must be made known through an act of "anamnesis," remembrance. According to the words of institution, the liturgy must not be silent, because a part of the *todah* is the proclamation of Jesus' death and resurrection. In addition to anamnesis, the early church observed "epiclesis," the calling on the Holy Spirit. If ever we need the presence of the Spirit it is in this observance.

4. At the beginning of the main prayer are the prefatory sentences and the Sanctus, preceding the words of institution. It is easy to show that the Sanctus came from the liturgy of the synagogue. The basic text of the Jerusalem temple liturgy, Isaiah 6:3 (in the Synagogue Ezek. 3:12 is added to it, as in the Apostolic Constitutions VII 35) is expanded in all the early Christian liturgies in a surprising manner: *"Heaven and* earth are full of his glory." This is appropriate for the heavenly Jerusalem and for a picture such as that given in Revelation 4, and it is not to be changed out of biblicistic reasons, contrary to all liturgical tradition. Through the Sanctus, heavenly and earthly worship become identical. Their unity is thoroughly biblical and guards against false spiritualizing as well as against the loss of a sense of worship.

The ancient Benedictus was apparently added first in the Gallic liturgy, but it is appropriate that it was adopted. Originally the wish for blessing on the one saved from deadly peril and now coming to the Temple to offer the *todah* (Ps. 118:26) was expressed in the Benedictus, according to Mark 11:1-10 (and parallels) on the basis of Zechariah 9:9-10, the welcoming praise for the Messiah of peace.

He is now the Easter victor, who in his sacrifice on the cross has overcome the sin and death of the world and given us in the Lord's
Supper a share in the kingdom. Thus the prefatory sentences and the
Sanctus, with the added Benedictus, rightly constitute the liturgy
prior to the words of institution.

5. It is certainly proper to regard the sacred meal as a real meal.
The bread should be real bread, the basic element of our nourishment, the "leavened" bread of thanksgiving eaten in our daily life,
but we must not mix the sacred meal with the agape or confuse the
one with the other. Nor should we think that abbreviating the sacramental dimension would be a help to contemporary men and wom-
en. Quite the opposite. Such abbreviations have already been around
for a long time and are responsible for many misunderstandings.
Only by making this central worship celebration fully accessible in
a positive way can we really be of help. In other respects the liturgy
of the Lord's Supper provides at least room for experimentation.
In reverence and humility we can open ourselves to that which is
mysteriously accessible to us as truth, and we can do this only in
attentive obedience to the word that has been handed on to us. We
will come to know that we have a part in the one eternal church,
which both permeates and transcends all historical forms, and which
encounters its crucified and risen Lord.

VI

The Messiah

THE BOOK OF ACTS RELATES how Paul, after his address on the Areopagus in Athens, in which he drew on the great Greek philosophical tradition for content and rhetorical tradition for form, went to Corinth, and there in the synagogue testified "to the Jews that the Christ was Jesus" (18:5). We are to understand this in terms of what was said of his earlier sermon in Thessalonica, "And Paul went in (to the synagogue) as was his custom, and for three weeks he argued with them from the Scriptures, explaining and proving that it was necessary for the Christ to suffer and to rise from the dead, and saying, 'This Jesus whom I proclaim to you, is the Christ' " (Acts 17:2-3). In Jesus' death and resurrection the Old Testament finds its fulfillment, and the knowledge that Jesus is the Messiah is the key to the Scripture.

In contrast to this view, it is often pointed out that the Old Testament includes much more than just messianic prophecy, and that messianic expectations did not play a decisive role. On an initial, superficial view this objection seems to have a good claim to being correct. The clearly messianic prophecies are not numerous, and it is hardly possible to understand the entire Old Testament in terms of such isolated passages. If messianism is only one line of thought among many in the Old Testament, perhaps it is only a secondary theme which assumed too great an importance in times of trouble

and oppression. Isn't it true that the Messiah is only rarely spoken
of in all the many eschatological texts?

But such statements as this express too one-sided a view of the
Old Testament, a view that examines individual texts and simply
places their contents alongside each other, seeking to measure the
importance of one against the other. This is to overlook the inner
connections of the whole Old Testament, in which traditions that
developed separately constitute an organic unity. Even if it is necessary to isolate a specific line of tradition for our theme, we must
not overlook the contexts in which it is found, its relation to other
material, and the functions which this tradition performs in the
whole of Scripture.

It would not be possible to speak of a messianic figure who is the
mediator of God's lordship over Israel, were it not for the basic
structure of biblical revelation, the personal and exclusive encounter
of God with his people. Without this the Messiah would be only
a special political or intellectual leader and could not be a mediator
of God's kingdom as the eschatological revelation of God. His role
as mediator developed out of the structure of revelation, in which
God discloses himself to humans, to this Israel, which God binds
to himself in an exclusive relationship. This is the ultimate personal
revelation within a mutual relationship.

At the beginning Moses represents the collective Israel as an individual confronting God, coming before God's "I" as a "thou," and
on the other hand he goes to Israel as God's representative, and with
God's authority transmits the revelation. This structure of mediation
indicates the nature of the revelation, and at the eschatological goal
of salvation history, revelation similarly consists in an act of mediation in a personal encounter of God with his people. This structure
left its mark on the figure of the Messiah which developed in the
history of revelation and which revealed God's eschatological kingdom.

The Davidic Son of God

Israel entered upon the stage of history through a slow process of
development. The coalition of tribes called "Israel" which worshiped

Yahweh existed at first in the stillness of a world almost devoid of history, lying on the periphery of the politically significant powers. Only when the Israelite state arose in connecton with the throwing off of the Philistine yoke, could Israel enter fully into the political and historical world of the middle-eastern states. This process of emerging into the world of nations, this formation of the state, reached its apex and its conclusion in the establishment of the Davidic kingdom. It was appropriate that Israel entered its life as a major power, the realm of external, historical power, in this way. (Of course Israel then transcended that world by its suffering in the experience of decline and bondage.) On this path into history, the entity Israel developed into a political factor of major significance, and revelation permeated the realm of human existence, extending even to the area of worldly power.

The Israel that had now attained historical significance had taken firm possession of the land, and this settling down in the land corresponds to God's choice of the land as an "inheritance" (*naḥala*). When the Ark of the Covenant was moved to Mt. Zion, God took possession of a piece of land, the sanctuary on Zion, as his dwelling place. The holy Ark already constituted a place where God was to be found, but it was the representation of the empty sacral realm. And when God appeared as the enthroned king, as Yahweh Sabaoth, the Ark represented God's dwelling, as the earthly foot of the heavenly throne. Through conquest by David's personal troops, Zion became the heritage of David's clan. According to Israelite ideas of the direct relationship of the clan to the land that was its heritage, the divine choice of Zion, which found expression in the moving of the Ark to Zion, became equivalent to a choice of the clan and of the person.

Consequently, the descendent of David who reigned in Zion as representative of the Davidic family became the "son" of God the moment he became king, because God himself was the real lord of Zion. When the Davidic king ascended the throne he became the recipient of the salvation oracle of the Ark of God: "You are my son, today (the day of his coronation) I have begotten you" (Ps. 2:7). Or, "Upon the holy mountain (Zion), from the womb, from the dawn (today as the king ascends the throne), I have begotten you" (Ps. 110:3 author's translation).[1] The coronation was his "birth" as the son of God, and Davidic kingship on Zion was vicariously the kingship of God. The Davidic king did not reign only as commissioned by God, but also with God's authority, and his rule was the counterpart of God's rule. "Sit at my right hand, till I make your enemies your footstool" (Ps. 110:1), is the statement of a coronation oracle, and the Davidic throne can be called the throne of Yaweh's kingdom, or the throne of Yahweh (1 Chron. 28:5· 29:23).

The concept of sonship, in its function as a designation of origin, was used in almost all forms of sacral kingship to express divine authority. It would thus be possible to assume, as has commonly been done, that the sacral kingship of surrounding nations was the origin of the biblical concept of son of God. Two factors must be kept in mind, however. First, the Davidic concept of son of God has a specifically Israelite form: it is based on the establishment of Zion as God's dwelling place through the moving of the Ark to Zion, and it is dependent on Israelite concepts of kingship and of the land as heritage. Second, a culture borrows ideas and points of view from surrounding nations, because it has developed something similar which can be interpreted and identified by such borrowing. Inasfar as an external influence has more than ephemeral significance, it must always correspond to internal developments.

It is superficial to explain the concept of the son of God on Zion as being derived from Canaanite culture. This would be to overlook the distinctively Israelite nature of the concept and the incomparability of Yahweh with the king-gods of other nations. We must understand divine sonship in terms of God's choosing and dwelling with Israel, and of the relationship of Zion and David's clan. In a manner that corresponds to the new nature of Israel after their full emergence into history, God approaches the world, and at one place, on Zion, discloses himself to the world, in the royal office of the Davidic king who rules from his throne on Zion. In consequence of this development in revelation history, such older Jerusalem

---

[1]For details of this translation see *Vom Sinai zum Zion,* pp. 121, 137f.

traditions as concepts of a highest God *(elyon)* who rules over all gods and who has created heaven and earth (Gen. 14:22), the tradition of the Melchizedek priesthood, the concept of Zion as the center of the cosmos and the world mountain, etc., were adopted. This constituted a consistent and legitimate expression of Israel's insights in terms of the Zion tradition, which had become a part of revelation history.

The concept of the son of God based on God's choice of Zion and his dwelling there is clearly expressed in the Old Testament in the oracles already cited, to which further texts could be added, e.g. Psalm 89:26-27, "He (David) shall cry to me, 'Thou art my Father, my God, and the Rock of my salvation.' And I will make him the first-born, the highest of the kings of the earth." It also is found in the Deuteronomic history, 2 Samuel 7:14 in the divine promise of salvation, "I (God) will be his father, and he shall be my son." The idea is paraphrased in a late text from the third century B.C., "My shepherd (a frequent traditional epithet for the king), . . . the man who stands next to me" (Zech. 13:7). The Old Testament, however, did not let the concept of the Davidic son of God become a neutral term, an ordinary royal title. God alone had the right to address the king in this way and thereby to give reality to the concept.[2]

There are two reasons for this reserve. First there was a possibility of confusing the term with a traditional term for divine beings subordinate to Yahweh, *ben el,* "son of God," "member of the category *el*" and the title could also be misused to deify the earthly ruler. Second, in secular usage the concept could lose its distinctive nature,[3] because "son of God" was freely used to designate beings created by God, and to express a strong personal relation to God. Israel could be called God's son, or first-born, etc. (Exod. 4:22; Deut. 1:31; 32:6, 18f.; Isa. 63:16; Jer. 31:9, Hos. 11:1 and other passages.

---

[2]Isa. 9:6 is no exception. Here Isaiah uses the term *yeled,* "child," but it is child in the usual sense of one just born. See *Vom Sinai zum Zion,* p. 140f.

[3]In late wisdom literature the wise and just man could be termed "son of God," e.g. Wis. 2:16, 18; Sir. 4:10; especially after death, Wis. 5:5; Sir. 51:10.

It should not be surprising that outside the New Testament the
title "son of God" is rarely used for the messianic king. Still there
is evidence that the title was known, as at Qumran the *Florilegium*
from Cave 4 I 10f. in the exegesis of 2 Samuel 7:11-14, "That is
the branch of David (a messianic title) who will appear with the
interpreter of the Torah . . . ," or in rabbinic exegesis of Old Testament texts dealing with the Messiah. But outside the Old Testament
the expression was avoided. Thus only God used it in speaking of
the Messiah. There is no need to allege, as some have done, that
there is anti-Christian polemic in the rabbinic texts. The New Testament designation of Jesus as *ho huios tou theou* is in the tradition
of the relationship of a son which God bestowed on the Davidic
king. Any other origin of the designation, from the non-Jewish
world, for instance, is excluded. The continuity with the Old Testament tradition is proven by the use of "son of David" and "son of
God" together (e.g., Rom. 1:3-4, Luke 1:32-33). We must note,
however, in the New Testament the importance of the testimony
given by God to divine sonship.

That the idea of the Davidic king as son of God was not borrowed
from Israel's neighbors is shown by what happened when the Davidic state collapsed as a result of the Assyrian conquest in the
second half of the eighth century. While elsewhere in Syria the kingship ideologies of political structure disappeared under Assyrian
suzerainty, in Israel the idea of kingship deepened and developed
into that of the Messiah. The prophets declared that this collapse of
the nation was God's judgment on it. The exciting institutions of na-
tionhood and politics, the official cultic practices of religion, as well
as conventional piety, observance of law, customary social relationships, in short, everything related to earthly power. was no longer
able to sustain the existence of an Israel based on the revelation of
Yahweh. This Israel that had become a nation-state was disclosed
as an external and false entity which under the judgment of God
was now crumbling, and from which the true Israel had to emerge.

In Isaiah 7:10-17 the important step from king to Messiah was
taken. God rejects the reigning house of David. The true son, with
whom God is present, Immanuel, will now be born. The concept

of son of God does not disappear, but it is transformed. No specific family can come forward as bearer of the promise given to the Davidic dynasty, but somewhere in the relationships of the great Davidic clan, not perceptible in specific detail, God will choose the bearer of the dynastic promise of eternal lordship on Zion. Even the reference of Ephrathah in Micah 5:2-4, provides a broad framework for the origin of the Messiah, while the late addition in Micah 5:3 refers to Isaiah 7:14 when it speaks of the unknown mother of the Messiah, "she who is in travail has brought forth."

It would be possible to try to see the distinction between king and Messiah in the promise given in Isaiah 9:6-7, especially in the four-fold messianic throne name, which surpasses even the figure of David—"Wonderful Counselor, Mighty God, Everlasting Father, Prince of Peace." What we have here is not merely an idealization of the ruler, but a revelation of God himself in an unrestricted revelation of righteousness and peace. In this the real concern of the original choice of Zion and David finds expression in a transformation of its nature, in which the boundaries of historical data are swept aside. The people Israel is no longer a fixed national entity, but consists of the *anawim,* the "poor," the oppressed and humble who submit quietly to God's judgment. Worship can no longer be complete in official governmental cultic activities, and the true Zion emerges from judgment as the shelter of those who beleive (Isa. 28:16 "Behold I am laying in Zion for a foundation a stone, a tested stone, a precious cornerstone, of a sure foundation: 'He who believes will not be in haste' "). So too the Messiah is more than the old ideal of kingship. In the late text, Isaiah 11:1-5 the Messiah's possession of the spirit, his establishing of laws and ordinances by a purely spiritual act in which he cannot be deceived, points up the spiritualization that has come about in this development of the tradition.

We can also find this spiritualizing tendency in a negative development of the figure of the Messiah in the exilic and early postexilic period—the division of the Messiah into two figures. Because of the sharp division between the holiness of the cultic realm and secular life (which we find especially in the concept of cult in the priestly document), and between the priestly office and the royal office (which of necessity was more concerned with the world), it was inevitable that the figure of the Messiah would be divided into two separate parts. For the old concept of kingship which was formed by the Zion theology, the high priestly office of the Davidic king as priesthood according to Melchizedek (Ps. 110:4) was determinative, and the connection between the divine choice of Zion as presented in the cultic transfer of the Ark to Jerusalem and the adoption of the king as God's son, which took place in the coronation of the Davidic king, had of necessity to be preserved.

This, however, could not be done in a concept of cult for which the world-transcending dimension of holiness was the dominant feature. In Ezekiel's draft constitution, the king (he is called "prince" in this context) is without any specific priestly functions, indeed, he is a layman. And in Jeremiah 33:14-18 there is placed alongside the choice of David and the covenant with David the choice of the Levites and the Levitical covenant of priesthood. And at the very beginning of the post-exilic period the figure of the anointed high priest appears along with that of the anointed Davidic king (Zech. 4:14). Does this mean that the figure of the Messiah is diminished?

In this two-part picture of the Messiah we must not simply ignore the priestly side and affirm that the figure of the royal Messiah has decreased in importance. Both parts belong together, and only when both are together is the figure of the Messiah complete, just as in the vision in Zechariah 4:3 the two olive trees that stand to the left and the right of the divine lampstand form in their symmetry a higher unity. It is also unclear to what degree this division is maintained in the depictions of the eschatological Messiah. This depends on the degree to which the presentation corresponds to a "realistic" view, that is, to current conditions. The basic context of the priestly and royal office is preserved even in the double form of the concept so that in any portrayal of the Messiah that included the transcendent dimension the unity is there a priori, as we shall see below. In any case it is characteristic of the usual, realistic concepts of the Qumran sect that they recognize the two messianic figures (1QS IX

11 where at the same time the prophet of the end time, an Elijah *redivivus,* so to speak, precedes the Messiah; cf. 1QSa II 12ff.; CD XII 23; XIV 19; XIX 10f.; XX 1).

In addition, in the late post-exilic period another deepening of the messianic concept is to be found. The first hint of it is found in the well-known messianic promise in Zechariah 9:9-10, from the end of the fourth century, B.C., the time of Alexander the Great. This promise took the form of a Zion hymn, that is a hymn which exults over the eschatological return of God to Zion (cf. Isa. 12:6; Zeph. 3:14-15; Zech. 2:10), but here the king who makes his triumphant entry is the Messiah. Now quite clearly the figure of the Messiah is in the full sense of the word an eschatological phenomenon, and with the arrival of the Messiah on Mount Zion the final reign of God becomes reality, in accordance with the proclamation made since the time of Deutero-Isaiah of the establishment of God's kingdom on Zion and in the eschatological enthronment Psalms.

The messianic tradition now merges fully with the main stream of the eschatological proclamation of God's kingdom, something that could perhaps have become possible only through the shattering of all the political hopes that had been in the foreground and in the Persian period had been attached to the family of David, e.g. Zerubabel. Now for the first time the beginning of God's eschatological kingdom, which includes the entire world and in which all peoples have joined God's servant people Israel, is brought together with the entry of the Messiah to Zion. In contrast to the old Davidic king, who imposed the world-wide rule of Zion with force and power through subjugating the powers of chaos, and whose dualistic nature was characteristic for the older view of the Messiah, the Messiah is now the king of peace for all peoples, and he needs no external instruments of power.

> Rejoice greatly, O daughter of Zion!
>   Shout aloud, O daughter of Jerusalem!
> Lo, your king comes to you;
>   triumphant and victorious[4] is he,

---

[4]Gese translates as passives, "justified and saved." Cf. *Vom Sinai zum Zion,* p. 224.

> humble and riding on an ass,
>   on a colt the foal of an ass.
> I[5] will cut off the chariot from Ephraim
>   and the war horse from Jerusalem;
> And the battle bow shall be cut off,
>   and he shall command peace to the nations;
> his dominion shall be from sea to sea,
>   and from the River to the ends of the earth.
>
> (Zech. 9:9-10)

His entrance riding on the royal donkey is in accordance with the old coronation rite (see 1 Kings 1:38), and the entire context underlines the peaceful, unwarlike character of the Messiah, even though he is coming as a victorious king. Yet his victory is God's victory in the apocalyptic establishment of his eternal kingdom. Thus the Messiah is the one who is poor and humble, the *°ani,* who since the time of the eighth century prophets has been regarded as one who passes through the divine judgment and is saved. The lordship of this Messiah in the universal kingdom of God brings eternal peace for all peoples, and human might is no longer necessary for the establishment of God's kingdom.

The New Testament made particular use of this striking messianic picture from the time of Alexander. Here with the combining of the basic apocalyptic tradition of the coming of the kingdom of God and the messianic tradition, we have a central passage in the history of messianic thought. Zechariah 9:9-10 is not merely cited in the New Testament as having been fulfilled; its fulfillment is portrayed. At the beginning of Passion Week Jesus entered Jerusalem, Mount Zion, in the promised manner and thus was manifest as the victorious Messiah who has passed through the judgment and who brings the eternal peace of the kingdom of God.

In the Ptolemaic period of the third century this deepening of the messianic concept went even further. In the apocalyptic framework where martyrdom plays a role in the eschatological struggle for the kingdom of God, the Messiah appears as the one who fights and, indeed, even as a martyr. The thought is expressed that the eternal

---

[5]According to LXX, "he" instead of "I"; note the direct connection with v 10a f.

kingdom of God can be born only in the pangs of the end time, that
in the final and greatest battle the powers of chaos must be defeated near, yes, in Jerusalem, and Israel itself must pass through the
purifying judgment of God, which is an analogy to the historical
judgment visited on Jerusalem by Babylon (cf. Zech. 13:7-9).
Since this deadly crisis involves everyone, even the Davidic king
of the end time is caught up in it.

> "Awake, O sword, against my (God's) shepherd,
> > against the man who stands next to me,"
> > > says the Lord of hosts.
> "Yes, I[6] will strike the shepherd,
> > that the sheep may be scattered . . ." (Zech. 13:7ab).

And in the following verses this event is portrayed as the establishment of a new covenant.

The "shepherd," the "man who stands next to me" (or "my kins-
man") is not presented here in the striking colors of the usual messianic picture, and it might even be doubted that he is a messianic
figure at all. But it seems certain that the mysterious title, which
hints at divine sonship, refers to the Davidic king, and this term
of honor, together with the quite positive royal title "my shepherd,"
can only refer to a ruler who is acknowledged by God. Although this
anointed one is not presented as the bringer of salvation but as the
one who has fallen in the battles of the end time, he still leads his
people on the way to the new covenant (v. 9b) even though this
road leads through suffering and death. We must not forget that
the concept of resurrection can be assumed here (cf. Zech. 12:10-
13, and the passage of Isa. 26:19-21, which dates from this period
at the latest) and it applies first of all to the martyr. In any case
we can speak of a Davidic king of the end time, Israel's king on
Mount Zion, who is acknowledged by God, who appears here
at the threshold of the new and eternal covenant as a martyr. According to the New Testament, Jesus quoted Zechariah 13:7 on
the way to Gethsemane (Mark 14:27; Matt. 26:31) and thus applied to himself the prophecy of the Messiah who suffers martyrdom.

---

[6]Read *hakke 'akke;* MT "strike the shepherd"

The Son of Man

With the third-century apocalyptic prophecy of the martyred Messiah, the development of the messianic concept in purely Davidic terms as the son of God reached its termination. In the second and first centuries B.C. we encounter a totally different tradition, which, however, must in some way be connected with the messianic tradition —the apocalyptic concept of the son of man.

The earliest text in this tradition is found in the vision in Daniel 7. In its present form this chapter dates from the year 164 B.C. In an initial vision (vv. 1-8), three empires rise out of the abyss of the ocean in the form of four powerful beasts. Then vv. 9-14 record a second, contrasting vision in which God's lordship is established. The thrones of the heavenly court are set up and God appears in the form of one that was ancient of days, with white hair and white raiment (which represent visually the splendor of the *doxa*), and he takes his place on the fiery throne on wheels, with which we are familiar from the well-known vision in Ezekiel 1. A stream of fire issued forth from before him, and the angelic beings who serve him stood before him. The court sat in judgment, and the books that contain all that has happened were opened. In this universal judgment the last beast is cast into the fire. A second section then describes how someone comes with the clouds of heaven and is led before the Ancient of Days. He looked like a "son of man." Dominion, glory, and royal power were given him forever, and all peoples served him.

The vision itself is to be distinguished from its interpretation in 7:15-27. There the son of man is explained as the "saints of the Most High," or " the people of the saints of the Most High." That means, as the context makes clear, the people of God, the true Israel, specifically the Jewish people who had remained true in the persecution of the end time. It is tempting to look for an original element in this explanation of the vision, in which the saints of the Most High are not the true Israel, but angelic beings. But since in Psalm 34:9 the expression, the "saints of God" means the true Israel, the truly religious, and the tradition of Israel as the holy people is of central importance in the Old Testament, this hypothesis cannot be maintained.

This unfounded hypothesis could serve to identify the figure of the son of man in the vision as an angelic being or a representative of the angels, so that here the lordship of the kingdom of the last days was delegated by God to an angel. A basis for this delegation of power could be found in the strongly transcendental nature of the concept of God, which strove to avoid any visible representation of God's eschatological kingdom. The similarity of the angel to a human should then be explainable in terms of the old tradition of the appearances of the angel of Yahweh in human form (cf. Judg. 13:2-20), a tradition that continued to Daniel 10:16, 18 (where the angel is Gabriel). This is clearly based on the fundamental concept of God and the concept of *imago dei:* God can be visualized only in human form.

This can be illustrated in even the sublime vision described in Ezekiel 1:26; 8:2. But can the figure of the son of man be explained in that way here? The following reasons are against it:

1. This cannot be a case of an extreme transcendentalism that endeavored to avoid an anthropomorphic portrayal of God's kingdom. Not only is such a portrayal given in detail in the vision itself, but God is described as the Ancient of Days, with white hair and wearing white raiment.

2. Both the old concept of the angel of Yahweh who represents Yahweh himself and the highly developed concept of angels encountered in the Book of Daniel reveal such an indirect association with God that it is impossible to speak of God and the angels working side by side. Instead the messenger of God carries out God's orders in a direct manner. A scene portraying angels is unnecessary; such a scene would confer on the angel an unprecedented independence.

3. The son of man takes the place of the beasts who arose out of the ocean. We should expect thus to encounter an earthly being, a human, and not an angel, especially since the son of man enters into the realm of the "clouds of heaven" and is brought before the throne.

4. The interpretation of the son of man as the true Israel would be a radical shift of meaning, while if a messianic figure is intended the collective interpretation is possible and meaningful, since the Messiah does represent the people of God.

We are obliged to find in the son of man, as the expression itself ("a member of the category 'human'") connotes, a human being, who as one exalted to heaven is now installed as ruler of the world. When this man appears with God "with the clouds of heaven" we are reminded of the occasion when Moses entered the realm of the transcendent (e.g., Exod. 24:18), except that the son of man now belongs forever to this realm of transcendence as the one who has been exalted. The installation of a human in the office of king of the world as representative of God's kingdom on earth reminds us so thoroughly of the Davidic conception of the kingdom on Zion that we must at once raise the question of the relationship of the two traditions, since in the Old Testament they stand in such direct relationship to each other.

Daniel 7 is concerned with the establishment and triumph of God's kingdom on earth through God's human representative, just as is the messianic tradition. In the messianic tradition this representative is the Davidic king on Mount Zion, while here it is an exalted "son of man." This ensures that this kingdom of the end time cannot be misunderstood as a mere historical power, but recognized as an eternal kingdom, truly of God. The historical limitation to the Davidic dynasty is replaced by the wider concept of a human person, in which, to be sure, (when we adopt here also the interpretation of the vision in Dan. 7:15-22) there is a special relationship to the true Israel as Israel's representative.

But the universal nature of the terms "son of man" and "saints of the Most High" and their freedom from restriction to one nation are clear. It is not historic and national categories that are determinative here but categories from revelation history. A father-son relationship between God and the Messiah is not mentioned here since the historical understanding of Zion is no longer present. Instead, emphasis is placed on the paradoxical manner in which humans belong to the heavenly realm in the midst of the angelic beings, while in this necessarily mythological scene the express designation of God as the Ancient of Days stresses the unique, absolute reign of God that transcends everything. A *deus otiosus* is not in the picture here at all.[7]

What we have here is a transformation of the old messianic concept. With the termination of the connection to the choice of David and of Zion the messianic circle is extended to include the exalted human who is brought before God's throne and given a task in the heavenly world. This enables us to identify a comprehensive Old Testament tradition which here extends the scope of the Davidic tradition—The Mosaic-prophetic tradition. Moses entered into the cloud, received the divine revelation, and was commissioned by God. Elijah appeared as the new Moses. Like Moses he was God's servant and mediated God's word to Israel, thereby establishing the true Israel of his time.

The Deuteronomic concept of prophecy (Deut. 18:15-22) places the true prophets in the Mosaic succession. Isaiah saw the One who was enthroned and was caught up to this highest circle of revelation by the purging of his sins. This provided the Deuteronomic theology with a mark of true prophecy, "Surely the Lord God does nothing without revealing his secret *(sōd)* to his servants the prophets" (Amos 3:7). The Hebrew *sōd* means the secret conversation that Yahweh the king carries out with his throne attendants. This is the highest realm of revelation, into which the prophet is admitted and then commissioned with the highest authority.

This line of tradition through Moses and the prophets should not be interpreted too narrowly as merely a prophetic influence on Israel. It is rather a transmission of revelation in the comprehensive sense of supplying a basis for existence, in which the mediator of revelation is also the representative of the revelation. Thus Jeremiah is more than a mere prophet; he is in and through his entire

---

[7]A comparison with the El of the Ugartitic texts does not clarify the passage, although appeal has been made to El's epithet of *ab shnm*, because that does not mean "Father of the Years," but "Father of the Heights" (*Die Religionen der Menschheit*, X 2,97f.). Moreover the interpretation of the coronation of Baal as a displacement of El is without justification.

life the representative of the true Israel of his day and to the world. As a consequence, in this tradition the concept could arise of a "servant of Yahweh," who in Deutero-Isaiah mediates the revelation of God to the entire world, not solely by proclamation, but through his total existence. In the original sense of the term, this servant in Deutero-Isaiah is the whole of the true Israel. This may cast a light on the way in which in Daniel 7 the son of man was explained in a collective sense, because true and full representation is involved. Here in the figure of the son of man the concept of the Davidic Messiah is enlarged through this basic and comprehensive line of tradition.

Ezekiel also belongs to this line of tradition, for there the term "son of man" was used to address a "man," who paradoxically appears as a man among the heavenly beings before the One on the throne (from Ezek. 2:1 on). Is it an accident that this unusual term is found also in Daniel, where in 8:17 Daniel is addressed in this manner when he is found among the heavenly beings? In this case this expression stresses the fact that in the heavenly realm of transcendence among the angels, a human appears and receives a commission from the Most High. The expression in Ezekiel has been regarded as a humbling term. It might be better to speak of a paradoxical expression which emphasizes the greatness and the significance of the revelation of a transcendent "secret" to a mere human.

It is important to note that in this tradition the son of man does not have a specific name. In contrast to the Davidic Messiah he is not assigned to any particular circle of a specific narrow tradition. Perhaps, however, it is more important that by such a designation expression is given to the idea that all humankind is represented in the transcendent heavenly realm. Any national or historical restriction of the messianic message is avoided. This agrees with the fact that in the place of any narrow and exclusive father-son relationship with the Davidic king on the basis of God's having taken up his dwelling on Zion, there is now the concept of an Ancient of Days who takes precedence over all beings. What we have here is the revelation of the transcendent kingdom of God itself, not some historical preparation or foreshadowing, but a revelation for all mankind, and with this the goal of the history of revelation appears.

Here in Daniel 7 it would be possible to discern a special meaning in the term son of man, because the kingdom of God, of which man is the representative, is placed in contrast to the historic empires of the beasts and their power. Although this interpretation of Daniel 7 is a significant one, the tradition of the son of man cannot be restricted to it, since a century or two later we rediscover the son of man tradition in the similitudes of Enoch, without any mention of the beasts, and since this special interpretation is not found at any later point in the tradition. This is not because the son of man as portrayed in Daniel 7 became a stereotyped figure, whose origin in the contrast to the beasts had been forgotten. In Enoch a wide range of terminology is used of the son of man. He is called *walda sab'e,* "son of man," *walda be'esi,* "son of a male," and even *walda 'egula 'emma-heyaw,* "son of the mother of all living (=Eve)." Although there is no reference here to the contrast to the beasts, the general human character of the figure is emphasized in striking fashion.

The son of man apocalyptic contained in the similitudes of Enoch (Chapts. 37-71), the main content of which could date from the pre-Roman period of the first century B.C. (although a later reworking of this section is probable), presents a further development of the vision of Daniel 7, even the details of which are presupposed, though the collective interpretation is not adopted. Thus the tradition regarded that interpretation as only one aspect of the full inerpretation of the passage, and in so doing was true to the basic distinction between the substance of the tradition and the interpretation given in Daniel 7.

There are three aspects of the further development of the son of man figure in the Book of Enoch.

1. In Daniel 7 the son of man is installed as representative of the kingdom of God only after the judgment of the world has taken place; he is now given the decisive active role in that judgment. The son of man carries out the judgment of the world and the establishment of God's kingdom as a single process, acting as the

representative of the fulfilled kingdom of God. His enthronement
is itself the judgment of the world (cf. especially Chapt. 62). He
pronounces the judgment and reveals all that is hidden; he leads us
to the resurrection and to the feast in the heavenly kingdom, where
God is eternally praised.

2. In the concept of the royal judge who destroys all God's enemies, we can clearly see the influence of the ancient Davidic messianism, and beyond doubt the son of man apocalyptic of the Book
of Enoch consciously drew on Davidic messianism, as is shown by the
title *mashiah* for the son of man (48:10; 52:4) and by the teaching
that the son of man is equipped with the spirit of righteousness, in
dependence on Isaiah 11:1-5. But this is intimately connected with
the view that the revealer possesses the spirit of wisdom and has
authority over all secrets. In addition to the connection of the king
with wisdom, there is the old sapiential understanding of the figure
of the revealer, which had been shaped by the Mosaic-prophetic line
of tradition. Just as even before his birth Jeremiah was "known" by
God (Jer. 1:5), so too the son of man, who is filled with wisdom, is
mysteriously bound to God from the beginning of time. Behind this
view is the teaching that wisdom existed before the creation; the
most eminent bearer of wisdom displays the very essence of wisdom.
As a consequence, the universal nature of the Messiah is recognized
in his role as the final revealer of the transcendent kingdom of God.
So here at the end we can combine the great Old Testament strands
of tradition—the Davidic expectation, prophecy, and the wisdom
theology—into the one figure that brings in the kingdom of God.

3. While it is correct to emphasize the transcendent nature of the
son of man, this should not be taken as standing in contrast to his
humanity. It is only in his humanity that his soteriological function
as mediator and his messianic role are to be found. The son of man
is not an angel, but a human who has been elevated. The circles
that produced the Book of Enoch taught the elevation of Enoch to
be son of man, but this probably developed only later (chapt. 70f.).
This supplementary identification is based on the view that the

authority figure, to which their apocalyptic revelation was subject, was the figure of the revealer *kat'exochen,* and consequently was to be expected to appear as the eschatological son of man. For the continuing tradition, however, this identification of the son of man proved to be less important than the collective interpretation in Daniel 7.

There is no need here to consider further developments and details of the son of man tradition, since the New Testament follows closely on the time of the Book of Enoch or even overlaps with it and at most presupposes only this identifiable end point of the Old Testament messianic tradition in Enoch. We might mention, however, that in 4 Esdras from the first century A.D. the figure of the son of man includes the Davidic Messianic concepts and does not stand alongside a Davidic Messiah, so that our view of the son of man as a transformation of the Davidic Messiah is confirmed here as well. In the interpretation of the (sixth) vision of the son of man, this figure is addressed by God with the Davidic title "my son" (13:32, 37) and mention is made of his appearing on Zion (13:35f). Thus Old Testament messianism does not divide into two parts, an original Davidic Messiah and a later belief concerning the son of man. Rather there is a single course of the development, in which the Davidic concepts are expanded to include those of the son of Man, without making the older form invalid or meaningless.

We come therefore to the conclusion that the son of man is the man who receives God's self-disclosure in its fullness, attains the highest circle of revelation, and transmits the revelation to mankind. He is the recipient of revelation who becomes the revealer, the one who brings God's final judgment and the eternal kingdom of God. This is fully in keeping with the biblical tradition and is not the result of foreign influence. Attempts to trace the figure of the son of man to Babylonian mythology or to Persian or Hellenistic teachings about a primeval man or something similar have proven unsuccessful. Hypotheses of this sort are unconvincing, because the tradition of the son of man involves a phenomenon of Old Testament tradition history, on the basis of earlier Old Testament traditions. At most it might be a question of borrowing individual motifs, which were then completely absorbed by the whole of the Old Testament, and which do not exceed the limits of similarities discernable elsewhere in the history of religion.

The son of man tradition is a transformation of Davidic messianism. It is not something that stands alongside the Davidic concept of Messiah as it was handed down, but embraces it by uniting the royal and priestly Davidic Messiah with the Mosaic figure of the prophetic bringer of revelation and by recognizing the general human mediator of God's revelation as himself being a revelation to mankind. The messianic kingdom is severed from any contemporary historic identity and is now the apocalyptic kingdom of God that will never end and that brings all human existence to its goal. So also the Messiah of this kingdom of God as interpreted transcendentally is not a merely historic phenomenon, but a human being who has been elevated, taken up into the realm of transcendence. The teaching of the son of man is therefore the necessary conclusion of messianism. It does not replace the older Davidic concept, but expands and elevates it, so that it can encompass the entire mediatory function of divine revelation to mankind. For in apocalyptic, the messianic kingdom of God has become the sum of the revelation of divine salvation as it proceeds from the eschatological judgment of the world.

Jesus the Christ

The proclamation and the work of Jesus of Nazareth were more than the eschatological proclamation of John the Baptist. Otherwise the historical relationship of the two figures and the distinction between the circles of their disciples would not be understandable. The forgiveness of sins pronounced by Jesus in his own authority, his fellowship with sinners and his abolition of all barriers between persons, his disciples' acting as if they were at a wedding, and the crossing of the boundary that separated Jews from Gentiles, all these indicate the arrival of salvation, and not merely the expectation of the imminent arrival of the kingdom.

The way in which Jesus' proclamation revealed all that had been hidden, the proclamation of the new Torah, the demonstration of an all-pervading holiness through his giving himself to the world in holiness, the abolition of the Sabbath rules, and making salvation available in true fellowship with God—all this goes beyond the limits of prophetic proclamation. It is the activity of the Messiah, especially because the kingdom of this Messiah not only went beyond the traditional views in every respect, but even reversed them. It is undeniable that these actions of Jesus, without a prophetic call, without "inspiration," going as they did beyond the entire tradition and leading to the absolute *telos,* could be performed only on the basis of ultimate authority, which showed itself to be that of the Messiah. Moreover, the sentence of death and the meaning which this death acquired are understandable only in terms of the messianic question.

The so-called "messianic consciousness" of Jesus is regarded as especially problematic, because Jesus' statements about the son of man point to the still future coming of the revealer of judgment. The expansion of messianism to include the figure of the son of man, which is assumed in the New Testament from the outset, brings with it the result that Jesus must speak of the future son of man, regardless of how he understands his own mission, for the work of the son of man is to be completed when he appears at the final judgment, that is, at his *parousia,* which is not to be confused with Jesus' appearing on earth.

On the other hand, in the tradition that is presupposed in the New Testament, there are not two messiahs. The tradition of the son of man, as we have seen, did not include a Messiah in addition to the son of man, because the figure of the son of man involves a genuine transformation of the figure of the Davidic Messiah, and not an addition to it. Therefore, if Jesus thought of himself as the Messiah, he must also have thought of himself as the future son of man. The usual assumption that what Jesus said of the future son of man excluded the possibility of his having a "messianic consciousness" is untenable, because the son of man is primarily the judge of the world who will come "on the clouds of heaven."

In his earthly life Jesus accomplished the messianic establishment of Israel for the imminent appearing of the son of man. He took on himself the responsibility for Israel and for all mankind, assumed the task of the Messiah (the Davidic Messiah) to represent Israel, in order thereby to be enthroned as the heavenly son of man. He is not the final exhorter and prophet, Elijah *redivivus* (to think of him in his manner is a major misunderstanding), but the one who brings Israel and the world to God; he is the one who brings the world to completion.

This activity is confirmed as the work of redemption by the opposition that it encountered. But it is not a chaotic uprising of the nations that leads to a hero's death, to the heroic martyrdom of the Davidic king, but an attack by Israel and by mankind on the one who fulfills God's will. The high priest and Rome condemn him to the shameful, ignominious, painful death of a criminal. But it is precisely in and through this worst of all deaths, in which the prototypical suffering is accomplished as portrayed in Psalm 22, that the turning point is reached: the resurrection is not a future event when the son of man appears as judge; the victory over death takes place here. The decisive movement had been made, a movement away from any mythological, that is, merely analogical, transcendence at the end of time to a real transcendence here and now in the event of the cross. Here the resurrection has taken place, being has swallowed up non-being, and life has conquered death. In this way the event of the cross has provided the basis for the saving event of overcoming the world; Easter has provided the basis for Christology and given the answer to the question of who Jesus was and what the Christ event is.

1. The breaking in of transcendence into this world accounts for the divine sonship of Jesus, formulated in the terms of the tradition of the Davidic Messiah, "who was descended from David according to the flesh and designated Son of God in power according to the Spirit of holiness by his resurrection from the dead" (Rom. 1:3b-4). Paul is citing here a confession that contains the original messianic concept—"adoption" as God's son, which took place through the enthronement (Ps. 2:7; 110:3[8]). The most varied strands of the

---

[8]Cf. also the expression "the day of thy might *(dynamis)*" as a designation of the day of enthronement.

New Testament (e.g. Matt. 28:18; Phil. 2:9-10, 1 Tim. 3:16) regarded the resurrection as enthronement, quite apart from the development of the special tradition of the ascension. Moreoever, in Acts 13:32-33 the messianic promise of Psalm 2:7 is said to be fulfilled by the resurrection of Jesus, who thereby is proclaimed as the Son of God: "And we bring you the good news that what God promised to the fathers, this he has fulfilled to us their children by raising Jesus; as also it is written in the second psalm, 'Thou art my Son, today I have begotten thee.' "

Baptism in the Jordan, the descent into the floods of the deep, represents death in a ritual manner, and the rising out of the waters represents the new birth out of death. Thus at the baptism of Jesus the proclamation that he is God's son follows logically as the prefiguring of the resurrection. "And a voice came from heaven, 'Thou art my beloved Son; with thee I am well pleased' " (Mark 1:11). Thus the use of the title son of God is expanded, but its use always implicitly presupposes the Easter event.

As a result the confession that Jesus is the Son of God can be found in material that does not contain Easter accounts. The story of the transfiguration is the presentation of the final "Sinai revelaion," in which Jesus himself becomes the divine word of revelation, "This is my beloved Son; listen to him" (Mark 9:7). There was good reason for the event to remain a secret until the resurrection (v 9). In any case, in the New Testament the Davidic-messianic designation as son of God was not used simply as a title, but was conferred on the basis of his being accepted by God in the resurrection, and prior to Easter it is surrounded by the "messianic secret."

2. In the sense expressed in the tradition of the Son of man, the risen one is acclaimed as Son of man, the elevated Messiah. This is the way he is seen by the first martyr Stephen, in his vision of glory. "Behold, I see the heavens opened, and the Son of man standing at the right hand of God" (Acts 7:56). The Easter event opened the way for the free use of the designation son of man for Jesus. This is in keeping with the gospel tradition, which not only mysteriously identifies the son of man with Jesus, but uses the title as the open

self-designation of Jesus, and formulates sayings about the suffering son of man. It is of decisive significance that the announcements of suffering are connected with the concept of the son of man. Here the pronounced difference between this usage and the identification of the exalted Enoch with the son of man becomes clear. Enoch is exalted only after a full and righteous life, while the accounts of the resurrection deal with the event of the cross as directly connected with the saving event of redemption, the beginning of the new creation.

The resurrection cannot be separated from the cross and is not a mere exaltation. In the formula of the resurrection, "on the third day," there is the direct connection with Jesus' death on the cross. In this expression from the Old Testament (cf. e.g. Exod. 19:11, 15-16; Hos. 6:2; Amos 4:4) it is not a matter of difference in historic time, but of the one, total day, here, the day of death. It is a matter of the total day as the "uncleanness" of time and the before and after that define it. It is the Sabbath that is sanctified by God, in which the old world is completed, and out of which there shines the Easter light of the new creation.

In addition, the earliest presentation of the death of Jesus under the themes of Psalm 22 allude mysteriously to the event of Easter.[9] The accomplishing of the resurrection in the Easter event marks the beginning of the new being. This is not something that takes place only at the *parousia* of the son of man. Thus the achieving of salvation through the event of the cross is the decisive difference from the older tradition of the son of man, and it is precisely for this reason that speaking of the suffering son of man avoids a possible misunderstanding. The reason the term son of man plays so amazingly insignificant a role in certain parts of the New Testament (e.g., the writings of Paul) could be that the previous understanding of the son of man would place too much emphasis on the event of the *parousia* as independent of the event of the cross.

3. A full explanation, a full understanding of the breakthrough of transcendence in the cross can be accomplished only in reference

---

[9]Cf. *Vom Sinai zum Zion*, pp. 180ff.

to the overcoming of the contrast of God and man, of God and world. Salvation is revealed in death, because we humans are in the sphere of death; it is revealed in the cross, because we stand under the curse of *hamartia*. The event of the cross portrays the way in which the transcendent kingdom of God breaks through into the realm of human sin. God's work through the cross brings about atonement. It is precisely because of this soteriological event of the cross that the incarnation was necessary. The doctrine of the incarnation is not a Hellenistic disguise of the man Jesus. On the contrary it is the acknowledgement of the true meaning and the profound nature of the event of the cross. The early church, by means of its emphasis on the doctrine of the incarnation, provided a comprehensive interpretation for the theology of the cross.

In Galatians 4:4-5; Romans 8:3-4; John 3:16-17; 1 John 4:9 there are quite similar formulas[10] which say that God sent his Son into the world (the Johannine form), "born of woman, born under the law," "in the likeness of sinful flesh" (the Pauline form) in order to bring about the work of redemption. The similarity of the formulas leads us to assume an early, pre-Pauline and pre-Johannine tradition that saw the Christ event as determined by the sending of God's Son. This necessarily implies the pre-existence of the Son of God, since the "sending" is not to be understood as a general commissioning which must be followed by a specific assignment of a task, but as an actual occurrence, that is, the entry into the earthly world. These formulas expressing a mission have been compared to the sending out of Wisdom to help and to save (Wis. 9:10, 17). But the sending of the heavenly son includes a self-commitment, a self-surrender, which, although containing differing nuances in detail in Paul and John, must be assumed as having been a part of the original theology of the commissioning formulas, and which mean a sending to suffering and death, when these statements are applied to the Christ event.

In these formulas, in the pre-Pauline traditions, as in the hymn in Philippians 2:6-11, in Pauline and Johannine Christology and in the forms in which these writers found it, the pre-existence of Jesus in heaven is presupposed. There are those who want to compare this with

---

[10]Cf. E. Schweizer, *TDNT*, VIII, pp. 376ff.

the pre-existence of the figure of the son of man in Enoch, but there is a decisive difference. In the statements about the pre-existence of Christ, we do not have, as in the tradition of the son of man, the pre-existence of Jesus with God, but the pre-existence of Jesus as God. In the man Jesus this pre-existent God enters into our world and offers his own being as a sacrifice on the cross. Only a Christology of incarnation, consistently expressed in its details, can adequately portray the soteriological dimension of the event of the cross, the revelation of God's glory in the ultimate depths of human existence.

The Old Testament supports this final profound expression of Christology by the presuppositions of tradition history and revelation history. Alongside the messianic traditions which we have examined, there is a further tradition that deals with the mediating of God to the world, the wisdom tradition. Everyone who knows the order of existence encounters the wisdom which God has placed before all people as the measure of being. Wisdom as the personal mediator appears in Proverbs 8:30 as a child sitting on God's lap and sharing his throne. According to Sirach 24:10ff. it is the revelation of God that dwells on Zion, foreshadowed in the Ark, present in the holy liturgy; it is the *shekinah,* which lets the kingdom of God shine forth from Zion. The wisdom teachings had a remarkable influence on the conceptions of the Davidic Zion. But as portrayed in the book of Enoch the son of man as the bearer of wisdom is also related in a remarkable manner to the pre-existent nature of wisdom. All these movements reach their goal in the Christology of incarnation. The Messiah, Jesus, the Son of Man is, as the Logos, wisdom itself. Through the Logos, God created the world, and the complete self-disclosure of God to the world takes place in the incarnation of the Logos in Jesus, the one who was crucified.

And so in Christology all the Old Testament traditions of God's revelation of salvation, God's self-disclosure to the world, to humanity, are brought together and completed. Jesus the Christ is the sum of revelation, and that which was revealed to Israel in the name YHWH, appeared in Jesus, the *kyrios.*

VII

The Prologue to John's Gospel

I N ORDER TO GAIN A VIEW of the Bible as a whole, we can attempt
to look at a particular aspect of the Old and New Testaments
together, or to trace a theme from the earliest parts of the Old
Testament through to the latest parts of the New. Or we can endeavor to understand the Old Testament background of a New Testament text, to interpret the New by the Old. Such attempts would
lend particular interest to a New Testament text that is generally
thought to be far removed from the Old, and almost to constitute
a contrast to it. In such a case, can the connections with the Old
Testament, if they are identifiable at all, be more than superficial?
Can it be shown that the text is fully rooted in the Old Testament?
That it does not merely relate to certain traditions, but contains
significant Old Testament material? That it brings Old Testament
concerns to their appropriate conclusion and even constitutes the
goal or *telos* of the Old Testament's development? In order to do
so we would have to show in detail that the biblical material is a
unit, that the Old in the New and the New in the Old constitute a
unity.

For such an undertaking it seems to me that the prologue to John's
gospel, John 1:1-18, is a suitable text, since it is a self-contained
unit, easily examined, and through its complex and compressed nature able to lead us to many observations about tradition history.
Moreover its contents appear to belong to the late strands of the

New Testament and to express the Christology of those strands. If we find in this text statements that appear to be directed against the Old Testament, this in itself will be especially significant for our point of view.

Within the scope of these observations it will be impossible to debate the quite varied, even mutually opposed evaluations of the prologue in New Testament scholarship. Although this limitation is regrettable, there are solid reasons for it in that in general the concern of New Testament studies has been to establish the position of the text in the time-frame of its development, and to leave to one side the question of how the text can be seen in terms of the Old Testament, that is, the question of a biblical theology. Often such a question is not raised at all. This question depends first of all on one's view of the Old Testament. In his commentary *Das Evangelium des Johannes,* 1968, p. 8 Rudolf Bultmann states, "it cannot be doubted that there is a connection between the Jewish Wisdom myth and the prologue of John's Gospel, but this does not consist in Jewish speculation being the souce of the prologue. Quite apart from the fact that the Logos title of the prologue would then take on a specific meaning, the Wisdom myth was not at all a living component of Judaism. It was merely a mythological and poetic means of expressing the teaching of the Law . . . . The Wisdom myth by no means had its origin in the Old Testament or in Israel but could only have originated in pagan mythology." To this he adds, "Attempts to trace the myth back to a specific origin have so far been unsuccessful" (Note 10).

Here we find quite specific a priori judgments that concern the prologue less than they do the Old Testament. The Wisdom theology of the Old Testament is regarded as something essentially foreign to the Old Testament. It serves only to produce a particular speculative interpretation of the Law, and the question is not raised whether the Law is anything more than a purely practical entity. The possibility is not even considered that there might be an inner relationship between "knowledge of God" and *torah* (Hos. 4:6). As a consequence, the "gnostic" character of the sapiential "speculation" must a priori be rejected as foreign to the Old Testament.

There are, to be sure, quite different voices that point to the many inner connections between the Gospel of John and the Old Testament, e.g. R. E. Brown, *The Gospel According to John,* Anchor Bible, 1971. But the question is not where connections with the Old Testament may be found in the prologue, but whether the text can be understood in terms of the Old Testament. The decisive matter is the nature of the "connections," the real relationship of the entire text to the whole Old Testament. For this reason New Testament scholars should not regard it as an invasion of their territory if we attempt simply to cast light from the Old Testament on a New Testament text. Biblical theology cannot put in an appearance if Old and New Testaments are treated as belonging to strictly separate realms. It is not surprising if, as the result of such a technical academic distinction, the content of such studies reflects the relationship of the two Testaments alongside each other and not their nature as each a part of the other.

Before we begin the task of studying the prologue to John in terms of Old Testament tradition history we must clarify a number of prior questions, which, however, will draw our attention to connections with the Old Testament.

Preliminary Questions

1. *Basic Issues*

The gospel of Mark, and thus the original gospel form, begins by introducing John the Baptist as the forerunner of Jesus. There are many reasons for this, but it is not necessary to go into them here. Mention may, however, be made of the fact that there is a historical connection between Jesus and John in that Jesus was baptized by him and there were relations between the two circles of disciples that went beyond superficial contacts. This historical datum is not enough to explain the positive acceptance of the figure of John as the basic witness to the surpassing and final significance of Jesus.

Of greater importance is the fact that John's proclamation and the institution of baptism constituted the introduction to Christ's career, something that was more than an eschatological proclamation. John the Baptist marks the direct entrance into the end or *telos* of salvation history, and thus the end of the old aeon. He is the end of the Old Testament and therefore can be understood as Elijah *redivivus* (Mark 1:2-3=Isa. 40:3, prefaced by Mal. 3:1). By beginning with John the Baptist, the gospel establishes a connection with the Old Testament, which in this way becomes for the first time "Old Testament."

The same pattern is followed by Matthew, Luke, and John. To be sure, Matthew and Luke preface to this material the nativity accounts, but they do this without obliterating the boundary constituted by John. The accounts of Jesus' birth and childhood are clearly set apart, and in Luke the figure of John is interwoven with Jesus' birth narrative. In the gospel of John, where the pre-history of the incarnation is taught and expressed with reserve and an air of mystery in the form of an already existing hymn about the Logos, the role of John the Baptist is given prominence in two passages inserted into this hymn, which are quite distinct from the rest of the passage. Today it is consensus that the gospel writer placed at the beginning of his book an already existing hymn about the Logos and inserted into it the two passages, vv 6-8 and 15, that speak of John the Baptist. The Logos hymn can be clearly distinguished from what follows by the poetic parallelism of its members, but vv 6-8 and 15 interrupt the context, despite their poetic form. Verse 9 continues directly what is said in v 5 ("the light of the world"), and 16 continues 14 ("we," "fullness," "grace").

The statements about John seem to interrupt, and so it is easy to assume that the Logos hymn was not only a finished, already existing unit, but was also something alien that was reinterpreted here. On the basis of this hypothesis it is possible to regard not only the reference to John as secondary, but also other statements which the gospel writer added as interpretation of a borrowed hymn, so that finally the identification of Jesus Christ with the Logos can be regarded as a secondary interpretation. As a result many more or less extensive hypotheses have been advanced for reconstructing the original Logos hymn. In addition to vv 6-8 and 15, other parts that have been regarded as secondary are vv 9, 12 (at least from *tois* on), v 13 especially, but also vv 17-18, and by some v 2 and finally vv 14 and 16.

Various arguments play a role in these hypotheses, especially the analysis of form, by which elements that disrupt the strict poetic form are excised. But where do the exegetes get their standard for strict poetic form? In order to avoid following their own choice of schematization they need to derive the form from the text itself, from a precise reconstruction of the poetic parallelism and the formulation of thought connected with it. In this parallelism we can already note the linguistic roots of the text in the Old Testament. In order to reconstruct this non-Greek poetic form that is so heavily stamped with the features of the Old Testament psalm tradition (extending as late as Sir. 24!), examples of which can be amply identified down to the Qumran material, it is necessary to render the text into Hebrew, regardless of whether or not it was originally composed in Hebrew (or Aramaic).[1] In form—the question of context must be set aside here—the passage shows that it was thought out and composed in Hebrew. In addition there is the well-known thoroughgoing influence of late Hebrew on the Greek expressions in the prologue, which can be fully clarified only by a literal back translation. Moreover, we can fully understand the structure of the verses only in the light of the metrical structure that emerges in a Hebrew translation.[2] (This also enables us to surmise the rhythmical form of the Greek text.) It would also be of interest if the Hebrew trans-

---

[1] In view of the relationships in Qumran (Hodayot, etc.) and some linguistic factors (metrical difficulties when it is translated into Aramic, construct state forms, syntactic features, Old Testament technical theological terms) it is my opinion that an original Hebrew form is possible, but not an Aramaic original. The question of the translation of a self-contained text like the prologue is independent of the question of the linguistic background of the gospel. Even in the unlikely case of a possible Aramaic original, the closeness of the passage to Hebrew is, because of the fixed Old Testament terminology, greater than would appear on grounds of language alone, so that in any case doing a back translation into Hebrew can give insights into the text.

[2] This is true in spite of the incomplete nature of our knowledge of the Hebrew metrical system. Independent of our theory we must consider whatever practical insights have emerged in the analysis of post-exilic psalm literature.

lation encountered difficulties produced by expressions which cannot be translated literally.

Another argument concerning the form that has been used in hypothetical reconstructions of the original form is the close resemblance to the language of the gospel writer. Anything that contains elements typical of his style has been termed secondary (e.g. v 2, 12 (from *tois* on), v 18). This argument is highly problematical. Quite apart from the assumption that the writer of the original hymn is not the evangelist or a member of his circle, the language used in the Johannine circle cannot be so precisely identified as to make it possible to distinguish in the prologue between non-Johannine (genuine) and Johannine (non-genuine) usage. In addition, the language of the original Logos hymn shows on the whole such closeness to Johannine language, that possible differences would not be strikingly noticeable.

Concerning the dubious passages, all we can say is that they *could* be additions to Johannine language. But that they *must* be such additions would depend on the conclusion that the poetic form indicated they were disruptive and therefore their content was to be reinterpreted. On the contrary, if portions that stand up to the critique of their poetic form and their content show Johannine linguistic features, this result must be respected. Indeed it would be quite aberrant if the gospel writer incorporated traditional material of such significance and was indebted to its content, without also having affinities with its language.

What follows is an attempt to bring together observations about form and several essential exegetical observations on the prologue to John's gospel in order to understand both the content and the form of the text and to be able to decide the question of the original form. I will occasionally consider the Hebrew formulations that lie behind the Greek text and therefore I have appended the Hebrew re-translation to the following English translation, which is as literal as possible.

A   a ¹In the beginning was the Logos
        and the Logos was with God,

b and God was the Logos;
  ²he was in the beginning with God.
c ³Everything was (made) through him
  and without him was not even one thing (made).
B a What was (made),⁴ in it he was the life,
  and the life was the light of men.
 b ⁵And the light shines in the darkness
  and the darkness did not overpower it.
  [⁶There was a man,
   sent by God;
    he had the name John.
  ⁷He came as witness,
   to testify about the light,
   so that everyone might believe through him.
  (⁸That one was not the light,
   but was to testify about the light.)]
 c ⁹He was the true light,
  which enlightens every man,
   (by) coming into the world.
C a ¹⁰He was in the world,
  and the world was (made) through him,
   and the world did not recognize him.
 b ¹¹He came to his property,
  and his own people did not receive him.
D a ¹²But those who accepted him,
  to them he gave power,
   to become God's children,
 b to those believing in his name,
  ¹³who, not by blood (of parents),
   and not by will of the flesh,
 c and not by the will of a male,
  but are born (begotten) by God.
E a ¹⁴And the Logos became flesh
  and dwelt (tented) among us,
   and we saw his glory,

b Glory as that of the only-begotten of the Father,
    full of grace and truth.
  [15 John bore witness to him
    and called out:
      "This one it was of whom I said,
    'The one coming after me
    is (someone who existed) before me,
    for he was before I was.' "]
c 16For out of his fullness we all have received,
    yes, grace upon grace.
F a 17For the law was given through Moses;
    grace and truth came through Jesus Christ.
  b 18No one has ever seen God,
    an only-begotten God, who is in the
    Father's bosom, he revealed (him).

וְהַדָּבָר הָיָה אֵת הָאֱלֹהִים		בְּרֵאשִׁית הָיָה הַדָּבָר 1	Aa	3+3
בְּרֵאשִׁית הוּא אֵת הָאֱלֹהִים 2		וֵאלֹהִים הָיָה הַדָּבָר	b	3+3
וּמִבַּלְעָדָיו נִהְיָה לֹא אֶחָד		הַכֹּל נִהְיָה בְיָדוֹ 3	c	3+3
וְהַחַיִּים (הָיוּ) אוֹר הָאֲנָשִׁים		אֲשֶׁר נִהְיָה בּוֹ חַיִּים הָיָה 4	Ba	3+3
וְהַחֹשֶׁךְ לֹא אֲחָזוֹ		וְהָאוֹר יִזְרַח בַּחֹשֶׁךְ 5	b	3+3
שָׁלוּחַ מֵאֱלֹהִים שְׁמוֹ יוֹחָנָן		[וַיְהִי אִישׁ אֶחָד 6		2+2+2
לְהָעִיד עַל הָאוֹר לְהַאֲמִין כֻּלָּם עַל יָדוֹ		הוּא בָא לְעֵדוּת 7		2+2+2
כִּי אִם לְהָעִיד עַל הָאוֹר]		(הוּא לֹא הָיָה הָאוֹר 8		3+3
הַמֵּאִיר כָּל אָדָם בָּא בָעוֹלָם		הָיָה הָאוֹר הָאֲמִתִּי 9	c	2+2+2
וְהָעוֹלָם לֹא יְדָעוֹ	וְהָעוֹלָם נִהְיָה בוֹ	בָעוֹלָם הָיָה 10	Ca	2+2+2
וְלֹא קִבְּלוּהוּ אֲשֶׁר לוֹ		וַיָּבֹא אֱלֵי אֲשֶׁר לוֹ 11	b	3+3
לִהְיוֹת זֶרַע אֱלֹהִים	נָתַן עֹז לָהֶם	וְהַמְקַבְּלִים אֹתוֹ 12	Da	2+2+2
וְלֹא מֵחֵפֶץ בָּשָׂר	אֲשֶׁר לֹא מִדָּמִים 10	לַבֹּטְחִים בִּשְׁמוֹ 9	b	2+2+2
כִּי אִם מֵאֱלֹהִים הוֹלָדוּ		וְלֹא מֵחֵפֶץ גָּבֶר	c	3+3

וַנֶּחֱזֶה כְבוֹדוֹ	וַיִּשְׁכֹּן בְּתוֹכֵנוּ	¹⁴וְהַדָּבָר נִהְיָה בָשָׂר	Ea	2+2+2
מָלֵא חֶסֶד וֶאֱמֶת		כָּבוֹד כְּדִי יָחִיד מֵאָב	b	3+3
זֶה אֲשֶׁר אָמַרְתִּי	וְהִזְעִיק לֵאמֹר	¹⁵[יוֹחָנָן מֵעִיד בּוֹ		2+2+2
[כִּי קֹדֶם לִי]	נִהְיָה לְפָנַי	הַבָּא אַחֲרַי		2+2+2
וְחֶסֶד תַּחַת חָסֶד		¹⁶כִּי מִמְּלוֹאוֹ לָקַחְנוּ כֻלָּנוּ	c	3+3
חֶסֶד וֶאֱמֶת נִהְיָה בְּיֵשׁוּעַ הַמָּשִׁיחַ		¹⁷כִּי הַתּוֹרָה נִתְּנָה בְּמֹשֶׁה	Fa	3+3ʳ
אֶל יָחִיד בְּחֵק הָאָב הוּא הוֹרָהּ		¹⁸אֶת־אֱלֹהִים לֹא רָאָה אִישׁ מֵעוֹלָם	b	3+3ʳ

Notes on the Hebrew text.

a. Instead of *nihyah* we could have here and in what follows, *naᶜasa,* but note the verbal correspondence that confirms the former (cf. 1QS xi 11).

b. Cf. C. Brockelmann, *Hebraische Syntax,* 1956.

c. Cf. Judg. 13:2; 1 Sam. 1:1; or it might read only *wayehi ish.*

d. The indeterminate participle form corresponds to the Hebrew predicate, *see* Brockelmann §103a.

e. Or *eleha.*

f. The literal translation *bene elohim* is not possible, since the expression is misleading because it means "gods," and it does not correspond to *tekna* which was used to avoid confusion with the Son of God. *zeraᶜ* is translated by *huioi* in Neh. 9:2; Sir. 46:10. On *zeraᶜ elohim* cf. Mal. 2:15 where it means spiritual fatherhood of the unmarried *(ahad)* parallel to kinship in spirit (instead of *ushe'ar,* read *ushe'er; she'er ruah* is the opposite of *she'er basar,* "blood kin," Lev. 18:6; 25:49; Num. 27:11).

g. Cf. Isa. 50:10.

h. The plural *damim* usually means "shed blood," "blood guilt," etc. but it can also serve to designate various types of blood (e.g. *Niddah* II 6) in the rare cases, such as this, where such a meaning is intended. To express the two types of blood which are meant here, the dual, which was so frequent in late Hebrew in contrast to Aramaic, would be used. Cf. Cf. M. H. Segal, *A Grammar of Mishnaic Hebrew,* 1937 §293. In New Testament Greek, of course, the dual was completely replaced by the plural.

i. It could hardly be *wannahaz.*

k. *kede,* "according to the measure of," "worthy of" corresponds exactly to the Greek with the genitive.

l. *Zᶜg* in the hiphil can mean a legally binding and charismatic summons, e.g. the mobilization of the army in a holy war. Cf. Zech. 6:8.

m. Also used of rank (Gesenius-Buhl, *Handwörterbuch über das Alte Testament*, 17th ed., 1915, see *pane* D3a, Sp. 648b.)

n. *we* "and that is" Gesenius-Buhl, 1d. Sp. 189b.

o. Juon's suggestions should also be mentioned (*Recherches de science religieuse* 22, 1932, p. 206). He saw in *anti* a *keneged* (cf. Gen. 2:18, 20) and translated "une grâce répondant á sa grace," that is, the grace received corresponds to the divine *charis,* which is revealed by this *doxa,* so that here the total, complete mediation of grace takes place.

p. The sign of the accusative is possible before nouns of category without an article, see Brockelman, §96. Moreover, *elohim* is a quasi personal name.

q. Cf. Lev. 14:57.

r. The last two verses are distinctly longer than the others. This feature can often be observed in the Psalms. A metric expansion to 4 + 4 or 4 + 5 would be possible, but does not seem likely, since in the proposed back translation there are never more than three unaccented syllables, and they must be taken into account in any case. The meter thus consistently contains six beats.

2. Exegesis and Analysis of Form

The parallelism of members, or so-called "thought rhyme," which is characteristic of biblical poetry, is no merely external feature. Here, in a dynamic progression, the content is presented and elucidated in doubled, intensified formulations. According to the view of early antiquity, something is complete only when doubled (cf. Isa. 40:2; the word for "double" means completeness), and a part of every sentence is its contrast, to the right as well as to the left, etc. Orderliness is created by revealing symmetry. Antithetic parallelism expresses the whole thought in terms of its contrasting aspects; synonymous parallelism does not merely repeat the same thing in different words, but adds to what was said by raising it to fullness and completion; and explanatory-synthetic parallelism builds up the whole thought out of its component parts. It is not, however, possible to draw sharp distinctions among these three traditional types. A parallelism that negates the contrasting term is, in content, synonymous. An intensifying of synonymous parallelism, whose two parts are not made syntactically absolute, becomes synthetic.

It is always the case that parallelism expresses an intensification, whether it is a contrast that belongs to the complete idea, or an intensification of the content by making it more concrete, or the attaining of the appropriate goal of the statement. The two-fold form can be expanded to a three-fold one, not by giving up the basic principle of duplication, but by making a half of it parallel to itself. This results in the following two formulations: a + (b_1 + b_2) or (a_1 + a_2) + b. Any analysis of the Prologue to John must identify the parallel formulations of the lines, which characterize the statements contained in this structure. Then it will be able to reveal the composition of the whole.

Vv 1-2. The words "in the beginning" echo the first word of the Torah (Gen. 1:1), which refers to the beginning of time itself. This specification of time gives the content of the realm before creation. Pre-existence in this sense means a direct relationship to the creator God as well as participation in the act of creation. The indication of time, "in the beginning" is continued and intensified by the parallelism to the indication of space, "with God." The two together constitute a completed, balanced line in which "in the beginning" naturally stands first in contrast to "with God," as in Gen. 1:1.

The second strophe (v 1c-2) passes from the statement about time and space into ontology. The consequence of the Logos being pre-existent with God is the deity of the Logos. The predicate substantive (without article) is placed first in the emphatic position (resulting in similar sounding line endings). The declaration of deity cannot be intensified, and so the parallel in v 2 repeats the full content of the first strophe (1ab). Such a return to the beginning indicates in poetry that a unit has been concluded, in this case, the statements about the self-existence of the Logos.

The view has often been expressed that v 2 shows traces of the gospel writer's style of definition and is a later addition. The real reason for wanting to strike v 2 is probably that it is regarded as a superfluous repetition (but why would something superfluous be added later?) V 2 is, however, quite necessary as a concluding and summarizing parallel. If we were to strike it, then v 1 would constitute a tristich, and this would produce difficulties in the back translation, in addition to being unique in the entire prologue, which consists entirely of six-beat lines. In addition the pleasing assonance of the two endings in v 1-2 would be lost, and the chiasmic structure of predicate-subject/subject-predicate would be disturbed, along with the repetitive summary of the absolute being in time and space that marks the conclusion.

V 3. Just as the description of the absolute transcendence of the Logos is consciously formulated in v 1-2 as a unit, so in the theological tradition of the Bible the statements of v 1-2 establish the connection to the creation which is subsequently expressed in v 3— everything came to be through the Logos. The parallelism, which consists in the total negation of its opposite, that is, of any exception, emphasizes the absolute preeminence of the Logos over everything that exists, including spiritual beings. The chiastic structure of the two lines and their quiet confidence bring v 3 into relationship to the preceding lines. His nature as God is joined to his work as creator, while the following verses move forward to new statements and lack the chiastic structure—they deal with creation.

The division between v 3 and v 4 is disputed. It is a priori probable that *ho gegonen* "that was made" goes with what follows, quite apart from the fact that if it went with *oude hen* "not anything" it would have to read *hōn gegonen*. With what goes before, it is unnecessary, while if it is connected with what follows we have the *casus pendens* construction, so common in Hebrew (cf. v 12a and also v 18b). Moreover, the following *en autō* instead of *en toutō* is quite correct, as shown by the *autois* of v 12. In addition it provided an example of anadiplosis, which in Hebrew serves to tie sections together (in discourse, for example, Gen. 3:1b-5 and in poetry, Ps. 121:1-5). It is also common in the prologue to John: *egeneto oude hen—ho gegonen; erchomenon eis ton kosmon—en tō kosmō ēn; auton ou parelabon—hosoi de elabon.* cf. also *charis* in v 16-17. The present verse division dates from the time of Jerome, but it is never found in the older Greek fathers, and is mainly connected with the ministerpretation of the *en autō* as referring to the Logos. This could then easily be taken to mean someone who had come to be in the Logos, with resulting doctrinal misunderstanding. On the other hand, a simple, "in him (the Logos) was life" would produce a clear text. It is striking how seldom, at least in the German language, the original verse division is followed. Below when v 4 is spoken of it is assumed that it begins with *ho gegonen.*

V 4. But now how is v 4a to be understood? Is "life" the subject or a predicate substantive? In favor of the latter is the absence of the article, in contrast to *hē zōē* in the following. The subject, however, cannot be *ho gegonen* ("what came to be, was life . . ."), because the *zōē* is no immanent biological life-force, but the "effect" of the Logos. Therefore the subject must be contained in *ēn* "he was" and mean the Logos, "in what came to be, he was the life." The *en autō* "in him" therefore resumes the casus pendens *ho gegonen.* If on the contrary, on the assumption of a transcendental understanding of *zōē,* the *en autō* is taken to refer to the Logos, we would not have a complete sentence: "what came to be, in him (the Logos) was life." The words "for it" would be missing. The fact that the subject is not explicit in the only possible interpretation of v 4a, "what came to be, in it he (the Logos) was life," is not a counterargument, just as it is no argument in vv 9, 10, where it twice reads *ēn,* "he was," or in what follows.

While *ho logos* in v 1 is explicit, and in v 2 at least referred to emphatically with the pronoun *houtos,* it does not appear explicitly in what follows until the decisive new beginning in v 14, finally to be identified as Jesus Christ in v 17. The Logos, the life principle of creation, is the light of men, that is, the light that gives consciousness to men, as we know on the basis of the Old Testament understanding of light. V 4b thus continues and intensifies 4a in terms of the innermost realm of humanity.

V 5. This light is now the subject of vv 5 and 9. The statement about the light shining in the darkness is coordinated with a negative explication, "and the darkness has not overcome it (the light)." The aorist verb is to be understood in the sense of "was not able to overcome it." The reference to the first work of creation in Genesis 1:3-5 is clear. The light is not swallowed up in the chaotic darkness or mixed with it in a half light, but in a cosmic victory it shines forth and sets a boundary to the darkness. Since in Genesis 1:3-5 the light is more than merely a physical phenomenon, and the Old Testament can have an intellectual concept of light, (which is not

to be separated from the natural phenomenon of light), the "light
of men" in v 4 should not mislead us into regarding the light and
darkness in v 5 as merely "allegorical" metaphors for a simple human
gaining of knowledge or into seeing in the attempt of the darkness
to overcome the light a merely human mental event of "compre-
hending," or "understanding." To be sure *katalambanein* can also
mean that, but the Johannine use of the word with *skotia* "darkness" as subject (12:35ff.; cf. 6:17 in אּ D) clearly has the meaning
of an overwhelming grasping and holding on to.[3]

Vv 6-8. The continuation of the statements about light is inter-
rupted in vv 6-8 by a section about John the Baptist. In 6-7 we have
two verses of three stichs each in the form $(a_1 + a_2) + b$. V 6 tells
how John made his appearance, and the statement that he existed is
intensified by saying he had a divine mission. The parallel is given
in terms of his name, which defines the historic person. V 7 states
the significance of the life of this man; he came to bear witness, and
this witness is immediately specified as witness to the light, while
the parallel line states the goal, to lead to faith (aorist). V 8 reverts
to two stichs. It takes up and explains the middle element in v 7,
that John the Baptist did not mean that he himself was the light.
The verse in itself seems to be superfluous, but since v 9 has the
statement "he was the true light . . ." it would be possible to fall
into the misunderstanding that John was the light, that is, we must
regard v 8 as a necessary element after the new beginning in vv 6-7.

V 9. Here we would expect a verse with three stichs, which would
complete the discussion of the light. The syntactic relationships are
not entirely clear. The frequent rabbinic expression "(all) who come
into the world" as a general designation of all mankind could be
taken at first glance as indicating that *erchomenon eis ton kosmon*
"coming into the world" modified *anthrōpon*. But in that case v 9c
is unnecessary, in fact it is nonsense to add an indirect paraphrase to

---

[3] *paralambanein* v 11 (which also means more than "comprehend") refers to the Logos and not to the light, and should not be restricted to the
meaning in v 5. Speculation about a pun between the Aramaic word *qabla*,
"darkness," and *qbl* (in the *pa'al*) "accept," is nonsense, because *qbl* does
not correspond to *katalambanein* but to *paralambanein*.

the concept that is expressed directly, and this sort of formulation is never found in rabbinic texts. *erchomenon* must therefore modify *to phōs to alēthinon* "the true light." John 3:19 and 12:46 (cf. 9:5; 12:35) also speak of the coming of the light into the world. It is moreover not possible to construe a periphrastic construction *en erchomenon*, "he was coming (into the world)" that would permit an entire relative clause to come between the two parts of the sentence. This would also destroy the structure of the verse in three stichs. As in v 4 it is a priori to be assumed that the subject of the sentence is contained in the verb *en*, "he was" and means the Logos.

Resuming the content of 4b, the verse says that he was the true light (the article is necessary with a predicate substantive in this case), and this identification of the true light is expanded in the following parallel (thus giving the form of a + [b₁ + b₂]) with the statement that this light coming into the world enlightens everyone. The entrance of the Logos into the world brings about the "enlightenment" of the human consciousness, and human awareness (of the light) follows. Thus v 9 summarizes the content of 4-5 in respect to the human experience and acceptance of divine salvation. Vv 4-5, which speak only of the shining forth of the light, thus do not make v 9 superfluous, especially since the emphasis on the entrance into the world announces the theme of the next section, the question of his being accepted by humanity.

V 10. With anadiplosis the verse in three stichs makes the transition, formulates the existence of the Logos in the world, and intensifies the connection between Logos and the world through the creation in order to contrast this close parallelism, in the form (a₁ + a₂) + b, with the failure of the world to recognize him. Here *kosmos* has the primary meaning of the world of humanity, for which v 9 has prepared us. But the person represents the entire cosmos (cf. Gen. 1), and the reference here to the creation underlines the implicit inclusion of the entire cosmos, which is subject to human beings. Just as in vv 4-5 the human and the physical are not to be separated, so here and in John in general *kosmos* is not simply metomomy for humankind. The cosmos can be seen in humankind and is represented in the human consciousness. The "knowing," which the cosmos could not accomplish, is to be understood in the meaning of the Hebrew *ydᶜ* as the acknowledgement, the knowing acceptance of the Logos, which must follow the enlightening, the seeing, the perceiving (v 9) as its answer. Human beings, and with them the cosmos, see, but do not acknowledge.

V 11. *hoi idioi* in John refers, not to humanity in general, but those with whom one has a special relationship (13:1; cf. 10:3-4, and "my own," 10:14; see also 17:6, 9-10). There is no question but that after the mention of humanity in v 10, this verse is speaking of God's own people, Israel, to whom the Logos "came" *ēlthen* a reference to the event in salvation history, in contrast to the "natural" occurrence signified by the verb *ēn*. "Receive" is the counterpart to "came" and gives stronger expression to the personal relationship than does the "knew" of v 10.

Vv 12-13. This new section begins with anadiplosis and speaks of the reception of the Logos in contrast to his not being received, as portrayed in vv 10-11. In v 12 (down to *genesthai*) we have a synthetic parallelism, which clearly consists of three stichs. The first major part expresses the reception from the human side, the second from the side of the Logos, and then in synthetic parallelism the "power" which is conferred is specified as that of becoming children of God, and the structure is a + (b_1 + b_2). The simple formulation of the reception of the Logos introduced by anadiplosis urgently demands and explication of its content, and the concept of being children of God, in the light of the old traditions of Israel as God's children (Exod. 4:22; Deut. 1:31; 32:6, 18-19; Hos. 11:1 etc.), remains a riddle, coming as it does after v 11 with its statements about Israel. It was necessary that these statements be further developed, and if identifying those who received him as those who believe in the Logos reveals a Johannine style (John 2:23; 3:18; 1 John 5:13), that is merely a use of Old Testament terminology (Isa. 50:10; Ps. 33:21) and is still no reason for deleting 12d.

The following relative clause in v 13 is probably, at least in part, the corresponding parallel and explains the nature of divine sonship. This is accomplished by the use of negatives—false reliance on belonging to the people of Israel is rejected. The sentence is composed of four parts, of which three are negative. From the time of Sirach 14:18 on, the expression "flesh and blood" was used with increasing frequency in the sense of "human" and to express the contrast of man and God, and it is thus clear that the first two and last two components constitute two pairs. The first pair is to be taken as parallel to v 12d, giving the formula $a + (b_1 + b_2)$, while the second constitutes a strophe in itself and expresses the decisive formulation of the non-physical, charismatic, divine birth.

Some have rejected the comparison with the expression "flesh and blood" *(basar wadam)* because the order of terms is reversed here. If, however, the terms were to be rephrased for the sake of poetic parallelism, then, in order to maintain the balance, their order would have to be reversed. More important is the fact that the traditional expression has been rephrased. By the addition of *thelēma*, "will," the human mental dimension is included and stressed, while the plural of blood[4] refers to the resulting mixture of the "blood" of man and woman (Wisdom 7:2; cf. also Job. 10:10). So a contrast is drawn between the physical and mental sphere of Israel *kata sarka* and the true divine sonship of Israel *kata pneuma*.

There is no reason to question v 13 because of similarities to the content of John 3:3-8 (note the differences in terminology). The only surprising feature of v 13 is the expansive style that contrasts to the usual brevity of this passage, where each line has its own function. It would have been quite possible to compress the content of vv 12-13 into two lines. In this an instance of an intentional expansion to three lines to conform to stanza structure? We will need to look at this question again.

V 14. This verse begins a new section, as is made clear by the explicit repetition of Logos. Then there is all at once the use of "we," meaning the apostle (cf. 1 John 1:1-4), which became in time the "we" of the New Testament church (v 16). And the absence of anadiplosis only serves to underline that this is the beginning of a new section. This casts light on the understanding of Israel *kata pneuma* in vv 12-13. Coming as it does after v 11 it must refer to

---

[4]See above p. 175, note h.

the true Israel of Old Testament times, which "trusted in the name of Yahweh" and not in its membership according to the flesh in the Israel of that day.[5] Thus it is only in v 14 that the prologue comes to the New Testament Christ event.

This is not contradicted by the fact that the New Testament achievement of salvation includes birth in the spirit and birth from God (John 3:3-8; 1 John 3:9; 4:7; 5:1-4, 18), as well as recognition of the "light of the world" (John 8:12; 9:5; 12:35-36, 46). Since the exegetes have not distinguished between the realms of creation and world, and Israel *kata sarka* and *kata pneuma* in the prologue to John, its content has been seen as involving an undifferentiated event of revelation of the Logos, so that ultimately vv 14-18 and the Christian character of the song as a whole came into question.

V 14 is to be divided into two lines. The repetition of *doxan* marks the beginning of the second line, with the description of the glory of Christ. Also *pleres* and the following words are taken up again at the beginning of v 16, so that here anadiplosis is a feature of both lines. The first line of v 14 gives "dwelling" (as in a tent) as a more specific parallel to the statement about the incarnation. In this figure of speech even the choice of the word is colored by Old Testament usage (σκν is similar in sound to *shkn*). Further parallels are given in the beholding of the glory as human knowledge of the event of revelation, in the pattern $(a_1 + a_2) + b$. The second line specifies that this glory, which was appropriate for the only son of the Father, is thus the true and complete glory of the Father, and therefore it can appropriately be described in the parallel line with the Old Testament expression, "full of grace and truth."

V 15. This verse is a pronounced interruption in the text. Two strophes of three stichs each, in the pattern $(a_1 + a_2) + b$, give the testimony of John the Baptist. The testimony given in the first line is parallel to the charismatic *krazein* "cried (out)",[6] and the

---

[5]It should be noted that according to the Old Testament the distinction between the true and the false Israel consisted in the contrast between trusting in God and trusting in human power.

[6]See above, p. 175, note 1.

testimony is identified as being about Jesus. The second line contains a beautifully worded paradox—the one who comes after John ranks before him, followed by the explanation that alludes to Jesus' pre-existence as the Logos, an indication that the precedence of the "follower" marks an absolute turning point.

V 16. The implications of the Christ event for salvation are stated in synthetic parallelism, where the second stich expresses the endless or complete nature of the gift of grace.[7] V 16 is the direct continuation of the two lines of v 14, and by summarizing them, it rounds out the implications for human salvation. This is strikingly similar to the relationship of v 9 to vv 4-5.

Vv 17-18. Just as v 9 was followed by two verses (10-11) that portray the failure to welcome the Logos, so here in vv 17-18 the revelation through Torah and that through Christ are contrasted. For the present the question can remain open as to whether this is meant as a contrast of the revelations given in the Old and the New Testaments respectively, or a contrast between the beginning and the goal of salvation history, between incompleteness and fulfillment. That will have to be determined in a larger context. V 17 is concerned with the gift of salvation to humans (revelation of God's will), while v 18 presents the revelation of God himself (revelation of his being). The gift of the Torah, through which salvation was first accomplished, is contrasted to the complete accomplishment of salvation ("grace and truth") and the initial mediator of revelation, Moses, is contrasted to the one who completed the saving revelation, Jesus Christ. Finally in this summary, the name of Jesus can be mentioned together with the name of Moses, and so the Logos is identified by name.

V 18 sums up the central Old Testament tradition of God's revelation of himself by permitting persons to "see God," from the oldest Moses traditions, through Ezekiel 1, and into the Apocalyptic writings. In the Old Testament this seeing of God is always veiled, and only in the *eschaton* will it be an encounter face to face. In contrast to this is God's revelation of his being through Jesus, the

---

[7] On the interpretation of *anti*, see above p. 175, note o.

revelation of an only begotten "God."[8] The clause in apposition here, "who is in the bosom of the Father," which modifies the "only begotten," does not express, as is often claimed, the picture of a friend lying on someone's bosom as at a banquet, for instance, but that of a child taken in the arms and held on the lap, which is explicitly indicated here in the Father-son relationship, and which, as we will see, can be derived from the Old Testament tradition history. The expression for revelation at the end of v 18, *exēgeisthai,* is a technical term for the proclamation of God's will through a soothsayer or similar functionary, and also for proclamations of the gods themselves (the Apollo of the Delphic oracle, Plato, *Republic,* IV, 427c) and can therefore be used for the revelation given through Jesus.[9] The absence of any specification of an object of the verb is appropriate here, because it lets the absolute nature of the event be expressed, "he has made known."

3. The Structure of the Prologue

Following the detailed analysis of the structure of the verses and lines, we can establish the structure of the whole passage. Let us draw together all the observations about the structure that were brought out in that analysis. What larger, comprehensive units (A, B, etc.) can we identify that consist of individual lines (a, b, etc.), if we leave to one side the sections that clearly deal with John the Baptist, vv 6-7, 8, 15? It is clear that the three lines of vv 12-13 hang together. They form a single sentence, dealing with the divine sonship of those who belong to the true Israel. Vv 10-11 clearly constitute a two-line unit, the failure of the world and of Israel to acknowledge the Logos. The same is true of vv 17-18, the contrast of the Old Testament and its fulfillment in the New. The three-line unit, vv 4-5, 9 is united by the theme of light, and the last line,

---

[8]The easier reading *huios* has weaker manuscript evidence for it. The repetition here at the end of the unusual declaration of *theos* at the beginning (v 1) could be explained on stylistic grounds, and in any case it is a frequent phenomenon in the poetry of the Psalms.

[9]Note the possibility that the verb *exegeisthai,* according to Lev. 14:57, could correspond to the Hebrew *hora.* This then would result in a chiastic reference here at the end of v 18 to the Torah at the beginning of v 17.

v 9, concludes by highlighting this general revelation to mankind and to the cosmos in reference to its reception by mankind. Vv 14, 16 constitute a three-line unit about the incarnation of the Logos, in which v 16 gives the human reception of this revelation of the *telos* of salvation history. Finally, vv 1-3 form a three-line unit that describes the Logos as God and creator. We have already seen that in structure, vv 1-3 constitute a contrast to 4-5, and have as theme the transcendent priority of the Logos to creation and the absolute being of the Logos, while the following section speaks of revelation in the cosmos.

This analysis disclosed a distinctive alternation of two- and three-stich strophes, and two parallel sequences in both of which two strophes of three stichs each are followed by a concluding one of two lines.

Aa-c The divine nature of the Logos

Da-c The human children of God

Ba-c The Light=general event of revelation
(c the human response)

Ea-c The incarnation=
The telos of revelation
(c the human response)

Ca-b The lack of fulfillment

Fa-b The fulfillment

It is obvious that the six sections constitute a larger two-fold unit, in which part B corresponds to E, part C to F, and in a certain sense, part A to D. In any case it is clear that part D was consciously formulated as a three-line section in order to fit into the larger pattern. The content of the entire passage follows a single path from the pre-existent divine nature of the Logos through the cosmic act of revelation, which on the one hand leads to rejection in the world and in the "natural" Israel, and on the other to acceptance in the "spiritual" Israel, and finally to the incarnation as a goal of revelation, ending with a backward look at the fulfillment and completion of the revelatory process. The double structure is appropriate to the revelation in creation and in the Christ event and is suggested by the polarity between fulfillment and non-fulfillment. In the poetic tradition of the Old Testament there are significant examples of two-fold structure of a composition, such as the creation hymn of the book of Amos, the song of the Ark of the Covenant (Ps. 132), and the structure of the account of creation (Gen. 1).

Once the double structure of the prologue is clearly in mind, it is obvious that the two insertions that deal with John the Baptist were placed at corresponding points, before Bc and Ec, that is, before the passages that speak of the human reception of the revelation of the Logos *asarkos* and *ensarkos*. In precise correspondence to the content of the context, one of these speaks of John's witness to the light, and the other of his mystery-filled proclamation of the incarnation. These originally two-line insertions (vv 6-7 and 15) bring all human reception of the Logos revelation into relationship with John's testimony and a priori give it his confirmation, so that the traditional beginning of the Gospel with John the Baptist can be reached. As far as the form is concerned, while the insertions disupt the context of units B and E, they still underline the importance of these two middle sections in their relationship to each other, with their common theme of revelation.

In summary, we conclude that apart from the insertions that deal with John the Baptist, the original Logos hymn does not contain any secondary material. Even the broader style of vv 12-13 can be explained in terms of the composition of the whole. The original hymn of the revelation of the Logos is a Christ hymn, which reaches its climax in v 14 with the portrayal of the incarnation of the Logos. The style of the hymn is reminiscent of the style of the gospel writer, and the origin of the song is to be ascribed to this circle of tradition.

The passages dealing with John the Baptist are clearly secondary, but they are appropriate to the original structure of the hymn. Poetically they fit perfectly into the total structure and are not the result of a redaction that was foreign to the original hymn or did violence to it. On the contrary, their presence here is evidence of how close the gospel writer was to the source of the hymn. The argument that material in the prologue which is stylistically close to the work of the gospel writer is secondary to the passage is not substantiated by the data. Thus from the point of view of Old Testament tradition history, we can assume the following form of the text for our study of the prologue.

A a ¹ἐν ἀρχῇ ἦν ὁ λόγος ——— καὶ ὁ λόγος ἦν πρὸς τὸν θεόν
 b καὶ θεὸς ἦν ὁ λόγος ——— ²οὗτος ἦν ἐν ἀρχῇ πρὸς τὸν θεόν
 c ³πάντα δι' αὐτοῦ ἐγένετο ——— καὶ χωρὶς αὐτοῦ ἐγένετο οὐδὲ ἕν

B a ὃ γέγονεν ⁴ἐν αὐτῷ ζωὴ ἦν ——— καὶ ἡ ζωὴ ἦν τὸ φῶς τῶν ἀνθρώπων
 b ⁵καὶ τὸ φῶς ἐν τῇ σκοτίᾳ φαίνει ——— καὶ ἡ σκοτία αὐτὸ οὐ κατέλαβεν
    [⁶ἐγένετο ἄνθρωπος ——— ἀπεσταλμένος παρὰ θεοῦ ———
    ὄνομα αὐτῷ Ἰωάννης
    ⁷οὗτος ἦλθεν εἰς μαρτυρίαν ——— ἵνα μαρτυρήσῃ περὶ τοῦ
    φωτός ——— ἵνα πάντες πιστεύσωσιν δι' αὐτοῦ
    (⁸οὐκ ἦν ἐκεῖνος τὸ φῶς ———ἀλλ' ἵνα μαρτυρήσῃ περὶ τοῦ
    φωτός)]
 c ⁹ἦν τὸ φῶς τὸ ἀληθινὸν ——— ὃ φωτίζει πάντα ἄνθρωπον ———
    ἐρχόμενον εἰς τὸν κόσμον

C a ¹⁰ἐν τῷ κόσμῳ ἦν ——— καὶ ὁ κόσμος δι' αὐτοῦ ἐγένετο ——— καὶ
    ὁ κόσμος αὐτὸν οὐκ ἔγνω
 b ¹¹εἰς τὰ ἴδια ἦλθεν ——— καὶ οἱ ἴδιοι αὐτὸν οὐ παρέλαβον

D a ¹²ὅσοι δὲ ἔλαβον αὐτὸν ——— ἔδωκεν αὐτοῖς ἐξουσίαν ——— τέκνα
    θεοῦ γενέσθαι
 b τοῖς πιστεύουσιν εἰς τὸ ὄνομα αὐτοῦ ——— ¹³οἳ οὐκ ἐξ αἱμάτων
    ——— οὐδὲ ἐκ θελήματος σαρκός
 c οὐδὲ ἐκ θελήματος ἀνδρός ——— ἀλλ' ἐκ θεοῦ ἐγεννήθησαν

E a ¹⁴καὶ ὁ λόγος σὰρξ ἐγένετο ——— καὶ ἐσκήνωσεν ἐν ἡμῖν ——— καὶ
    ἐθεασάμεθα τὴν δόξαν αὐτοῦ
 b δόξαν ὡς μονογενοῦς παρὰ πατρὸς———πλήρης χάριτος καὶ ἀληθείας
    [¹⁵Ἰωάννης μαρτυρεῖ περὶ αὐτοῦ ——— καὶ κέκραγεν λέγων
    ——— "οὗτος ἦν ὃν εἶπον

»ὁ ὀπίσω μου ἐρχόμενος —— ἔμπροσθέν μου γέγονεν ——
ὅτι πρῶτός μου ἦν«"]

c   ¹⁶ὅτι ἐκ τοῦ πληρώματος αὐτοῦ ἡμεῖς πάντες ἐλάβομεν —— καὶ
χάριν ἀντὶ χάριτος

F a   ¹⁷ὅτι ὁ νόμος διὰ Μωυσέως ἐδόθη —— ἡ χάρις καὶ ἡ ἀλήθεια διὰ
Ἰησοῦ Χριστοῦ ἐγένετο

   b   ¹⁸θεὸν οὐδεὶς ἑώρακεν πώποτε —— μονογενὴς θεὸς ὁ ὢν εἰς τὸν
κόλπον τοῦ πατρὸς ἐκεῖνος ἐξηγήσατο

The Prologue and the Old Testament Tradition

1. Wisdom Literature

Beyond any doubt, the texts that provide the closest comparison to the
Logos poem are the Old Testament didactic poems about wisdom.
They express praise of wisdom in a variety of forms: Wisdom prais-
ing herself in the first person (e.g. Prov. 8; Sir. 24), praise of wisdom in the third person (Job 28; Wis. 7:22ff.), and a sermon in deuteronomic style (Bar. 3:9-4:4). The fact that wisdom, which rules
the whole of creation, which is prior to creation and then can also
be identified with the Torah, can be praised in such a variety of
forms shows the living significance of this tradition for the Old
Testament.

This is not the place to show in detail how in Israel wisdom developed into a stream of tradition that was determinative for the
nature of the Old Testament and that in the post-exilic period (in
contrast to the development of wisdom outside Israel into philosophy) wisdom became distinctly Israelite. We can only indicate briefly the following points. The wisdom of early antiquity, an international phenomenon that is identifiable from a specific stage of human
culture onward, and that naturally has many antecedents, is the early
form of science. People investigated the regularities and laws of
nature and of human life, and in an inductive manner accumulated
experiences and observations, primarily in the form of proverbs.
The possibility of discovering the fixed laws by which the world
operates leads to knowledge of the world and a cognitive mastery of
it, which was represented by this early stage of science. Even though

these human efforts are religious in the wider sense, because those with understanding seek to work with what they encounter as an ordinance with divine authority, this "wisdom" is not tied to the national traditions of cult and religion. For example, the wisdom texts do not speak of individual gods, but of God.

In the Solomonic age, when the people of Israel came into full contact with the cultures of the ancient Middle East, they consistently adopted this general, cultural, scientific wisdom. Now the wisdom tradition took its place alongside the priestly and prophetic traditions. It did not cultivate the specifically Israelite tradition of salvation history, but it was still specifically Israelite and became more so with the passage of time, in that the new human condition that resulted from the revelation of Yahweh was also expressed in this body of knowledge. Some of the individual proverbs stress the transcendence of God over against the natural order of the world, and later writings deal with the relationship of God to the world order, not merely as a too-narrowly-understood question of theodicy, but in a specific manner in Israel under the influence of the Yahweh revelation, for example in the Book of Job.

After the exile, a theological wisdom literature arose, which cannot be ignored in the total picture of Old Testament theology. It exerted an influence beyond the specific realm of wisdom, and affected the entire realm of spirituality, as the Psalms show. The world order which was constructed out of the knowledge accumulated by early wisdom literature could never be regarded as an alternative to God's revelation to Israel, and it could not for long remain separated from that revelation. If the God of Israel was the creator, then experience of the order of creation was experience of Yahweh. In the biblical tradition there was never a separation of "natural" theology from revealed theology, and certainly never an opposition of the two. The created world reveals the order established by the creator in the nature of the cosmos, and in this manner it bears witness to the creator himself.

> O Lord, how manifold are thy works!
> In wisdom hast thou made them all (Ps. 104:24).

The Lord by wisdom founded the earth;
  By understanding he established the heavens;
  by his knowledge the deeps broke forth,
    and the clouds drop down the dew (Prov. 3:19-20).

Through such an understanding of the world order, knowledge of wisdom becomes knowledge of God, and what was originally secular wisdom becomes theological wisdom.

No confusion could arise between God and world, creator and creation, because the world order, wisdom itself, was regarded as transcending the world. A hymn in praise of wisdom was inserted into the Book of Job (Chapt. 28) in the Persian period. This hymn raised the question of where the "place" of wisdom is. The answer given was that wisdom existed before anything was created and constituted the presupposition for the work of creation, in that God created the world according to this cosmic law (vv. 23-27). This preexistent and transcendent wisdom as an independent being, as a "hypostasis," stands in a remarkable contrast to God (cf. Job 28:27). It is also distinguished from the creation which is the object of the creative act. As a result wisdom occupies a mediating position between God and the creation; wisdom mediates God to the world.

The role which wisdom plays before God as a hypostasis, is connected with the similar role wisdom plays before humanity. How is this to be understood? Reference to foreign deities that outside Israel represent conceptions similar to Israelite wisdom—for example the Egyptian Maat, and later Isis or the Syrian Astarte—is of little help, even though some individual features may correspond. Neither does the relationship of Maat to humans take on the specific forms portrayed in Proverbs 1-9, nor can Maat be described as being enthroned or as playing before God, as pictured in Proverbs 8:22-31. And a cult of Astarte could at most have served as model for the counterpart of wisdom, Dame Folly (Prov. 7:5-23). Basically, explanations of this sort from the history of religions are unsatisfying, since the question remains of how such borrowings were possible in the quite different Israelite thought-world.

Even though certain individual features may have been borrowed, we must start from the realization that the distinctive nature of the

personification of wisdom in Israel is related to the personal structure of the revelation of Yahweh, in which God reveals himself to
Israel, or to Moses, as an "I" to a "Thou," as one person to another
(cf. Exod. 33:11). The world order which humans discern is not
encountered merely as an external revelation, but as wisdom which
humans have perceived. When, for various reasons, in the relationship of God to man, a represention of his revelation appears instead
of God himself, the personal experience of the revelation can give
a distinctive character to the representation. Thus the word of God
is "hypostatized" when because of the statement of its immediate
nearness to man it is regarded as something separate from God
(Deut. 30:14), or when there is a description of the power and
might that belong to the word (Wis. 18:14-16). How much more,
then, is this true of wisdom, which, as a truth encountered in the
realm of human knowledge is a counterpart to God, and possesses
its own essence and an absolute authority.

Because of the personification of wisdom, the urgent nature of
wisdom's admonitions is experienced as a personal demand. When
the results of knowledge take the form of admonition and advice
and not those of an order or an apodictic command, this is not to
be explained as due to a lack of urgency, but to one's participation
in the truth, which is a part of the knowledge, and which is expressed
in a personal sense of responsibility. With the passage of time,
however, wisdom literature took over more and more the forms of
prophetic speech and sermons (e.g., Prov. 1:20-33) and of priestly
instruction (e.g. Prov. 3:1ff., cf. 6:23), and the wisdom admonition
to obedience, like the Torah, came to confront humans with the
decision for life or death (e.g., Prov. 8:35-36).

In wisdom literature, this authority which lays its demands on the
whole person is seen in personal knowledge, in an ultimate personal
realm. Thus the meaning of the personification of wisdom as feminine is clear—the wise man is united with wisdom in an intellectual
eros (Prov. 4:6, 8; 7:4; 8:17, 21, 34; 9:1-6). By the same token,
the evil of human actions and intellectual activity is personified as
a woman (Zech. 5:5-11, as a female idol, and in Prov. 1-9 as folly).

Here we are involved in the inner, intimate realm of personal encounter.

By analogy with the experience of revelation in Israel, the personal character of the knowledge of the world order leads to the personification of wisdom. Moreover, the exclusive relationship to God in the function of wisdom as mediator also becomes clear. The experience of the transcendence of an order that lies at the basis of all being can only be the experience of a God who mediates and reveals himself in this manner. Knowledge of the created world becomes knowledge of God, without confusing God with creation or identifying them with each other, because it is wisdom that is the mediator between God and the creation. It is this mediation that makes the absolute and total nature of revelation possible.

The question of the nature of wisdom, of its personal character, and its function as mediator, of its pre-existence in contrast to all that has been created, and of its transcendence which consists in its intimate relationship with God, is as a consequence rightly an object of theological teaching about wisdom. To be sure it is an "object" that can be presented only in hymns of praise, wherever possible as wisdom presenting herself and revealing herself to humans in this manner, not by placing herself alongside God, but by appearing as God's revelation.

The high point of the introductory chapters of the book of Proverbs (Chapts. 1-9) is the so-called self-commendation of wisdom in Chapter 8. In a framework of admonitions to hear (vv. 4-11, 32-36) .wisdom reveals her true nature. She is the spiritual principle of all human virtues (vv. 12-21; even divine attributes can be ascribed to her, cf. 14 with Job 12:13, 16) and of all the order that sustains the universe (vv. 22-31). Formed in amazing manner before the creation as the "beginning" (*reshith* of Gen. 1:1)[10] she was present at the creation itself. Her participation is stated as, "Then I was beside (*'mwn*) him (the creator God), v. 30. Some have wanted to interpret the difficult word *'mwn* as *'amon* or *'amman,* meaning "master workman" (cf. Jer. 52:15; Song of Solomon 7:2).

---

[10]Cf. *Vom Sinai zum Zion,* 139.

Wisdom 7:21; 8:6 speaks of wisdom as *technitēs*. The context of Proverbs 8:22-31, however, speaks against this. God himself made the created world. It is therefore preferable to interpret the word as the passive participle of *'mn,* "to hold on the lap, or in the arms," and to interpret it as meaning "nurse" or "attendant." (In what follows wisdom is seen as the child of God.) But *'amun* should not be translated as "beloved child." The text means rather, "I was (held) on his lap." Here too at the creation God is portrayed as sitting on his throne, and he lets the personified world order share his throne by sitting on his lap. Similarly Wisdom 9:4 calls wisdom "one who shares God's throne." In contrast to the feminine hypostasis of the wisdom, *'mwn* is not given in feminine form, because the resulting picture would be offensive.

The conclusion of the chapter praises wisdom's function as mediator:

> I was daily his (God's)[11] delight,
> > rejoicing before him always. *(Time category)*
> rejoicing in his inhabited world
> > and my delight (delight over me) was among
> > > the sons of men.
> > > > *(Space category)* vv. 30b-31.

Wisdom's activity is presented in the form of play, while delight over this play unites God and man. Humans who know what has happened participate in God's joy over the world order. In the order of creation God mediates himself to the world, and in the knowledge of wisdom this mediation attains its goal.

A further step in this significant theological development can be found at the end of the third century B.C. in Sirach 24, which corresponds to the "self-commendation" of wisdom in Proverbs 8. Wisdom, the order of creation, is now identified with the revelation of God to Israel through salvation history. After the account of the founding of the cosmos (vv. 3-6) all that is said deals exclusively with Israel (vv. 7-12), a matter that we must return to later.

> [3] I came forth from the mouth of the Most High,
> > and covered the earth like a mist.

---

[11]Cf. LXX.

> [4] I dwelt in high places,
>   and my throne was in a pillar of cloud.
> [5] Alone I have made the circuit of the vault of heaven
>   and have walked in the depths of the abyss.
> [6] In the waves of the sea, in the whole earth,
>   and in every people and nation I have gotten
>   a possession.

The beginning of the cosmos is mystically portrayed on the basis of Genesis 1. Wisdom begins her speech by introducing herself as the word of creation (v. 3a), and in the parallel statement her existence before the world, following Genesis 1:2, is portrayed as the dark, primeval "cloud," [12] and behind the following parallel lines (v. 4), with its statement about the world-transcending dwelling place, there stands the report of the creation of the light (Gen. 1:3-5), which was already understood in Genesis 1 as also "intellectual light." Corresponding to the dwelling in the heights that transcend the world (the firmament is not mentioned until later) is the epiphany on the throne above the columns that uphold the clouds, where the "consuming fire" is to be found.[13]

Then, following the account in Genesis 1:6-8, there is the description of the delimiting of the cosmos by the firmament and the abyss, which wisdom accomplishes alone by walking through them (v. 5). Finally there is the establishment of the lordship of wisdom within the world, on land and sea and among all peoples (v. 6). On the basis of Genesis 1, wisdom is thus described as the one who carries out the work of creation and *expressis verbis,* as the Logos of creation. And wisdom is able to express this self-praise among the angels, the heavenly hosts (vv. 1-2), distinguishing herself from them all in comparable manner.

Let us stop here. There is no doubt that the source of the praise

---

[12]*homichlē* corresponds to *hoshek* in Isa. 29:18 (and not to *ʿanan* in Sir. 43:43:22). The statement of Sir. 24:3b is carefully formulated as only a comparison. The use of *ed* in Gen. 2:6 (and the role of *homichlē* as the original state of the cosmos in Sidonian mythology; cf. Damaskios, De. princ. 125c.) may also have contributed to the figure of speech here.

[13]Cf. v. 4 with the description of the appearance of the glory out of the heights by means of the column of cloud in front of the Tabernacle, Exod. 33:9, or in it, Exod. 40:34.

of the Logos in the prologue to John's Gospel is to be found in this tradition of the praise of wisdom. We can understand the *en archē* (cf. Prov. 8:22; Sir. 24:9) at the beginning of the prologue, which echoes the *bereshit* of Genesis 1:1, as well as the statement *pros ton theon*. The step from there to the statement that the Logos is *theos* is a small one, and if in Sirach 24:1-2 wisdom can boast before all the angels that surround God, the preparation for this step had already been made.

In the light of the theme that is presented in Proverbs 8:22-31 and in the first six verses of Sirach 24:1-12, it is completely understandable that the description of the absolute being of the Logos (John 1:1-2) moves toward identifying him as the creator (v. 3). And the fact that the following section deals especially with light, can be explained in terms of the intellectual background of this light, and Proverbs 8:30b-31 moves on to the theme of the soteriological role of wisdom. Sirach 24:7ff. makes the relationship of wisdom's cosmic activity to revelation history clear and provides thereby the prototype in tradition history for the further step taken in the prologue to John.

The only difficulties seem to be those created by the expression Logos itself. Does this title contain an element foreign to the Old Testament? Attempts to derive the title from a philosophical tradition or from the theology of Philo are not convincing. The rationalistic features of the title in those traditions are lacking in the prologue to John, where it, encompassing as it does, both creation and salvation history in their full meaning, cannot be termed rationalistic. It is clear that wisdom as the order of creation belongs a priori in the closest relation to the Old Testament's theological statements about the word of creation, and wisdom's presentation of herself as the Logos of creation in Sirach 24:3a marks the two as identical. The tradition prepared the way for wisdom to be understood as the Logos. The question, however, remains, of why the title of Logos completely replaced that of Sophia in the prologue to John.

We might think first of all that Sophia was displaced by the Logos because the feminine gender of *hokma* and *sophia,* which corresponds to a feminine hypostasis, is not suitable for Christological statements, at least when they refer directly to the incarnation. But that is merely an external reason which corresponds to an inner reason that involves the content. In Sirach 24:7-12 the cosmic effect of wisdom had already been superceded by the aspect of salvation history in the revelation to Israel, and the more strongly this aspect is stressed, the further the content is removed from the original concept of wisdom. This is, to be sure, no cause for concern, because the concept of wisdom was broadened and modified according to the theological development.

In Sirach 24 the identification of wisdom with Torah (cf. v 23) presents no problem at all. But if the concept is regarded primarily in terms of the appearing of Jesus Christ as an event in salvation history, a theological concept is required which can bring together creation and salvation history, and that concept is that of the divine word, which is equally determinative for the doctrine of creation and for that of history, and which had already been used to express the theological union of both, as, e.g. in Deutero-Isaiah (Isa. 44:27-28):

> "(Yahweh), who says to the deep, 'Be dry,
>   I will dry up your rivers';
> who says of Cyrus, 'He is my shepherd,
>   and he shall fulfill all my purpose';
> saying of Jerusalem, 'She shall be built,'
>   and of the temple, 'Your foundation shall be laid.' "

When therefore the truth was recognized that the Christ event, the *telos* of salvation history, is identical with the cosmic order of the world, which further expressed itself as the giving of revelation to Israel, then a concept from salvation history had to replace the primarily unhistorical concept of wisdom. Or to put it more precisely, it was necessary that in the presentation of wisdom that component should come to the fore which long since had united creation and salvation history, the divine *dabar*. It is not that the concept of Logos is introduced there in order to give wisdom a new philosophical coloration—that is not what the Logos poem intended, but rather it is introduced in order to unite fully and completely the historical event of Christ with the nature of wisdom. The question from the history of religion concerning the possibility of the borrowing of a foreign concept is to be replaced by the question from tradition history, Why is wisdom the Logos? The answer is, Because the historical appearing of Jesus Christ is the revelation of the original order of the universe.

2. The Saving Event of Revelation

The development of the doctrine of wisdom in the Old Testament shows that this strand of tradition became united with the elements of the salvation history tradition, resulting in a distinctive merger and the illumination of each strand by the other. God's revelation to Israel came to be identified with wisdom. Let us clarify the basic features of the salvation history tradition of the revelation to Israel.

The core of the Old Testament tradition formation may be said to lie in the tradition of the revelation at Sinai. It is here that we encounter the name "Yahweh," and the concept of the entity Israel as Yahweh's partner. This tradition asserts that God reveals himself to an "international" partner, comprised of tribes that he binds to himself. It is a revelation in an exclusive mutual relationship, and the exclusivity of God is also the exclusivity of Israel. God reveals himself in that he binds himself to his partner, to his "people," that he brings into being by his act.

Since the revelation is revelation of God's person, the person who represents Israel, Moses, takes on special significance, and every future recipient of revelation was measured against Moses. God spoke with Moses "mouth to mouth" (Num. 12:8), "face to face, as a man speaks to his friend" (Exod. 33:11). And yet this does not mean that God did not reveal himself in his majesty in his divine nature, but rather Moses encounters the *kabōd,* the glory of the consuming fire. This Sinai revelation was even ritualized in the cultic institution of God's revelation in the Tent of Meeting (*'ohel mo^ced,* Exod. 33:7-11).

This tradition of the revelation was significantly deepened by Israel's emergence as a nation. When Israel had settled in the land, had become under King David a political state in this world, and had entered fully and completely into the world of nations and states of the Near East, then along with the change in Israel's being, God's being for Israel had been transformed. Zion took the place of Sinai, and there God acquired a piece of the land of this world as his heritage, his own possession *(naḥala),* and there the Ark of the Covenant, which represented God's presence, had found a resting place *(menuḥa).* There with the Ark on Mount Zion, Yahweh Sabaoth, the king of the world was present, there he had taken up his dwelling *(shkn),* and from Zion the splendor of the revelation of the divine *kabod* went forth to fill the world *(melo kol ha'aretz kebodo,* Isa. 6:3, cf. Num. 14:21; Ps. 57:6; 72:19; Hab. 3:3) as the royal principle of order in this world, which was also represented by the reigning Davidic king, who as son of God was the deputy of the real lord of Zion, and who, as senior member of the family dwelt on the family's heritage chosen by God.

This tradition of the event of revelation became united with the doctrine of wisdom no later than the end of the third century B.C., after wisdom and the revealed Torah had in the Persian period been placed in the same intimate context (cf. eg. Ps. 19:1-6 with vv. 7-14 or the concept of Torah in Prov. Chapts. 1-9, especially 6:23).

In Sirach 24, wisdom says of herself after the description of how she established the cosmos,

> [7] Among all these (nations) I sought a resting place;
>   I sought in whose territory I might lodge.[14]
> [8] Then the Creator of all things gave me a commandment,
>   and the one who created me assigned a place for
>   my tent.[15]
>   And he said, "Make your dwelling in Jacob,
> [9] From eternity, in the beginning, he created me,
>   and for eternity I shall not cease to exist.
> [10] In the holy tabernacle I ministered before him,
>   and so I was established in Zion.[16]

---

[14]*aulizein* indicates an original *lin,* cf. Sir. 14:26; 51.23 and the poetic use of *lin* in the Psalter: only at night does one "dwell" in the narrow sense.

[15]Behind the unidiomatic Greek expression *katepausen tēn skēnēn mou* we can detect a literal translation of *hinniaḥ mishkani,* a formula that builds on the use of *menuḥa.*

[16]On *stērizein* cf. *ysd* in the *pi'el,* Sir. 3:9.

11 In the beloved city likewise he gave me a rest-
    ing place,
    and in Jerusalem was my dominion
12 So I took root in an honored people,
    in the portion of the Lord, who is their
    inheritance.

The transition from the work of creation to salvation history was achieved in such a manner that wisdom desired to take up her dwelling in the world to which she had brought order. Through borrowing the theological terminology used of the transfer of the Ark to its new site in Jerusalem (cf. Ps. 132), the statement was formulated that wisdom sought her resting place *(menuḥa)*, her inheritance *(naḥala)* (v 7). So God assigned her to dwell in Israel (v 8). This resulted in the portrayal of revelation in salvation history that we find in the following verses. Although wisdom was pre-existent and endures from everlasting to everlasting (the idea of the beginning from Prov. 8:22-31; used here in Sir. 24:9), she first found her home in the Tabernacle of Israel's wilderness wanderings—she is the "liturgy" of the Tabernacle cult, and thus identical with Torah —and then became firmly settled in Zion (v 10), and thereby closely connected with the Jerusalem of the Davidic dynasty (v 11), and with the nation that received the revelation (v 12).

On the basis of the identity of wisdom and Torah, the tradition of revelation in salvation history is transferred in an impressive manner to wisdom, which can now be spoken of in the same manner as the cult of the Ark of the Covenant. Indeed wisdom is the *doxa* itself which shines on Israel in revelation, the *shekinah*, which took up its dwelling in Israel on Mount Zion. Clearly all this is not merely a poetic or intellectual presentation of Sirach's. In the later literature we find a general identification of wisdom with Torah, and thus the adoption of the tradition of revelation history (cf. Bar. 3:9-4:4 and the abundant rabbinic material on this theme). Therefore in any evaluation of John's prologue in terms of tradition history we must begin with this stage of the formation of tradition.

There is still another important strand to add to this—the transfer into the eschatological dimension of the theme of wisdom taking up her dwelling (Sir. 24). According to the metaphors of Ethiopic Enoch (Chaps. 37-71), which represent a final stage in apocalyptic tradition prior to the New Testament, wisdom was unable to find a dwelling among humans and therefore she returned to her place in heaven among the angels, while unrighteousness spread more and more among mankind (Chapt. 42). Wisdom will appear only in the revelation of the Son of man (Chapt. 49), and she will permit only the saints and the righteous who have hated the world of unrighteousness to recognize the Son of man (48:7). We have here a remarkable parallel to John 1:10-13, but it would be best not to begin with this late apocalyptic use of the wisdom motif in our explanation in terms of tradition history, since we have here, not a text from wisdom literature which fully represents a specific stage in this tradition, but only a borrowing of content that is then totally subordinated to the apocalyptic aspect of the document.

In Sirach 24 the song of praise of wisdom in its role in creation from the beginning on (Prov. 8:22-31) has become the song of praise of the revelation of wisdom. This revelation extends from the creation of the Torah, which appears in the Zion cult, and has become an entity in cultic history. John 1:1-18 is the song of praise of the revelation of the Logos from creation to the incarnation in Jesus Christ. The basic structure of the Logos hymn was already at hand. In a hymn in praise of wisdom, God's revelation can be presented in a universal manner. Just as according to Sirach 24:7 cosmic wisdom wills to take up its dwelling in the world as the revelation of Torah in salvation history, so also does the Logos in John 1:10-11.

The step from doctrine of creation to salvation history is taken, according to Sirach 24, in the borrowing of the theology of revelation in terms of taking up one's dwelling, as colored by the traditions of Zion and the Ark, while John 1 speaks directly of recognition and acceptance, of the recognition of revelation. Sirach 24 places more emphasis on the objective factors of cult history (tent of meeting, Ark on Mount Zion), while John 1 emphasizes the human and subjective acceptance of revelation, but the form and the structure given to the content are the same in both instances.

Sirach 24 can rest content with the objective factors of the cult institution as the event of revelation, because there the critical separation between the Israel that accepts the revelation and the Israel that rejects it is not involved. In John 1, however, the subjective acceptance of the revelation, Israel's response, must be included. Thus it is spelled out that the world, although it was created by the Logos and therefore is in its inner nature dependent on him, did not recognize him (v. 10), just as in Sirach 24:7 wisdom did not find a resting place among the peoples. The revelation to Israel in salvation history (cf. *ēlthen* in contrast to *ēn*), to God's own people (in Hebrew originally usually expressed only with *ᶜam* + suffix designating God; here because of the distinction, the concept of people is understandably avoided), does not lead to acceptance in the case of Israel *kata sarka* (v 11), but only among those who are "children of God" (vv 12-13).

This new feature of an Israel that closes itself to revelation, in contrast to the picture in Sirach 24, is not to be rejected as "contrary to the Old Testament." On the contrary, this rejection agrees with the prophetic proclamation of judgment and is also a living tradition in the post-exilic parts of the Old Testament (cf. especially Third Isaiah and apocalyptic literature in general), so that even the wisdom literature makes use of this language (Prov. 1:20-33). If we bring into consideration here the metaphors of Ethiopic Enoch, we see that because the world of this present aeon, including Israel is rejected, the apocalyptic spirit produced statements similar to those in the Logos hymn: Wisdom cannot find a place to dwell, and makes her first appearance with the Son of man; it is only to the holy and just that wisdom reveals the Son of man. But we also see that the Logos hymn is more than a mere apocalyptic version of the wisdom tradition, and that the Logos hymn portrays primarily an ultimate retracing of the whole of revelation history and not merely a judgment on this aeon, even in reference to wisdom doctrine.

The goal, the completion of revelation, is attained in the incarnation of the Logos. In contrast to an appearance of the Logos in a spiritual realm only, and to human reception, as it is described in vv 12-13, v 14 formulates in unmistakable manner, fundamentally and precisely, that the Logos became "flesh," thus taking up the Old Testament term *basar,* which designates the earthly corporeal nature that constitutes our human nature.

It will not be possible in the scope of our theme to trace even in outline the Christological development which led up to the affirmation of the incarnation. The path to a full statement of the incarnation can be traced in pre-Pauline and pre-Johannine form of the so-called commission formulas (Gal. 4:4-5; Rom. 8:3-4; John 3:16-17; 1 John 4:9) or in a hymn such as that in Philippians 2:6-11. The first step on this path had already been taken in the Old Testament when the statements about the pre-existence of wisdom were adopted into the doctrine of the Son of man (Ethiopian Enoch 48:3, 6). This understanding of the incarnation was basically determined by the understanding of the event of the cross as the atoning descent of the "Son" to the lowest depths of humanity and does not have the contrasting meaning of an apothesis. This revelatory nature of the incarnation will be underlined in the following sentences, formulated entirely in Old Testament terminology.

The incarnation is called a *skēnōsai* (cf. *shkn*) and thereby brought into the great tradition of the revelation of God's having taken up his dwelling on Zion, a tradition represented by the conception of the tabernacle in the priestly document as far back as the early period of the Sinai revelation, and also in Sirach 24:10a. In the statements parallel to *sarx genesthai* this passage poetically expresses an additional intensification and takes up the Old Testament teaching of revelation in a fundamental manner, showing in this way that the Christ event completes the truth of what the Old Testament presents as the history of revelation.

One feature of God's taking up his dwelling is the shining forth of the *doxa,* the brilliant light of revelation. Derived from the old theophany tradition, the *doxa* motif was characteristic of the Zion theology and was expressed in a distinctive way in the theology of the priestly document (cf. Exod. 40:34-35). In John 1:14 the beholding of the *doxa* is, in keeping with tradition, the experience of revelation, but now not a revelation in a derivative sense, of, say, angelic glory, but the revelation of the Father presented directly and completely through the only Son. In the parallel stich its content is specified as "full of grace and truth." It cannot be denied that behind the expression *charis kai alētheia* lies the expression so well known and so significant in the Old Testament, *ḥesed wa'emet*. Even the argument that in the LXX it is regularly translated as *eleos kai alētheia* is not convincing. Quite apart from the fact that in later writings *charis* came to be used more and more as the translation of *ḥesed*,[17] Symmachus translates it this way in 2 Samuel 2:6; Psalm 40:11.

In the double expression *ḥesed wa'emet*, the first element *ḥesed* is the more significant, and consequently it alone is used in v. 16. The dispute over whether *ḥesed* connotes gracious generosity or an attitude appropriate to a specific human relationship of close friendship is unproductive. *Ḥesed* presupposes an on-going, more or less close community relationship and connotes the friendliness and goodness appropriate to and distinctive of this relationship, but in attitude and practice it goes considerably farther than what would normally be customary in terms of that specific relationship. *Ḥesed* therefore expresses the superior nature of a positive human and personal relationship, that is, friendliness, kindness, graciousness.

This concept was undoubtedly determinative for Old Testament theology to the degree that in the revelation in which God disclosed himself to Israel, this special relationship of God to Israel was experienced as *ḥesed*. It is not possible here to examine the wealth of expressions used in the Psalter to designate the *ḥesed* operating in Israel's relation to God. It should, however, be noted that the concept was used as a standard attribute of God (God who shows *ḥesed*, Exod. 20:6; Deut. 5:10 etc.; "abounding in *ḥesed*" Exod. 34:7; "who delights in *ḥesed*" Micah 7:18; "abounding in *ḥesed* and *emet* "Num. 14:18; "abounding in *ḥesed*" Joel 2:13; Jonah 4:2; Ps. 86:5; 103:8; Neh. 9:17 [Exod. 34:6; Ps. 86:15], "abounding in *ḥesed*" Ps. 145:8).

---

17 Esther 2:9, 17; Sirach 7:33; 40:17; 2 Sam. 2:26σ; Jer. 31:2α,σ,ϑ; Ps. 31:8σ; 31:17 Sexta; 33:5ε; 33:18 Sexta; 40:11σ; 89:25σ; Prov. 31:26ϑ (Greek letters indicate the ancient Greek translations: α = Aquila; σ = Symmachus; ϑ = Theodotion; ε = Quinta [fifth column of the Hexapla]. Sexta indicates the sixth column of the Hexapla).

The word added to *ḥesed, emet,* "truth" emphasizes the full, constant, sure nature of *ḥesed.* The Hebrew concept of truth does not stress (as does the Greek) human uprightness, "reliability," but rather the validity and reliability of something. *Ḥesed wa'emet* is therefore that which is constant, fully valid in the goodness and mercy of human relationships. This double expression, sometimes in slightly different form, is widely used for the relationship of God to humans. It connotes the kind, wholesome, direction of human life (Gen. 24:27 Abraham; 32:11 Jacob; cf. Micah 7:20, and especially Ps. 25:10); that which guards and protects persons (Ps. 40:10; 61:8; Prov. 20:28); that to which a person looks (Ps. 26:3) and which a person particularly praises (Ps. 40:10; 115:1; 138:2. Even in the early texts it is an expression of the wholeness, the gracious *shalom* which God bestows (2 Sam. 2:6; 15:20).

In the magnificent *shalom* oracle of Ps. 85:9-13 we even find the expression *"ḥesed* and *emet* will meet" (v. 10). It is especially interesting that this concept is closely connected to the thought of the cosmic order (cf. alongside the general significance in the concept of order in wisdom literature, Prov. 3:3; 14:22; 16:6, note its significance for the king, Ps. 61:7; Prov. 20:28, and especially Ps. 89:14.) In summary we can say that *charis kai alētheia* represents the Old Testament concept of total divine salvation, which humans may partake of as God's eternal graciousness disclosed in his revelation to Israel. It is the grace which in revelation is the basis of the covenant; it is the inviolable, enduring truth.

The fatherly *doxa* which shines out from the Son is described as being "full of grace and truth" (v. 14), and this is returned to in the expression of "his (the Son's) fullness" (v. 16). There is a great wealth of statements about the abounding richness of God's grace (cf. the attribute of God mentioned above, "Who is rich in *ḥesed* and *emet";* the statements of abundance of God's *ḥesed,* Ps. 5:7; 69:14; 106:45 *kethib;* Lam. 3:32 *kethib;* Isa. 63:7 pl.[18])

---

[18]Because of these passages which use *rab* or *rob,* it is tempting to hold that behind *plērēs* and *ek tou plērōmatos autou* lie the expressions *rab* and *merubbo,* but I do not know of a single Greek version that translates thus. Therefore in John 1 we must retain the wording that has come down to us.

and of its eternal duration (cf. Ps. 89:2; 103:17; 138:8 and the refrain "for his loving kindness endures forever" Ps. 136 and elsewhere.

The idea that this grace fills the cosmos is striking; *ḥesed* reaches to the heavens (cf. Ps. 36:5; 103:11, "for thy steadfast love is great to the heavens, thy faithfulness to the clouds" Ps. 57:10=108:4); Yahweh's *ḥesed* fills (*male'a*) the earth (Ps. 33:5; 119:64). Note here the close relationship of the concept *ḥesed wa'emet* to the concept of cosmic order. In a way similar to that in which the Zion theology *doxa* goes out from the place of revelation to fill the earth, here the fullness of grace is spoken of in the context of the appearing of the *doxa*. Since the Hebrew term *ml'* has both intransitive and transitive force, "be full" and "fill," we can understand the statement "we have all received (v 16) with the stress on "all," and in the light of v 12 it is not self-praise. The apostolic "we" (v 14) has become the "we" of the ecclesia that represents the new "world." In v 16b the endless fullness of grace is effectively expressed.[19]

The Logos hymn reaches its climax with this description of *doxa* and in vv 17-18 concludes with a summary that looks back on the revelation event. V 17 deals with the objective content of the revelation—salvation, and v 18 with the one who reveals himself—God, and the revelation events of the Old and the New Testament are contrasted in both instances. Even these concluding verses with their apparently negative attitude toward the Old Testament stand squarely in the Old Testament tradition of revelation.

V 18a does not refer to a general experience of the invisibity of God, but to the Old Testament tradition of God's being seen by Moses and the prophets. The Old Testament teaching about seeing God is remarkably vague. Although basically it is the case that to see God means death, since what is unholy is destroyed by the holy (Exod. 19:21; 33:20; Lev. 16:2; Num. 4:20 etc.) it says in the old Sinai material which wanted to stress the revelation to Israel that the elders saw God(Exod. 24:10-11), while the Deuteronomic theology teaches that the one who reveals himself cannot be seen

---

[19]Cf. above p. 175, note o. In this less-likely case the statement would be appropriately related to the full mediation of grace.

(Deut. 4:12, 15-24), and in later times the invisibility of God is generally assumed (Sir. 43:31).

On the one hand the revelation to Moses can be distinguished from all other revelation in that he saw God (Exod. 33:11; Num. 12:8), but in the other hand this is limited to God's "passing by" and to seeing his back (Exod. 33:22-23; 1 Kings 19:11), or the covering is mentioned with which Moses (Exod. 3:6) and Elijah (1 Kings 19:13) covered themselves. Yet even so the greatest prophetic inspiration consists in the vision of God on his throne (1 Kings 22:19; Isa. 6; Ezek. 1). But in the eschaton at the revelation of God's kingdom every covering and veil will be taken away (Isa. 25:7).

All this, however, is only apparently contradictory, and if the differing degree of spiritualization and the differing intentions of the statements in the revelation are taken into account, they fit together well and can be summarized in what is meant in John 1:18: The revelation of God himself which took place when he was seen by Moses and the prophets who followed him (cf. Deut. 18:15-22) was necessarily hidden by a covering which separates humans from what is transcendent (according to Deut. 4:15-24 the reason for the rejection of images of God), but in the eschatological event of revelation the covering will be removed. In this aeon there cannot be an unveiled revelation of the transcendent God. Only the transcendent Logos, who, as we learned from Proverbs 8:30, was enthroned before all time like a child on the lap of his father, this son could—by virtue of his incarnation—accomplish this revelation in unlimited, absolute manner.

V 18a is not intended as a denial of the Old Testament tradition of the highest revelation in the vision of God, but it underlines the teaching of the Old Testament itself that even the highest revelation to Moses and the prophets was veiled. Here, as in the Old Testament, stress is laid on the distance between us and God even in the highest revelation, and on the covering which keeps us from seeing God, when the vision of God is granted. On the other hand, the doctrine of the Logos includes the teaching of the transcendence of wisdom and its intimate relationship to God in contrast to all that was created.

V. 17 presents the contrast between the gift of Torah and salvation through Moses, and the accomplishment of full divine salvation, in *ḥesed wa'emet,* by Jesus Christ. We must insist that this text in the wisdom tradition understands the gift of Torah as the content of the Sinai revelation in a full and positive sense, and this is what makes the text distinctive. For if the Torah of Moses was the doctrine that was identical with wisdom (Sir. 24:23), then Torah must also be the doctrine of the Logos (cf. John 5:45-47).

The contrast then is between the doctrine of the Logos given through Moses and the Logos himself, of the Torah, the fulfillment of which was to accomplish salvation, and the completed divine salvation itself. The two parts of the verse to not constitute a contrast in content (and we should not use an adversative particle in v 17b), but their relationship is that of allusion and reality. The New Testament is not superior to the Old Testament in the sense that it is its contrast, but in that it is the completion and fulfillment of the Old. So, just as Torah could only allude to the salvation to be accomplished in Jesus Christ, just as the Old Testament awaited the removal of the covering, so the Old Testament stands at the beginning in contrast to the goal of the New Testament, as expectation in contrast to fulfillment.

3. Light, Life, and Divine Sonship

Verses 14, 16 of the Logos hymn deal with the incarnation, that is, God's coming to dwell in the world, and describe the appearance of the *doxa* in the same way that the Old Testament describes God's presence, the *shekinah,* as the fullness of the *doxa* (Isa. 6:3; Exod. 40:34-35). In the total composition, stanza E corresponds to stanza B (vv. 4-5, 9), which deals with the light. We have already pointed out that the presentation given here is oriented to the significance ascribed to the creation of light in the creation story in Genesis 1:3-5, and that a formulation such as that in v 5 is based on the story of driving chaos back and placing cosmic limits on it through a division of light and darkness, that is, a "victorious" shining of the

light out of darkness. We noted that the concept of light in the prologue contains a remarkable overlap of the physical and intellectual
concept of light, of cosmic and spiritual aspects, of light and enlightenment. In order to understand vv 4-5, 9 correctly, we must
look at what the Old Testament says about light.

The view that the contrast of light and darkness represents that
of cosmos and chaos was current not only in Israel but throughout
the ancient world. Cosmos results from the light setting limits to the
darkness. There remains in the cosmos a remnant of the element
of darkness that results from chaos, but in the cosmos it is limited
to its proper place by the light. In each night the remembrance of
chaos is present. This cosmic significance of light was not simply
taken over in Israel as an element of myth, but was worked out in
distinctive form. It is not only that according to Genesis 1:3-5 creation begins with light, not only that in the eschaton the alternation
of night and day ceases, because there is then nothing but light
(Isa. 60:19-20; Zech. 14:6-7, etc.). Even when in this world the
chaotic powers seem about to overwhelm Zion, the center of the
cosmos, yet with the dawning of the day the order of the cosmos is
established anew, and at morning God makes the victory of the
cosmos evident (Isa. 17:14; 29:7; Ps. 46; cf. also Isa. 26:9; 33:2;
Zeph. 3:5; Ps. 5:4; 90:14; 143:8). In Zechariah's apocalyptic night
visions the troubles are announced at evening (1:8-17); at midnight,
in the time of crisis, the divine light shines forth (Chapt. 4); and at
morning the world is awakened to new life (6:1-8).[20] The morning
is the time when the created world shines with light, and the Easter
event becomes known with the rising of the sun (Mark 16:2).

These ideas are not artificial myths but are based directly on the
perception of reality, so directly that light as such is regarded as a
primal phenomenon (not as "electromagnetic radiation"), while the
bearers of light, the lights of the heavens, presuppose the existence
of light. The light of the Bible does not come from the stars, as
they merely reflect it (cf. Gen. 1:3-5 in contrast to vv 14-19, and
Isa. 5:30; Jer. 4:23; Ps. 74:16; Job 38:19-20 etc.). Sight is the most
important of the human senses. *r'(h)* means "perceive" in general,

---

[20]Cf. *Vom Sinai zum Zion*, pp. 207ff.

and only the one who perceives exists, so that perception constitutes existence. For life and perception then, light is determinative. Light forms the essence of life, and the phrase "light of life" is frequent (Ps. 56:14; Job 33:30). To be unable to see the light is to be dead (Job 3:16), and to give light is to give life (Job 3:20). "He has redeemed my soul *(naphshi)* from going down into the Pit, and my life shall see the light" (Job 33:28).[21] God brings "back his soul from the Pit, that he may see the "light of life" (Job 33:30).

By the same token, death is the extinguishing of light (Job 18:5 and often elsewhere). Since the biblical concept of life does not mean mere existence but "living," a wholesome, full life, the concept of light can be used for life. "Yea, thou does light my lamp; the Lord my God lightens my darkness" (Ps. 18:28). It should be kept in mind that light, as an expression for life, includes the concept of perception and therefore means not the mere fact of being alive but the intellectual side of life, less being than being conscious. Thus light comes to mean truth, and there is a great wealth of Old Testament passages that present the intellectual effect of light. "Oh send out thy light and thy truth; let them lead me" (Ps. 43:3). "Thy word is a lamp to my feet and a light to my path" (Ps. 119:105; cf. Isa. 42:16; Job 22:28; on the absence of light, Deut. 28:29; Job 12:24-25 etc.). Revelation, God's truth, is light, and the servant of God becomes the light of the nations (Isa. 42:6; 49:6; and so does the Son of man, Ethiop. Enoch 48:4).

Here we must consider the special relationship of God to the light. If light is being and truth, then God's revelation of his *doxa* is the transcendent light, the "consuming fire." This direct manifestation of the divine revelation is not a logical inference, but it is something that stands at the beginning of all perception. God's presence which brings blessing is seen in the light of his countenance. Those are blessed who walk in the light of his countenance (Ps. 89:16), and they live by means of God's light ("for with thee is the fountain of life; in thy light do we see light" Ps. 36:9), and blessing is bestowed in the light that shines from God's countenance (Ps. 4:7; 31:17; 67:2; 80:4, 8, 20; cf. Ps. 118:27; 119: 135, etc.).

---

[21] Following the *kethib*.

Because the *Doxa* is of the nature of light, the Old Testament can say that light is God's garment (Ps. 104:1b, 2a). Light can even be an epithet for God. Of the servant of God it is said, "He shall see light[22] from the travail of his soul and be satisfied by his (God's) knowledge" (Isa. 53:11; cf. 2 Sam. 22:29; Ps. 27:1). And the apocalyptic redemption occurs when the light of God's shines forth (Isa. 60:1-3; cf. 40:5; 62:1; 66:18-19).

In the Priestly account of creation (Gen. 1:3-5), light existed before the stars were created, and it came into being by God's word alone, not by his action like all the other created things. This is an expression of the sublime character of light, which is not something that was "made," and this corresponds to the nature of light as representing the *doxa.* In and with physical light, this passage includes the general cosmic nature of light and its intellectual aspects, the total perception of light, inwardly and outwardly, as is the case elsewhere for the Hebrew concept of light. The best commentary on this interpenetration of outward and inward is Paul's word, "For it is the God who said, 'Let light shine out of darkness,' who has shone in our hearts to give the light of the knowledge of the glory *(doxa)* of God in the face of Christ" (2 Cor. 4:6).

Since in the Old Testament, light is always in such close proximity to God, is the cosmic power *kat' exochen,* and is coordinated with the category of the spiritual, wisdom of course is in a close relationship to the light. It can be said of living in the light, "But the path of the righteous is like the light of dawn, which shines brighter and brighter until full day" (Prov. 4:18), and of instruction in the wisdom tradition (in which the concept of Torah is included) "For the commandment is a lamp and the teaching a light, and the reproof[23] of discipline is the way of life" (Prov. 6:23). In Wisdom 7:25-26 is can be said of wisdom in reference to the divine *doxa* itself,

> For she is a breath of the power of God
>   and a pure emanation of the glory of the Almighty;
>   therefore nothing defiled gains entrance into her.
> For she is a reflection of eternal light,

---

[22]Cf. 1QIsab (Qumran Isaiah scroll), LXX.
[23]Read *sgl* LXX.

a spotless mirror of the working of God,
and an image of his goodness.

In wisdom literature, life is spoken of more often than light, since
here it is possible to apply the teaching directly to the individual.
We have already seen that *ḥayyim* does not mean life in the biological sense, but the "liveliness" which is proper to animal life and is
always bestowed by God; it is true, wholesome human life. This life
can be attained only by living in accordance with God's ordinances,
which are made known in creation and through revelation. Therefore, in the Old Testament life is promised, on the one hand, to
those who follow the commands, the cultic and legal ordinances,
and the prophetic exhortations, which often take the form of Torah
instruction (Lev. 18:5; Deut. 4:1; 30:15-20; Amos 5:6, 14, etc.),
and on the other hand it is wisdom that promises life. "For he who
finds me (wisdom) finds life and obtains favor from the Lord"
(Prov. 8:35), "Whoever loves her (wisdom), loves life (*zōē*)"
(Sir. 4:12). It is not necessary here to spell out in detail the extent
to which this concept is permeated by a spiritual depth that extends
even to a transcendental "eternal life," as can be traced from Psalms
49 and 73 down to Wisdom 3-5.

The fact that an entire strophe (vv 4-5, 9) in the prologue to
John is devoted to the nature of the Logos as light (at the place in
the total composition that corresponds to the description of the *doxa,*
vv 14, 16) expresses fully the cosmic and human-intellectual meaning ascribed to light in the Old Testament. After v 3, which speaks
of creation through the Logos, this strophe speaks of the activity
of the Logos in creation. In the created world the Logos is the
life that is the light of men (v. 4). The wholesome life of all that
was created (in the specific meaning of *zōē*, wholesome human life)
is the direct effect of the work of the Logos, for this God-given
life appears in and through reliance on the eternal ordinances of
creation and revelation as they are taught by and embodied in wisdom literature and Torah.

According to the concept of Logos presupposed by the prologue
to John, the Logos himself represents the wholeness of life. Two
examples have already been given for the relationship of the con-

cepts of life and light: to live is to see light, and thereby the side
of life characterized by perception and knowing is made manifest.
This is expressed here poetically as an intensification from life as
existence to life on a spiritual level, to consciousness, the specific
human quality.

Now that light has been mentioned by name the bringing of
salvation can be spelled out in a fundamental cosmological statement about the light shining in darkness (v 5) and in the statement about enlightening humans (v 9). We have already pointed
out that the statement in v 5 is not limited to spiritual components,
and according to Old Testament ways of thinking cannot be so
limited. Light here means the entire light of the whole cosmos, which
is not only created by this cosmic principle of victory over the chaos
of darkness, but is continuously sustained.

Light and darkness are to be interpreted in spiritual terms as well,
but not to the exclusion of direct perception in physical and cosmic
terms. To be sure, light here means intellectual light, which is not
extinguished by the darkness of ignorance and insensitivity or by
lies and deceit; to be sure it means the evidence of wisdom that cannot be overcome no matter how much opposition it encounters; but
in addition the cosmic dimension remains. And it is totally incorrect
to exegete v 5 as a statement with the same meaning as vv 10-11,
that is, unfortunately, the darkness did not accept the light. Verse 9
must also be understood in a positive sense: every(!) one is enlightened by the light of the Logos, inasfar as one participates not
only in being but also in consciousness. And it is in this enlightening
of the consciousness that the light comes into the world. Verse 5
formulates in physical terms the cosmic work in which the shining
of the light brings wholeness, and v 9 formulates it in spiritual
terms.

Is it possible to say that this strophe on the light of the Logos,
which speaks in this way of the enlightening of every person, presents a natural theology of the Logos *asarkos* as a counterpart to the
revelation of the Logos *ensarkos* in vv. 14, 16? The concept of a
natural theology, which in its specific formulation is post-biblical,
is out of place here. Quite apart from the fact that the statements,

which encompass the entire cosmos, go far beyond consciousness, and that they would have to be reduced to a concept of reason, they also include the basic features of the realm of Old Testament revelation, even though the revelation still requires a special event in salvation history, the "coming" of the Logos (v. 11), for the Torah is revealed wisdom, the answer to all the questions about wisdom (Job 28:28). But even though the concept of natural theology does not fit here, doesn't the concept of light, understood in this comprehensive way and not merely as an appropriate symbol, lead to an uncritical "universalism" of the truth, which we would hardly expect in the Bible?

On the contrary, the key is in vv. 10-11. The crucial issue is that through truth (which in the Bible is always to be understood in as universal terms as possible) the Logos was not recognized, that knowledge of the truth cannot be complete, because it is not knowledge of God, and that by it no one becomes a child of God (cf. John 3:19). From Isaiah (e.g. 29:13-15) to 1 Corinthians (1:17—2:16; 3:18—4:13) the distinction between true and false wisdom constitutes, as in the prophets, a constant motif.

Biblical theology possesses unsurpassed breadth. A wisdom tradition that from its beginnings accepted foreign wisdom as legitimate (cf. Prov. 22:17—23:11 with its borrowings from the Egyptian "Instruction of Amenemope" and other sources), tested everything, and held fast to what was good, was aware of the general significance of its study and its tradition for all mankind. It became most profound in the doctrine of the Logos, who is all truth, who is the light of all perception and knowledge, and who must be known if the truth is to be known.

The objection might be raised to this exegesis of John's prologue in terms of its structure, that the insertion in vv 6-7(8) is intended as a testimony to Jesus, and that as John 8:12 shows, the light simply means Jesus. This, however, fits so poorly with the interpretation of vv 4-5, 9 as referring to the cosmic and human-intellectual working of the Logos, that even when the secondary character of vv 6-7(8) is taken into account such exegesis is unlikely. This line of argument

overlooks first of all the fact that the identification of Jesus with the
cosmic light in John 8:12, which is also the case here in the prologue, does not say anything as to how this light, which has meaning in itself and not only as the proclamation of Jesus, is to be understood in the first part of the prologue.

It has already been pointed out that in the gospel Jesus can speak
of birth by the spirit and from God and of the light of the world,
even though the prologue connects these thoughts with specific stages
of realms of the revelation of the Logos before Jesus appeared. It
is not a matter of superceded revelation, but of a unique, developing revelation that unfolds toward a goal which includes all that has
gone before. Since the reference to the witness born by John the
Baptist is given in two parts and comes at two different points in the
prologue, these two parts will probably have a specific relation to
each other. Both deal with John's witness, but only the second (v
15) identifies Jesus with the pre-existent Logos. This means that
this identification is not presupposed in the first testimony, where
only the light is spoken of.

Then what is the concrete meaning of the testimony to the light
that leads to faith? It is not by chance that in the presentation of
John the Baptist's testimony immediately following the prologue
(1:19-34)[24] two clearly distinguished testimonies are recorded. In
vv 19-28 John replies to the inquiries of the official sacral-religious
delegation from Jerusalem consisting of priests and Levites and to
the Pharisees who had been sent to him. When on the next day John
sees Jesus coming to him, he spontaneously gives testimony to Jesus
(vv 29-34). This second testimony (v 30) contains a verbatim repetition of the identification in the second insertion of material dealing
with John the Baptist (v 15). But this identification is not explicitly
assumed in the first testimony (v 26). Since the second insertion
about John corresponds to the second testimony in the following
passage, we can assume that in similar manner the first testimony
(vv 19-28) refers to the first insertion in vv 6-7(8). In his first

[24]Only 1:19-34 represents the actual testimony of John the Baptist; cf.
1:19, 32, 34 with 3:26.

testimony John rejects the question of whether he is a figure who will usher in the eschaton (Messiah, Elijah *redivivus,*[25] or the prophet of the end-time[26]) and describes himself as one who prepares the way, with reference to Isaiah 40:3. John also refutes the Pharisee's objection to the eschatological baptism he is administering, by a reference to the appearance of the one who is coming after him—one who is already secretly present, though unrecognized—as the one who brings in the consummation of the world. As for his eschatological preaching and baptism as a preparation for the Messiah, as a preparation for faith (that is, the messianic expectation and apocalyptic proclamation prior to the encounter with Jesus, which contain the sum of the Old Testament) these would then be understood in terms of the testimony in v 7 to the light, testimony that leads to faith. And in an interpretation of the original text this could easily be understood as a full experience of the Light, which is limted only by the appearance of Jesus, and which leads to belief in the Logos and to birth as God's children (vv 12-13), accomplishment of which is ritually symbolized in John's baptism.

The light of the Logos that shone in human consciousness did not lead to recognition of the Logos (v 10), and Israel, which received the revelation in its role as a contemporary entity as a nation in history, did not welcome the Logos. Only those welcomed him who believed in the one who revealed himself[27] as a person, those who believed in "his name." They are the ones who by receiving the Logos shared in the birth as God's children, the transcendent basis of their being.

During the exile Israel-Judah kept a genealogical record in order to preserve the integrity of God's people and to have a documentary claim to their homeland, and such records played varied roles in the early post-exilic period in the framework of the reestablishment of Judah. These records were testimony to their union with Yahweh

---

[25]I am not able here to discuss the question of whether Elijah *redivivus* was an eschatological figure or one who preceded the eschaton.

[26]See above, p. 149.

[27]For an application of the name, see H. v. Stietencron, *Der Name Gottes,* 1975, pp. 75ff.

(cf. Exod. 32:32). The striking concept that at the New Years festival God would compile a register of the births in Israel was expressed in the cult, as Psalm 87 indicates, and in modified form this is still of importance today in the Jewish New Year's ritual. God keeps a record of the births of all humans, and he finds among all nations those who acknowledge him. Although in the natural sense of the word they were born in a foreign land, spiritually they were really born in Jerusalem (Ps. 87:4-6). Jerusalem is the true mother of all those who know God.

The Psalter expresses in many ways the idea of unity with Zion, the spiritual dwelling where God's presence is found in the world, the place of safety under the wings of the cherubim. Zion becomes the great mother, from whom all who believe trace their descent, and from whom they are born (cf. Isa. 4:3-6). When God reveals his eschatological reign as king, Zion will have many children (Isa. 54:1-3), and apocalyptic terms are used to portray how God will make his appearance in the final judgment when the people of God are born from Mother Jerusalem (Isa. 66:6-11). The Isaiah apocalypse teaches that this birth is something which we cannot achieve by ourselves, but it will be a birth out of death, it will be a resurrection (Isa. 26:17-19).

In the wisdom literature there are certain parallels to the concept of child of God which had its origin in the cultic piety associated with Zion and which then developed in apocalyptic. The wisdom tradtion also had its sons—a pupil is a son—but with the increasing theological dimension of wisdom the wise man came to be the son of God (cf. Sir. 4:10 and especially Wis. 2:13, 16, 18). In the late forms of devotion that had been influenced by both sapiential and eschatological forces, these two strands could merge, and in John 1:12-13 both roots can be identified.

John's baptism is important in this connection, since, if we examine the New Testament description of the rite, it is clearly a ritual enactment of rebirth. It is customary to derive it from the Jewish ritual immersion, but the basic differences should not be overlooked. The ritual bath serves the purpose of attaining Levitical purity, but

John's baptism goes far beyond a cleansing in this sense.[28] The ritual bath is repeatable, while John's baptism is an initiation rite performed only once. The ritual bath takes place without a confession, while confession of sins is a pre-condition (cf. Mark 1:5) for John's baptism. The ritual bath is possible anywhere, John's baptism only in the Jordan.[29] The ritual bath lacks any eschatological meaning, while this is fundamental for John's baptism. Morevover the ritual bath does not have any direct ethical dimensions, but a totally new way of life is demanded in John's baptism. Reference to the first proselyte baptism that can be cited after the destruction of the Temple does not lead us any further, since it is the initial ritual bath and thus serves to confer Levitical purity.

Do the ritual baths of the Qumran community (1 QS III 4f., 9; V 13f.; cf. Josephus, *War,* II 129, 138, and also 149f., where he is speaking of the Essenes) bring us any closer to John's baptism? Here too the purpose of the frequently repeated baths is basically Levitical purity, and there is no tie to the Jordan (cf. 1 QS III 4f.). The observation is often made that baptism at Qumran involved confession of sin and included the forgiveness of sins. The data, however, are not entirely clear. In Qumran the effect of the various sprinklings and washings that have effect on the body are distinguished from true, inner repentance, and a sinner was not permitted contact with the water used for washings by the circle of those who lived in great holiness. In principle such ritual baths had the same nature as the customary Jewish ritual bath, except that

---

[28]This is not refuted by the fact that in John 3:25 baptism is connected with the concept of cleansing. In any water baptism that goes without saying, even though here it appears to be a third element in contrast to the ritual bath. In spite of the fact that the understanding of Christian baptism goes far beyond a cleansing, the New Testament speaks of both washing and cleansing (e.g. Acts 22:16; 1 Cor. 6:11; Heb. 10:22).

[29]There are two traditions concerning the location of Aenon (John 3:23), and the Madeba map identifies both sites. Because it is said to be in Judea the tradition is probably correct which locates it east of the Jordan near the ford in the vicinity of Jericho. In addition, the Bethany where John baptized is said to lie east of the Jordan (1:28). The other possibility is that Aenon was a point south of Scythopolis in the western Jordan valley, where there is a spring that feeds into the Jordan, so that here too "Jordan water" would be used.

they were incorporated into the holiness system of this community and were used along with other rites in the initiation of new members.

It is not possible to derive John's baptism from this type of ritual bath, not even as an intensification or specialization of it. The evidence against it includes the unrepeatable and eschatological nature of John's baptism, the place it was performed, and the confession of sins originally connected with the baptism ritual. How is John's distinctive baptism to be understood? We can begin with John's citing of Isaiah 40:3, which is firmly anchored in the tradition. John is the one who prepares the way. This eschatological way by which God comes to set up his kingdom on Zion corresponds to the prototypical event of salvation, the Exodus.

This correspondence can be first seen in pre-exilic prophecy as it developed in an early form, when the great judgment results in the restoration of the primordial period of salvation history and so becomes a renewal of that history. With the beginning of eschatological prophecies of salvation in Second Isaiah, however, the correspondence to the primordial time of the Exodus (and the wilderness wandering) is worked out consistently (43:16-21; 51:10-11; cf. also 48:21; 52:12). This was taken up by a related tradition (Isa. 11:15-16; 63:11-13) and came to permeate the late prophetic tradition in general (cf. Micah 7:15; Zech. 10:10-11). The vitality of this understanding of the eschatological event is seen in the exegesis of Isaiah 40:3-5 in Baruch 5:7-9.

The Jordan is the boundary of the holy land, through which the entry to the land took place, and for this reason it was here that the event at the Sea of Reeds was reenacted (Josh. 3-4; the miracle at the Sea of Reeds was repeated at the Jordan by Elijah, the Moses *redivivus* 2 Kings 2:14). The waters of the Jordan have their eschatological and also protological meaning. By passing through them the true people of God accomplished its entry into the kingdom of God.[30] As waters of the Sea of Reeds and waters of chaos (cf. Isa. 51:9-11) they are less waters of cleansing than waters of death. All

---

[30]Note the unusual place of baptism, beyond the Jordan (John 1:28; cf. the preceding note).

that is at enmity with God is submerged by them. Following here on the confession of sin, being immersed[31] has the ritual and symbolic significance of dying, but on rising out of the waters, one enters into the new being—a rite of rebirth, yes of a new creation. John's baptism is the ritualizing of the eschatological birth of which Isaiah 26:17-19 and other passages speak.

On the basis of this understanding of baptism as the symbol of the primeval redemption Paul's exegesis in 1 Corinthians 10:1-5 becomes understandable.[32] Mark 10:38-39 where the baptism of death is spoken of alongside the cup of judgment, can be explained in terms of the symbolic judgment and death in baptism. Baptism with fire (cf. Isa. 43:2; Ps. 66:12) can be understood in the same way, since fire must be interpreted as the eschatological sacrifice in judgment (cf. Mal. 3:19), while the out-pouring of the spirit when one emerges from the water of death is a distinctive expression of the gift of new life.

The experience of rebirth in the rite of passage of baptism is, in the Christian understanding of baptism, participation in the death and resurrection of Jesus (Rom. 6:3-4). Christian baptism is distinguished from that administered by John by being in the name of Jesus (cf. Acts 8:16; 10:48; 19:5; 1 Cor. 1:13; Gal. 3:27). If the one baptized by John dies symbolically, the Christian becomes the follower of Jesus—ritually and symbolically he suffers the death and resurrection of Jesus. Because of the connection with this original event even the ritual connection with Jordan could be dropped. The usual interpretation of John's baptism as a ceremony of cleansing must undergo a thorough reinterpretation for Christian baptism, in which the ritual event is interpreted allegorically in terms of the Christ event of death and resurrection.

It must be asked how this interpretation is possible in an unbroken

---

[31]The often-expressed skepticism as to whether baptism in the Jordan involved a ritual immersion is incomprehensible in view of the meaning of the word and also in light of the description of the baptism of Jesus (Mark 1:9-11) and the interpretation given in Rom. 6:3-4.

[32]The cloud naturally means the cloud that conceals the theophany fire and into which Moses entered. Representation and substitution lead to the statement about being baptized "into Moses."

ritual tradition. Granted the understanding of John's baptism as a rite of new birth from death, the new Christian interpretation evolved of itself, and the characterizing of baptism as being performed in the name of Jesus expresses it simply and clearly without concealing the allegory. The motif of birth as children of God could be thus expressed at the end of the Old Testament in a ritual that brought about the entry into the new aeon.

We have reached the end of our investigation of the prologue to John's gospel in terms of tradition history. It has been shown that the relationship of the prologue to the Old Testament is extensive and intimate. Even in its apparent critique of the Old Testament and its emphasis on the lack of fulfillment and completion, the prologue is oriented to the Old Testament tradition with its references to the provisional nature of all present reality and its movement toward the eschatological goal. The prologue is not dependent on various details of the Old Testament. It is related to the Old Testament tradition itself, and the total conception of the prologue grew out of this tradition.

The Johannine prologue demonstrates that a separation of the theology of the Old Testament from that of the New is impossible, and that exegetical work on the New Testament that is restricted to historical considerations cannot do justice to the facts, because of the connection with a realm of intellectual history that is determinative for the text. By the same token, study of the Old Testament that does not take into account the organic growth of tradition down to and into the New Testament is incomplete and leads to false conclusions, for example, in reference to the theological significance of the wisdom tradition.

That which is distinctive in a text such as the prologue to John can be discovered only against the background of a tradition that binds the two Testaments together. That is more than can be undertaken here. Our presentation also suffers from being unable to investigate New Testament passages dealing with the wisdom tradition that preceded or were contemporary with the prologue to John. All that could be done here was to pose for a text selected from the New Testament the basic questions of its relationship to the Old Testament.

VIII

The Question of a World View

I F WE ASK THE QUESTION, "Does faith need a world view?"
we are assuming that faith and world view are separate from
each other, because when we say "need" we assume that in the
long run there is a necessary connection between the two, but that
at the outset faith exists by itself, independent of a world view.
While this question may contain a positive evaluation of world
view as something that supports faith and contributes to it, we must
keep in mind that for a long time there has been a tendency to
emphasize the independence and absolute nature of faith. A *Welt-
anschauung,* as the summary of all metaphysical concerns and con-
victions, includes also the evaluation of all forms of being and life.
A world view *(Weltbild),* by contrast, is the summation of a total
objective view of the world, a point of view that a person con-
structs or accepts as something given, but which in any case is independent of a specific personal attitude or position, free from any
specific values or commitment, at least inasfar as objective knowledge
can be free from these things.

Faith, which is usually understood as an inward religious position,
maintained by personal commitment, is often contrasted to this
objective character of a world view. A world view is based on perceptions that maintain a certain distance from the visible appearance
of the world as we find it; faith, however, relates to what is unseen,
is an expression of trust, and involves personal commitment. The

tendency, not only to make a sharp distinction between the two but to separate them as fully independent of each other and to deny any inner relationships is understandable and can be observed in a variety of forms. Let us begin by examining these concerns in order to gain a genuine understanding of the question of faith and world view.

The awareness that one has a new world view that contrasts to what has been handed down and is in opposition to tradition did not appear until the modern period. The consciousness of being separated from the past by a new world view is not really the result of the wide-ranging discoveries and experiences that took place at the beginning of the modern period—the Copernican revolution, the discovery of America, the new access to the ancient world through direct examination of literary sources, because all this was simply a case of the new replacing the old, the true replacing the false, the far-reaching taking the place of the narrow. These factors produced a new general feeling toward the world but not the knowledge that one had a quite specific, definable view of the world.

This consciousness of having a world view has been with us only since the Enlightenment, and it presupposes two factors. The first of these is a significant mass of assured scientific knowledge, and the second is the knowledge of the historical distance from past human views and prejudices, the knowledge of the manifold and historically quite varied restrictions on human concepts in past ages in contrast to the freedom we have through present-day knowledge, and the feeling that we have advanced from fantastic errors to fixed, unassailable insights.

The natural sciences have accumulated such a mass of knowledge and through their assurance of objectivity have attained such authority and such power to convince, that science has been able to construct a complete and assured world view. Rationality, having established itself in this manner, became the criterion for judging all traditional material, and thus the world view that was guaranteed by reason and was derived from and proved by natural science came to take the place of the fantastic and biased world views of earlier times. It is out of this scientifically established position of conscious objectivity in historical distance to past views and mere traditions that world view came to be defined as the view of the whole of objective reality. When regarded as a basic contrast to earlier traditional interpretations of the world this comprehensive world view has great value for our historical understanding. The more extensive and detailed historical knowledge became in the nineteenth century, the easier it was to identify the world view presupposed by past cultures and historical periods, and even by specific data from human life in the past. It was possible to use the world view to measure the inner historical distance and at the same time to demonstrate the limited validity of traditional material. In the outdated world view we had evidence of the limitations imposed by time, and we had our present world view as the valid standard.

As a consequence it is easy to see how faith—which as a religious expression of the subject was in each instance colored by the presuppositions of the current world view and could without ado be articulated in terms of that world view—came to be separated in principle from it. This is illustrated by the fact that in any interpretation of an old confession of faith, the interpreter is concerned to separate the prejudices due to the world view from the actual statements about the faith. This enables the interpreter to arrive at the existential verities contained in the statements permeated by the world view and thus allows the pure statement of faith be heard.

The so-called demythologizing program of Rudolf Bultmann represents the attempt to provide an interpretation that would separate the historically derived "mythical" world view of the New Testament from the statements of the New Testament. This separation of faith and world view, however, can also be seen in the concern of modern persons to purge concepts of their faith—often they can only speak of "feelings"—from any metaphorical expression. Such "concretizations" are regarded as childish at best and the pictures and concepts marked by the old world view are not directly valid, while the valid, scientific view of the world has nothing to do with faith.

Then what pictures and concepts are appropriate? Is it possible to deal with the philosophical concepts of God, freedom, and immortality without letting religious existence in its fullness shrivel to a mere moral attitude? Is it possible to express oneself in purely existential terms without losing the contents of the biblical tradition, the historical content of faith? How can we still have today the *fides qua creditur* alongside the *fides quae creditur,* when, in the tradition of faith, world view and faith are so closely intermeshed that the postulated separation between them cannot be accomplished in a convincing manner? If the concept of the world view as the human experience of the world cannot be accepted, must it perhaps be modified or reformulated?

Since the concept of world view was formed by both the natural sciences and the experience of historical distance, two points of view emerge, from which the biblical tradition, especially the Old Testament, can be approached in relation to the question of world view and faith. First we will consider the problems raised by natural science and the aspects of the question that involve the theory of knowledge, and then the historical problems and the aspects of the question raised by the history of revelation, in the hope that in the end we can arrive at a comprehensive answer.

The Ancient World View and Human Perception

The contrast of the modern, valid world view and a multiplicity of out-moded, error-ridden world views from past ages and cultures is reversed in our intellectual situation when we approach the biblical tradition. There never has been a time when there was so little agreement about a philosophical world view as there is today. Between Heidegger and Popper there is a range of possible world views that is hard to measure, and the disagreements that arise today between the individual philosophical conceptions are far more numerous than those known in earlier centuries. Just as in the world of art today, in contrast to earlier times, there is no single style or even stylistic framework that is dominent, so too there is no contemporary world view that even comes close to having universal validity. Since the collapse of metaphysics there are only individual disciplines, the sum of which might represent a totality of knowledge, but the great number of contradictory aspects involved cannot be reconciled or unified.

In contrast to this multiplicity and to the vast inner differences, the biblical tradition, indeed the entire ancient tradition gives the impression of harmony and unity. In spite of the extremely great historical and cultural distinctions that existed in the ancient world, it is possible to discern a unified world view. The most varied philosophical representatives that appear in a Ciceronean dialogue, for example, show so much inner kinship, even in their opposing philosophical positions, that we can say that while there are different interpretations these representatives are expressing the same content, and while there are various aspects they are viewing the same picture. The pronounced historical differences that existed in the ancient world between the early period, the so-called classic period and the Hellenistic period, are related to each other as far as their view of the world is concerned, as evolutionary stages that reveal a consistent development of an identical world without destroying the wholeness of this world.

Modern scholarly developments, however, seem to produce explosive changes in the way we view the world. That this view of the ancient world as a closed unit is not just the result of our distance from that world, but that it was so regarded in ancient times, can be established by appeal to the ancient tradition itself. Egyptian texts of the Old Kingdom could be studied in later times with the same zeal as always, but we can approach a scholastic text of the Middle Ages, for instance, only as something of historic interest. Herodotus could identify his gods with those of ancient Egypt, while today we have trouble accepting the early Lutheran confessions as our own. All of ancient intellectual life depended on tradition, on the humble, respectful transmission and re-interpretation and development through extension and deepening of tradition. We regard anything from the previous century as out of date. "Traditional" has become a negative concept, and "original" a positive one.

When we consider the outer, material, and spatial aspects of the ancient world view, the unity is especially impressive. With scarcely a ripple the mythological world view was sublimated into natural philosophy, and in spite of considerable growth of knowledge from the natural sciences the world view of late antiquity was only a refinement of the old concepts. These concepts always arose from the direct perception of the material world. And the world views of cultures that never had contact with each other, whether that of Homer, or the Bible, or the Babylonians, or the Indians, were essentially the same.

The world view of the Bible was the same as that of all other people of ancient times. It is an original world view that arose from direct perception. Modern natural science has nothing that corresponds to it. Even though the continuity of discoveries is overwhelming, this is not merely a matter of completing a structure in an accepted framework, or a mere refinement of knowledge, but of a basically new understanding. Above all we are dealing with the advances of the individual sciences, which in the case of the exact natural sciences have a close inter-relationship in terms of scientific methodology, but do not encompass the total place of mankind in the world. It is because of this non-human character that a comprehensive world view cannot be derived from this knowledge, and we have instead the precise description of realities that are not directly human reality, with which we are not really involved, and which in a real sense do not belong to the world of our perceptions.

What then is the given framework beyond which the prescientific world view of the ancients did not progress? It is defined by human sense-perception, our vision, hearing, etc. The material of the ancient world view is the world of nature as perceived by the human senses. It is this that unifies that world view. Indeed we can have only this one world view if the term "view" is to be interpreted in human terms. The limits of sense perception were never exceeded in the ancient world, but in modern natural science they are violated, not merely in the case of necessity, but as a matter of principle. The material for the natural sciences is not provided by subjective human perception, because material so supplied is so complex and subjective that it could not be processed. Instead it is provided by precise measurements. Scientific instruments for measurement take the place of human perception, because human perception is limited and subject to error. More importantly, however, it is complex, that is, objective perception is always tied up with interpretations of what is perceived, with emotional reactions, for instance.

Most important of all, however, natural science is concerned with establishing quantitative regularities, while human sense perception is directed toward qualities, and only under certain circumstances can it by a rational act of counting deal with quantity. We are accustomed to regarding scientific measurements as greatly superior to our sense perceptions. We should remember, however, that we are dealing with two basically non-comparable types of perception or information about reality. The reality perceived in both cases is connected, but each is also to be distinguished from the other.

Let us take as an example the perception of light. It is a basic, direct experience of the ancient world view that the light of human perception exists as such, and from it we perceive the appearance of visible objects. For natural science light is a segment, a small part of electromagnetic radiation, and the light which humans perceive exists only as a limited portion of that radiation. It is easy to say that the human eye is an inadequate instrument for perception and that physical instruments are the only means for measuring this reality. But in such a judgment human perception, despite its scope that far transcends physical measurements, is simply shoved aside, reduced to physical reality.

There are two ways in which human perception goes beyond physical realism. First, human perception includes an intellectual realm, that is, with the perception of light is becomes possible to perceive things as "light." The idea of physical light and that of being in the light shape each other. Every perception is open to an intellectual interpretation, which is something essential for humans and not merely something extraneous. We can illustrate that with our perception of space. Humans think in terms of up and down, right and left, front and back, and this indicates qualities in addition to mathematical dimensions. Up is qualitatively different from down; heaven cannot be down and hell up. By this qualitative perception of space humans are able to distinguish between height and depth. These are not merely abstract evaluations of postive and negative qualities.

Heaven is "high" but people can also be "haughty." Why is wisdom "deep," and not "high"? In physical terms there are no entities "up" and "down," but only spatial relations; human perceptions, however, discern qualities that go beyond spatial relations, and are open to metaphorical usage. Each perception makes a metaphor possible. It is not possible to say that in each case the metaphor grew out of a conscious transferal of meaning, but an inner perception suggests itself with each outer perception, as when light is perceived as enlightening and height as that which is high. There is an intellectual element in perception. The almost inseparable connection between the two is not the product of a higher, more refined culture, but of primitive human perception, of a naive view. It is the refined culture that distinguishes between the physical and the intellectual, because it is accustomed to the independent production of artificial intellectual concepts.

The second thing that can be said of human perception is that it is the basic element in and the standard for all knowledge, however abstract it may be and however far removed it is from direct perception. *"Wissen,"* to know, comes from *videre,* to see. The Greek *oida* "know" is related to *eidon* "see." That is to say, human knowledge is bound to the concepts and views that correspond to perception. And the more profound and inward the knowledge is, the more strongly it lays hold of the whole person, and the more subject it is to perception, in which it can be intellectualized into a symbol. The more knowledge is concerned with outward forms, the more easily it can substitute a schema for a perception. In any case perception and idea belong together, and that reality which can become truth is known and "perceived" only in human terms. The physical reality of the natural sciences is connected with this reality, but it should not be identified with it or confused with it.

But this has happened and the change is permanent. It results in a bad distortion of our view of reality, which then all too often takes the place of a total world view. Inadequate education in the natural sciences, and thus erroneous upbringing, comes about because children are introduced to the results of the natural sciences at all too early an age without being able to grasp the nature of this knowledge. This leads them to transfer their scientific knowledge to the world of perceptions in such a way as to falsify that world. While the perceptible world is true to our human senses, it is by no means true to the reality which we discover through measurements. These can produce conceptual models, that is consciously artificial transferences into the perceptible world, which make certain knowledge "perceptible," but do not express its true essence. These models, however, are then taken without further ado as representations of reality. Models of atoms and molecules are presented to students, who then conceive of matter in terms of these preceptible models and not in terms of the knowledge which they represent.

Modern physical insights, however, lie completely beyond what we can perceive. The popular "explanations" of the theory of relativity, for example, are of necessity inadequate distortions, because they continue to present reality through the usual perceptions of time and space, in an area where there can be no relationship between time and space. The concept of absolute velocity has to struggle against a view of velocity according to which it can always be increased. As a matter of principle the exceeding of quantitative boundaries must always play a significant role for human perceptions, so that the speed of light can no longer be grasped by our perceptions as "velocity." Anyone can measure the curvature of the earth by seeing a ship "appear" in the distance. But however easy it may be to construct a sphere with a specific curvature, it is impossible to picture the earth on the basis of the observation of its curvature in a manner that corresponds to our perceptions, without reducing the earth to the size of a model. The quantitative limits of our power to perceive are not merely something negative, but they are of essential significance for the structure of perception.

Instead of allowing the knowledge of the natural sciences to stand alongside concrete, meaningful human perceptions, these perceptions are systematically hemmed in and restricted. We speak of the "apparent" movement of the sun in the sky. This is true, because this is the only way the sun "appears to us." But it is false to combine this with a negative judgment, which produces in today's men and women, so estranged from the world of nature, the idea that they must basically mistrust their senses because the senses communicate to them a world of deception. The impression of the rising and setting of the sun is then replaced by the concept that the earth races around the sun at dizzying speed. Human ideas of speed derived from life on earth are simply transferred to things not perceptible in earthly terms. We take no notice of the fact that the "apparent" movement of the stars in the sky constitutes a boundary of human perception. That speed which is perceived as a continuum appears to our fleeting observation as standing still. So there are many and various mysterious relationships between the human capability of subjective perception and objective earthly situations. Instead of leaving scientific knowledge in the mathematical form that is appropriate to it, and so being conscious of the reality that it represents, we try to transfer it to the world of human perceptions under the naive assumption that there can be only one reality and that it restricts or "corrects" the world as perceived by our senses. This world that we perceive, however, is that of the ancient world view. It would also be ours if we would be willing to allow—correctly, in accordance with scientific theory—the reality grasped through human perception to stand alongside the reality mediated to us through instruments.

But doesn't this ancient world view contain obvious errors? An example is the concept of the sky, which is perceived as a dome. This is merely an optical illusion, since the stars are so far away that perception of them in terms of parallax and space is not possible. They appear to be all the same distance away, and this gives the impression that there is a hemisphere above the observer, because a sphere is the geometric location of all points equidistant from the center. First of all, the concept of optical illusion is in need of correction here. An optical illusion is not a false perception, but one that indicates the distinctive nature of human vision, which is much more than mere "photography." Such well-known examples of optical illusions as parallel lines that appear not to be parallel, or lines of the same length that appear to be of different lengths, arise because the individual lines involved are not seen as such. We see a total picture in which other lines contradict the impression of being parallel, or of the same length. Vision involves the whole, and this is more than the sum of the parts. The impression of the sky as a dome, which arises by day as well when humans look at the unending reaches of space, results from seeing things in a way that has significance. The "sky" is the human perception of unending space. When humans confront this endlessness they experience, in a manner appropriate to their perceptions, the sky as a boundary. Perception of the sky is perception of the boundary between us and transcendence.

We bring children up with the prejudice that people of ancient times were simple-minded, not to say, stupid, to a degree that we can scarcely imagine. We like to look at the old picture that shows how a man sticks his head through the firmament and then looks at the world "outside." This picture is, first of all, a modern one, and certainly does not represent the ancient concept of the firmament, which, whether naive or intellectual, was far removed from such a simplistic and coarse view of reality. We have evidence of how the ancients regarded the firmament in various periods. There are the highly intellectual speculations about the nature of the firmament in Midrash and Talmud[1] or the quite ancient concepts of the sky derived from mythological ideas of perception, which are much more profound than our realism.

For example, according to the Babylonian creation myth, the sky is described as the upper half of the body of the chaos goddess Tiamat, who was cut in two "like a fish on dry land." When anyone is unable to accept any longer the concept of the ascension of Jesus as it is described in Acts 1:9-11, because of the "primitive" views that the account presupposes ("Jesus travels on a cloud, as if on an elevator, toward a firmanent that was thought to exist in the sky") the difficulty does not lie in the ancient account but in our inability to understand this "sky" as a perception of transcendence, so we reduce it to a "primitive" view. We fail to understand what the cloud is, a concept that dates back to the tradition of the revelation on Sinai, where it constituted the cloak concealing the divine glory—

---

[1]*Genesis Rabbah* IV 2ff; *Pirque Rabbi Eliezer* 4; *j Berakot* 2cd, and many other passages; cf. M. D. Gross, *'osar ha'aggada,* III, Jerusalem 1961, pp. 1304ff.

the cloud took him up "out of their sight." Of course we can find in the Bible a wealth of early concepts, but it is our blindness to the deep intellectual nature of these early thoughts that gives rise to what at first sight appears "primitive" and which we must then find unacceptable.

The ancient world view, which we can confidently speak of as the world view of human perception, is our world view too, when we are not instructed otherwise, and it is the only one that enables us to have a completely human relation to the world, an intellectual understanding of the world. The openness of our sensual perceptions to intellectual perception, the metaphorical nature of perception on the one hand, and on the other the basic importance for all knowledge of the fact that the material world is accessible to our senses, show that the intellectual structure of the human mind corresponds to its ability to process the data of the senses. For our human understanding of the world, the world view that corresponds to our perceptions is indispensable, will never be out of date, and can merely be supplemented through the knowledge gained by the exact sciences through indirect means not dependent on the senses.

Depth psychology teaches us that even our unconscious is structured by the world we perceive through our senses, and that here past states of the soul and mythical experiences of the world are preserved. If we are to be fully human, we cannot reject or fail to acknowledge this spiritual substance. Neither can we, when dealing with deeper human knowledge, exclude the mental intensification of our experience of the world through our senses. For humans, art is not a mental "superstructure," but a basic expression of our being in the world. Only in art is it possible to give form to our experience of the world in a manner that we can fully identify with. It is obvious that art is fundamentally tied to our sense perceptions, and therefore to the world view that corresponds to our perceptions. It would seem that the obvious crisis of art in the present day—a unique development in human history—is connected with modern man's profound alienation from the world. We should remind ourselves too that in the ancient world the purpose of art was not merely to reproduce something beautiful: art had an aesthetic function in the original sense of the word and was in the service of the intellectual perception of the world.

Poetic speech did not have the function of taking a true statement and then providing it with a beautiful form, but in and through the poetic form it served to lay hold on truth. True and beautiful (that is proper order) were ultimately one and the same. So many of the biblical texts are poetic, because it was only in this form that the truth could be expressed. Poetic language brings a statement closer to what our senses can perceive, while at the same time intensifying it metaphorically. Knowledge is made more profound, not by abandoning sense data, but by intensifying our sense perceptions until they express what is original, underived, and general, and become symbols rich in meaning.

Let us look again at the example of light. The biblical account of creation in Genesis 1, tells of the creation of light before that of the stars, in fact, creation begins with light. It is ridiculous to think the ancients were so simple-minded that they had not noticed that light came from the sun and stars. But just as light is not a partial phenomenon (as it is in the physical sense), so it is more than the stars, the "lights," as they were called. It would be absurd to explain this sequence of light and stars in terms of natural science by the hypothesis of a fog. The account of creation is not natural science in our sense of the term.

In Hebrew, "to see" is the word to "perceive" in general, and we might compare it with the etymology of *"wissen"* and *"videre"* cited above. In biblical language "light" can have the semantic content of "life" in the sense of "perception," or of "consciousness." "And the life was the light of men" (John 1:4). This is no artificial, abstract concept. Light is not an allegory for consciousness, but it is a "symbol." It goes without saying that Genesis 1 is speaking of the real light of sense perception, which physically corresponds to a specific electromagnetic shining, but this primal phenomenon of absolute perception also includes that light which a blind man can see and which brings enlightenment.

The symbol transcends physics. It is that light which can be termed the garment of God (Ps. 104:1b, 2a), that is, the external aspect of the form in which God appears. It is the light of the *doxa,* the divine splendor of majesty that will shine forth at the end and goal of being, when sun and moon are no more. The biblical text gives expression to the mystery of the intellectual meaning of this light. The rest of the account expresses two ways in which creation is accomplished, on the one hand through the word, and on the other through forming, through the deed. But in reference to light, only the creative word is spoken of, "And God said, 'Let there be light'; and there was light" (v 3). This light takes precedence over the activity of making and comes into being only through the intellectual process of the word. In contrast to the perception through which the subject sees, which is also a part of the process of creation, ("And God saw that the light was good," v 4 etc.), the word proceeds from the subject, becomes audible, and expresses the pure will of the creator, the act of creation.

In this concept of word we have a phenomenon of both the senses and the mind, a symbol, in which the process of creation can be brought to expression, in which it is conceived, is "perceived." This holds true on various levels. There is an account of creation through the word that comes from an earlier time of mythological thought. (There are those who like to speak of a magical concept of word, but are unable to establish precisely what "magic" is supposed to mean.) On the other hand it appears here in a relatively late biblical text which has all the marks of intellectualized points of view. The ancient world view, that is based on human perception, can thus encompass this vast historic span of intellectual history.

At the beginning of the Sabbath, the Jewish wife lights the Sabbath candles. (The light which humans perceive symbolically does not come from electricity, but from the flame of fire, which has accompanied all human culture from its beginnings.) She holds her hands before the flame while she utters the blessing, "Blessed art Thou, O Lord our God, King of the universe, who hast sanctified us by thy commandments and instructed us to light the Sabbath candle." Then she looks for the first time into the flame and perceives the blessed light of the Sabbath. Perception and ritual belong together. Only in the world view of human perception is perception possible, that is, a holy carrying out of actions through a perceiving person in this world, actions that point to truths, represent them symbolically, and make it possible for humans to enter into relationship with them. A merely passive perception is intensified to active re-enactment, a primal human event that can take place only through the world view of human perception.

Christian worship includes sacraments. The water of baptism and the bread and the wine not only mean something, they are something, not merely an outward sign, but a true sign and symbol. To be sure, they cannot be this without the word. But all thought, all intellectual activity requires the word, normally the spoken word, and only in exceptional cases the word that is merely thought. Worship also includes prayer. Speaking to God presupposes a relationship of sense data and intellectual activity, even their unity. It is really possible only with the presupposition of the human experience of reality through the senses, through which the intellectual world constantly reveals itself. The anthropromorphisms of prayer do not reflect primitive, unenlightened limitations, but rather the transcendence appropriate to human experience, which does not avoid the perceptions available to our senses, but rather permeates them.

Ever since the Enlightenment, people have increasingly turned away from the world of their perceptions. They have combined the data of the senses with the knowledge that is obtained through natural science, and have constructed purely formal, schematic, one-sided intelligence at the expense of deeper, fully human sense perception. This has led to such impoverishment of our intellectual and spiritual life that meditative practices, which, to the extent that they involve meditation on objects, are exercises in experiencing the ancient world view and are felt as something liberating.

After all that has been said, it is clear that men and women need for their own well-being the world view that is formed through human perception and rests upon it. We may absolutize faith as much as we want; it is still faith only when it is fully human faith, and therefore it can be articulated only in the language and the experiences of this world view. Limiting faith to the existential takes human self-experience seriously, but it makes people one-sided in that they refer everything only to themselves. Thus their relationship to the only world in which they are human is severed. Faith as something preeminently human is in need of the human view of the world.

World View and Revelation

The points clarified above are not specifically concerned with the biblical tradition, but with the general tradition of the ancient world. How does our investigation of the relationship of world view and faith change when we look at it from the point of view of biblical tradition? It is here that we have our particular historical connections and here that we see the historic differences that developed from the earlier to the later Old Testament and to the New Testament. Can permanent norms be established for our quest, and how are they to be understood?

The starting point for the biblical revelation is God's self-disclosure in the events at Mt. Sinai. In the earliest days of Israel, as the event that constituted Israel's existence, God's self-revelation took place in his self-disclosure to a human counterpart, binding himself to this counterpart and that counterpart to himself. "I am YHWH thy God." It is God's disclosure of himself as a person, an "I" to Israel's "thou." While the previous forms of God's revelation involved only the revelation of a specific divine "utterance" with reference to the original revelation in primeval time and involving coordination in a world of gods, a pantheon, now God reveals *himself,* without his being coordinated with anything else, in an exclusive relationship to his counterpart. It is revelation in a relationship, the ultimate binding together of God and his people; and the exclusive commitment of God involves the exclusive commitment of his counterpart, Israel.

The transcendental nature of the events surrounding the revelation is presented to us in terms of extreme disturbances in the atmosphere and on earth—storm, earthquake, the volcanic activity. Such perceptions of transcendence, however, are known to us from other ancient traditions, because they correspond to the ancient world view. The decisive feature is the close relationship between

God and the world, the linking of transcendence and immanence. God himself spoke with Moses as a man speaks with his friend (Exod. 33:11). God binds himself to Israel, and by so doing enters the realm of this world.

The immanence that is characteristic of this revelation was made even greater when God bound himself to David and his clan and to Jerusalem, with its cultic site. In contrast to ancient parallels, this too has the exclusivity of a personal relationship. The transcendence of revelation is strengthened even more in the tradition of Elijah in 1 Kings 19, when the purely intellectual realm of the inaudible word takes the place of storm, earthquake, and fire, and the bonds established by the revelation at Sinai are rejected. The truly human realm of word in its intellectual form is the medium by which revelation comes.

The combination of transcendence and being-in-the world that is characteristic of revelation is especially clear in the experience of death in Israel. In contrast to the rest of the ancient world, there is no sacral relationship to the realm of death. The dead have, as such, no share in God, because wherever God is, there is life. Neither, however, is there any relationship to the dark powers, by which the dead would be hidden among these anticosmic powers of the depths. No, the dead belong to God, but without being bound to him, because that would presuppose the intellectual realm of life constituted by consciousness.

Out of this tremendous tension between not being alive physically but still not belonging to the mythical transcendence of the depths, there developed in the history of revelation a new, intellectual transcendence of being with God eternally—beyond all physical reality. This grand knowledge is described in Psalm 73:17 as entering into the sanctuary of El, and formulated later in the psalm as follows:

> Nevertheless I am continually with thee;
>   thou does hold my right hand.
> Thou dost guide me with thy counsel,
>   and afterward thou wilt reecive me to glory.
> Whom have I in heaven but thee?
>   And there is nothing upon earth that I desire besides thee.

> My flesh and my heart may fail,
>   but God is the strength of my heart and my portion for
>   ever.   (vv 23-26)

The personal bond between God and the individual Israelite is interpreted in transcendent terms, and community with God constitutes the realm of a new transcendence, which goes beyond all limits of human existence. However much the Old Testament faith is concerned with this world as it overcomes the mythical transcendence of Hades, it just as greatly transcends worldly being. Eternal community with God does not begin after death, but is present here and now in life, and it never ends, since it transcends both life and death. Much is said today about the secular nature of the Old Testament, but most people look at only one side, immanence, and do not see that this being in the world consists in the overcoming of the world.

To be sure Israel participated in the early form of science, the wisdom literature of the ancient world, that magnificent effort of the human spirit to grasp and understand the world and to order human life according to this knowledge of the world, that movement which outside of Israel led to philosophy and in Israel to theology. In an early form of this wisdom movement it was recognized that those who lived in a manner appropriate to the order of the world were in a realm of that which is right, orderly, and whole, and that they exerted a healing and wholesome influence on the world, which, reflecting that wholesomeness, enabled them to be in a state of wholeness. It must be admitted that this wholeness that is the result of human effort is often conspicuous, while the wholeness that humans should receive remains concealed. But that does not change the basic correctness of the conception of an order that is experienced as well-being by those who submit themselves to it.

The Socratic concept of righteousness held that people are truly just only if they receive no reward for their actions. This ontological transfer from a realm of wholeness to a justice that exists independently and demands no reward, makes its appearance in Israel in the Persian period in the Book of Job. Job is the person who gains nothing from being righteous. He loses all his possessions and even his physical health, but he clings to God, even though in his deepest experience of suffering he wishes his existence could be snuffed out. But this new view was opposed by his three friends, who represented the older point of view. For them salvation and well-being could be experienced only in this life. Through humble petition and submission to suffering, while confessing their guilt, they wait for things to take a turn for the better. But Job is not concerned with salvation in this life—he has moved beyond that. He desires only one thing, not to be rejected by God. Job's argument is based on the transcendence of his life, and here there is only the communion with God which results from justification. So he cries out—and we are reminded of the confession of Psalm 73.

> For I know that my Redeemer lives;
>   at last he will stand over the dust (of my body),
> and after my skin has been flayed,
>   and without my flesh I will see God;
> yes, I will see him for myself,
>   my own eyes will see him, not those of a stranger,
>   even though my reins faint within me.
> (Job 19:25-27, author's translation.)

For Job this justification is accomplished by God himself acting as Job's advocate against Satan.

Here in this wisdom tradition we see in Israel a world-transcending process of revelation, in which human existence in the world is freed to become fully human and cannot be violated by any of the forces of evil, whether it be death or the devil. In all these stages of the history of revelation, in which what we call faith is set forth in many different ways, human life is grounded in this world in constantly new ways, and at the same time freed from this world. In communion with God that transcends this world, humans attain the freedom to be in the world and yet not of the world. They are then able to understand their this-worldly existence in the light of their understanding of God.

In this second part of our discussion it is necessary to turn from the external world view to a consideration of the more inward world view that mirrors our human existence in the world. No sharp distinction is possible, however; the world view of human perception, the "ancient" world view, fits well with this revelation, for it is God's revelation in the specifically human realm, that is, God's self-disclosure in his personal relationship to his chosen people. It is the relationship of God to the individual who lives under the threat of death, and to the person who leads an imperfect existence. Here, where we are completely ourselves, God reveals himself as the "I." Just as the physical is united with the mental in human perception, just as language is structured metaphorically, so this perception corresponds precisely to this revelation, and the revelation can take form in this language. However much the content of revelation leaves myth behind as a stage in the history of religion, it is unable to abandon myth as the form of speech and knowledge. We can observe a cultivation of the possibilities of human knowledge and speech in the manner in which the biblical tradition grasps intellectual reality (and not beside or behind) perceptible reality.

This is especially striking in the apocalyptic literature of the later parts of the Old Testament. Here it is often the case that what was called symbol in the foregoing discussion, that is, transcendence in the world of perception, comes to the fore in a manner that we can scarcely recreate in our day. This is the reason why our contemporaries generally reject this apparently wild and fantastic world of imagination. But we must not forget that this late layer of the Old Testament is also the basic layer of the New Testament, and it is a questionable undertaking to attempt to deal with the new Testament by trying to eliminate its world view and the form of its language as something conditioned by the time in which it was written, especially before making the effort to understand it properly.

The earliest apocalyptic material is contained in Zechariah's seven night visions from the year 519 B.C. early in the Persian period. We cannot here go into the concepts, views, and perceptions found there, but as an example of the material we may take the middle vision, which corresponds to the hour of midnight. There it is reported that the angel once more awakens the prophet, who had already seen apocalyptic visions. For the climax of this series of visions it was necessary to have a special intensification of consciousness, a special awakening. What is then shown to him is pure symbol—a lampstand with forty-nine (that is, seven raised to its highest potency) flames. In mysterious manner the prophet is informed that these are the eyes of God, which survey and range through the whole world.

Here we again have light as the "appearing" of the Godhead, a pure theophany, expressed now in a cultic symbol. And we can understand why this is interpreted as signifying the eyes of God: no one can see God, as he is not an object; anyone who sees him is seen *by him*. This world of apocalyptic concepts that appears so bizarre to us is a world of highly-developed biblical knowledge and language, which we have trouble dealing with because we no longer understand what a symbol is. We regard it either as a secret language that then can be translated into allegory, or interpret it realistically in a literal manner, which is as foolish as trying to discover the zoological species of the fish that swallowed Jonah.

In the Old Testament the ancient world view is retained as a basic element and not as something that is forced upon it. The ontological transformations that occur in the history of revelation find their expression in this human understanding of what is perceptible by the senses, and they cultivate this understanding. In the unity of human knowledge the succession of the various stages of human understanding of the world and of revelation can be fully preserved. The formation of tradition does not replace the old by the new, but includes the old in the new. For example, in Psalm 19 we can distinguish three stages:

1. vv 1-4a.

> The heavens are telling the glory of God (E);
> and the firmament proclaims his handiwork.
> Day to day pours forth speech,
> and night to night declares knowledge.
> There is no speech, nor are there words;
> their voice is not heard;
> Yet their voice[2] goes out[3] through all the earth,
> and their words to the end of the world.

---

[2]Compare the versions. Heb. "line."
[3]The verb should be read as an imperfect.

In the form of a wisdom riddle the poet speaks of the Logos of creation, who represents the cosmic order. The passage presupposes highly developed wisdom concepts that express the transcendence of the work of creation by the Logos, to which the order of time and space correspond.

2. In contrast to this, vv 4b-6, almost as an example of the creation Logos, present the sun in completely mythological language. (One is almost tempted to say, the sun god.)

> In them he has set a tent for the sun,
> which comes forth like a bridegroom leaving his chamber,
>   and like a strong man runs its course with joy.
> Its rising is from the end of the heavens,
>   and its circuit to the end of them;
>   and there is nothing hid from its heat.

Because of the unified world view, it was possible to preserve earlier concepts at a later stage. The ability of our senses to perceive the world is the basis on which the various stages of tradition rest.

3. Finally, the creation Logos is presented as identical with the Logos of revelation through the law, vv 7-8.

> The law of the Lord is perfect,
>   reviving the soul;
> the testimony of the Lord is sure,
>   making wise the simple;
> the precepts of the Lord are right,
>   rejoicing the heart;
> the commandment of the Lord is pure,
>   enlightening the eyes.

The order of nature and the specifically Israelite revelation of human existence, before God and with God, can be identified with each other, since nature as known by humans has a structure that is appropriately related to humanity. Only a world that humans encounter through their senses can correspond to human existence as characterized by the senses. In concluding this part of the discussion we can say that the revelation which corresponds to faith will always involve a world view which includes an openness to the transcendence contained in human existence as perceptible through the senses.

After having worked through from two angles our question of the relationship of world view and faith (in as far as it is possible to do so within the limits set here) we can combine our positive summary with the special point of view of the Christian faith. On the one hand we have seen that only one world view is appropriate or even possible for humans—that which is transmitted by our sense perceptions, which are open (precisely in their limitation to the world of the senses) to intellectual interpretation. Faith, as something essentially human, stands in need of the knowledge that can be gained of the world through human perception. Worship, prayer, and the language of faith are grounded in our human relation to the world, a relation that is both sensory and intellectual. On the other hand we have seen that the biblical revelation is revelation in terms of God's binding relationship to humans, and that it opens up divine transcendence wherever humans come to themselves. Just as the world view based on perception corresponds to human existence in the world, so can it also be the area where this revelation can be known and can find verbal expression. Faith as biblical faith requires that there be in each of us a capacity for knowing the transcendent. While still in the world, we are no longer of the world, but in our humanity we are with God.

When we turn to the events of the New Testament, we see that here the goal of the biblical revelation is reached and its fulfillment, that, is, God's entering fully into the human realm, is attained. The New Testament is the direct continuation of the Old, and the attempts to separate the two cannot be justified in terms of tradition history. The only thing that can be regarded as distinctive of the New Testament in terms of the history of revelation is its nature as *telos*, the fact that here the goal of revelation has been reached. But what could bind the Old and New Testaments more closely together than this?

In the Christ event transcendence becomes reality in our own death, and God's holiness is united to that which is alien to God—human sinfulness. Here and now we move from mere analogies of transcendence to real transcendence. In the one who was crucified—in the final depth of our own reality—God appears to us. The infinite distance between the heights of God's holiness and the abyss of human guilt and distress, of human suffering and death, is abolished, and in our darkness there shines forth the Easter light of the new creation.

The faith that perceives this secret would be reduced to absurdity if it were translated into a world view that lacked transcendence. It would be reduced to mere subjectivity or lose itself in working for social goals. Therefore with our senses alert we must perceive our world anew, and in this way learn to understand the world view of the Bible. It is much truer than we think.

Index of Subjects

Index of Biblical References

Index of Greek and Hebrew Terms